TEACHING/DISCIPLINE

A Positive Approach For Educational Development

FOURTH EDITION

D1484579

Clifford K. Madsen
Charles H. Madsen Jr.

The Florida State University
Tallahassee, Florida

CONTEMPORARY PUBLISHING COMPANY OF RALEIGH, INC

5849 Lease Lane, Raleigh, NC 27617 · (919) 851-8221
www.contemporarypublishing.com

To our parents—lifelong teachers,
unwitting behaviorists,
wonderful people

Portions of this book first appeared in Teaching/Discipline: A Positive Approach for
Educational Development, Expanded Second Edition for professionals by Charles H.
Madsen, Jr. and Clifford K. Madsen, Copyright 1974, 1970 by Allyn and Bacon, Inc. and in
Parents/Children/Discipline: A Positive Approach by Clifford K. Madsen and Charles H.
Madsen, Jr., 1972 by Allyn and Bacon, Inc.
Teaching/Discipline: A Positive Approach for Educational Development, Third Edition,
Copyright 1983, Charles H. Madsen, Jr. and Clifford K. Madsen.

Library of Congress Catalog in Publication Data:

Madsen, Clifford K. 1937-
   Teaching/Discipline.

   Includes bibliographical references and index.
   Classroom management. I.   Madsen, Charles H. Jr., joint author.
II.   Title.
LB3011M25 1980   371.1'024   80-19772

ISBN 0-89892-178-3

Copyright © 1981, 1974, 1970 by Allyn and Bacon, Inc., 470 Atlantic Avenue, Boston,
Massachusetts 02210

Copyright © 1998, 1983 Charles H. Madsen, Jr., and Clifford K. Madsen

Printed in the United States of America

10   9   8   7   6   5   4

Contents

Preface

This edition of Teaching/Discipline represents an expansion and reorganization of the Third Edition. It is written especially for teachers, prospective teachers, counselors, therapists, and other professionals who interact with students. It is specifically intended as a classroom discipline and subject matter presentation.

This edition is presented in four parts. Part I is organized in question and answer schemata designed to help clarify the central issues that have arisen from the authors' interactions with children and teachers in the schools. Part II represents a selected summary of scientific and professional practices deemed relevant, transferable, and directly applicable to teaching. One hundred twenty examples are arranged developmentally for the convenience of the reader. Part III treats the effect of teacher responses on student behavior in an attempt to help facilitate a positive approach. Part IV provides an observation manual, techniques for consequating behavior, and an introduction to behavioral designs. A glossary including explanations for those with little background in behavioral research is presented to serve as a transition from this volume to the published research found in scientific journals.

We are deeply indebted to the researchers whose studies are summarized as Scientific Applications in Part II and more specifically to their unnamed scientific progenitors. We are especially grateful to Christopher M. Johnson who provided the new material found in Part IV. We are hopeful that this edition will help teachers apply systematic procedures to increase social and academic learning in the classroom. We also urge teachers to take fuller advantage of the benefits being produced through continuing scientific research.

PART I

TEACHING AND DISCIPLINE

Teaching—
The Art of Discipline

A FIRST DAY?

As she approached the school, she wondered why all schools look the same. Why couldn't someone be imaginative enough to disguise the telltale landscape and those separate rows of windows that indicate the time-honored concept of individual classrooms? Why were all the buildings that didn't look as though they were designed by school boards called experimental? What about those experimental programs, anyway? Were there communities that really cared enough about education to pay for all that? It was obvious this wasn't one of them. Notice the dull color of the paint; that Quonset hut must be new, but what a poor excuse for an education site. Oh yes, that must be a "portable classroom"—a nice euphemism for lack of planning or no money. Money—this job didn't pay that well. Why was she here? Parkside had a better program, or perhaps she should have stayed in school. The graduate assistantship could have come through, and why even teaching? But then, why think about all that nonsense anyway? This is the day, the first day for the students. She felt her stomach skip and her throat tighten. Was it this bad for everyone? As she walked into the building she wondered why those other people looked so calm? She stopped at the restroom. Wasn't this the third time since getting up this morning? Her eye caught a limerick, and she wondered why students were not as creative in class as they were on bathroom walls. Why were all these wild thoughts so vivid this morning? "Okay, face it—you're scared. Just plain scared!"

Her mind wandered back to a discussion with her father. There was a teacher—fifty years in the public schools. She had gone home especially to talk to him those two weeks before the planning session. She remembered her father smiling as she asked him many questions. She remembered getting no answer day after day until the last evening before she was to leave. "But Dad, what makes a good teacher?" After a long silence his brow furrowed, and his bright eyes narrowed.

"Every teacher goes out with a golden apple of knowledge the teacher wants to share, but some students don't want that knowledge, and their attitude becomes, 'Teach me if you can, but I'll make it as difficult as possible.' Remember two things. When it is as difficult as it can be, don't give up. You might think that it can't get worse, but it does when you give up. The second thing—*you can't even get started without discipline.*" As she looked in the mirror after washing her hands, she became suddenly angry with her father and that discussion. Cliches, cliches, that's all she needed now—two more cliches: "Don't give up. Discipline." She remembered her professors—more cliches. "Motivate the students, captivate their interests, recognize individual differences." Great, great, but how? No one ever says how. As she approached her room, she felt guilty about her thoughts concerning her father. Sure, he *was* a fine teacher—years of compliments, awards, letters, everything a teacher could want. Then she suddenly realized that even her father didn't know why. The art of teaching—is it really that elusive?

When she got to the door, she stopped for a long moment. "Please, please let me be a good teacher." Then it happened. The door knocked against her face as a student ran out. She watched the boy run down the hall as the students inside started laughing. She wondered quickly if she should go after him. "No, I'd better stay with the class." She had rehearsed an opening joke; that wouldn't work now. She felt her face flush as she tried to decide what to do. After a long pause she muttered, "Good morning," but instantly realized that it was a mistake when one boy softly mimicked her. Again, laughter. Why, oh why couldn't she start all over again? She looked over the sea of faces. Where was a friend? She quickly picked up a piece of chalk and began writing her name on the board. With her back turned, she tried frantically to think of some way to gain control. She heard some small noises, then a girl's louder voice, "Quit it." Was it this way everywhere? From kindergarten through twelfth grade, was this what teaching was all about? Finally she spoke. "Students, please take your seats so we can get started. As you notice on the board, my name is . . ." Two boys were standing in the back. "Would you please take a seat?" The class turned around to see. One boy shrugged, "OK, OK, OK." The class burst out laughing again as he dropped into a chair. The other boy started to move, but then stopped as the class laughed louder. "Would you please sit down!" The class grew quiet. She felt her heart pounding and mustered the sternest look she could. Student and teacher were now staring at each other. The classroom became not only quiet, but also electric as students looked from teacher to troublemaker and back again. After these thousand years of silence, she heard herself say angrily, "Now, you sit down this instant." Nausea came into her stomach as she watched the muscles tighten in his face, his lips curl sarcastically. "Are you goin' to make me?"

A first day? —A large majority of teachers who leave the teaching profession do so because of what they term "inability to discipline."

WHAT IS OUR INTENTION?

It should be obvious that the above teacher wanted to be a "good teacher." It is also obvious that she was not successful, at least on her first day. One of the most important aspects for teachers concerns the difference between what we intend to get and what we actually get, or what we intend to achieve and what we actually achieve. The issue of *intention versus function* is important for many aspects of our lives; it is extremely important for teachers. It is assumed that most of us have had what we consider to be "bad teachers," or at the very least, one "very bad teacher." Several questions can be asked regarding these "bad teachers." What are the motivations of these teachers? Why are they teaching? Should we assume that they all entered the teaching profession because they wanted to make students miserable? Or perhaps to make themselves miserable? Did these teachers get up every morning and look forward to being in a classroom in which they were ineffective academically and socially? After the negative experiences that they encounter with students on an ongoing basis, do they gloat with happiness about the unpleasantness they have caused? Does it seem reasonable that a person would enter the teaching profession looking forward to being ineffective and upsetting students? The answer to all of these questions is—probably not.

Unless a person starts out with a love of inflicting damage on others, or after a period of time grows to enjoy it, then perhaps what happens to beginning teachers is that they do not achieve the results that they *intend*. It is assumed that most teachers go into the profession because they want students to get excited about the subject matter, to be successful, to learn how to get along with others, and to be nice people. Additionally, many teachers would like their students to feel about them the way they feel about important past teachers who have had a great influence on their own lives. Often a past positive role model is the main reason that a person becomes a teacher. While different teachers stress different things, it is assumed that all teachers desire to be "good teachers." *The problem is not in the intention; it is in the function.* Most things that do or do not happen within a classroom have to do with the *effect* of certain behaviors from the teacher, or the effect of other aspects of the student's total environment, not because of the teacher's bad intentions.

Think for a moment about one of the worst teachers that you have ever had. What do you think this teacher's response to you would have been if you had *genuinely* asked to spend time outside class to learn more about the subject matter? What would this teacher's interactions have been with students who already were well behaved regardless of all other circumstances? What do you think this teacher's responses would have been if the teacher had previously established a strong positive rapport with you as well as with every other student in the classroom?

A *functional analysis* that investigates the behavior of both student and teacher most often reveals things that the teacher could do in order to achieve different or better results. Most of the material in this text concerns what it is that teachers can do in order to achieve desired outcomes. At any point in our own lives we can count many, many times when our intentions did not result in positive outcomes. We intended to do something, but forgot to do it; we wanted something to happen, but it did not happen; we expected someone to give us something that we did not get; we intended to study, but never got around to it, and so on.

Intentions *are* important. Sometimes it is the intention of a person that matters most. In our personal relationships we often judge the intent of our significant other's actions. We want to know the motivation behind the action; we want to know *why*. Yet, while this may help establish a degree of true involvement and concern, it does not obliterate the effect of an action. Suppose a close friend says something in public that hurts our feelings. The function of this behavior has hurt our feelings, and our feelings have indeed been *hurt*. Later we might find that our friend did not mean (intend) to hurt us—we are still hurt. The effect of this hurtful action may have already resulted in extreme disapproval from our point of view. Our friend may apologize and be very sorry—we have still been hurt.

Sometimes consequences can be devastating and even life threatening. Assume a situation where the only information we have concerning a particular situation is that a man is somehow responsible for his wife's death and his car has been involved. If this situation came to court and you were on the jury, what would you want to know concerning his *intentions*? Suppose the man took out a very high paying insurance policy on his wife's life just a few days prior to her death. Suppose that he was intoxicated and completely oblivious to anything at the time of her death. Suppose that he lost his temper, lost all control—and backed his car into her causing her death. Suppose that his car broke down when they were out together in a remote area with freezing temperature—that he left to get help but did not return in time to halt her demise. Suppose that he was driving on the highway at an extremely high rate of speed and caused an accident in which she died. Suppose that he allowed his car to malfunction, and at a crucial time it failed, thus causing an accident. Now suppose that the deceased was not his wife but another acquaintance with whom he was having an affair. Suppose . . . suppose . . . but a person is still dead.

While this may seem like an extreme case, the major point is that, regardless of our intentions, certain things result from our behavior. Most often these effects are small; sometimes they are large. Sometimes a child is physically hurt while in the care of a teacher; sometimes a child's feelings are irrevocably hurt because of an insensitive remark made by a teacher. It is the *effect* of certain actions that determine important aspects of human behavior. Knowledge of intentions may help us assess responsibility, and this knowledge may also help us to "understand." It may even provide the rationale for our "judgement," yet the effect of the previous behavior is still the same; it has already happened and it cannot be undone. We all enjoy knowing that we matter. When working with others, we matter perhaps more than we intend, so we must learn to make our every action thoughtful, meaningful, and equal with its intent. Indeed, what a teacher does is what the student gets.

What is our intention? —As far as the student is concerned, it is that which functions.

WHOM DO WE DISCIPLINE?

Many teachers and parents have drawn an artificial line between love and discipline. Some make a point for love, others for discipline. The wise think they solve the problem when they say it must be both, and all are perhaps equally naïve. The essential point is that we, as teachers, must understand precisely what we mean by love and/or discipline before we begin. The major thesis of this book is that we must be concerned with how people *act* in order to assess behavior or to define terms. How should we know that we are loved but by the way people act toward us: what they say, how they look, how they touch, in a word, what they *do*? Attention, praise, kind words, and physical contact have been demonstrations of love for years. Who cares if someone loves them if they never receive evidence through attention, contact, or by the spoken word? While it may be possible for love to exist in total abstraction, most people are not content with such little personal involvement, especially over an extended period of time. One often hears the phrase "I'll love you no matter what." This is a good example of a meaningless cliché. Indeed, very few, if any, really believe it, especially over long periods of time. "No matter what" remains an abstraction that has little meaning until it is eventually violated. That is, I'll love you until you desert me, find someone else, treat me cruelly, violate my trust, and so on. Most people do stress overt behaviors. A more fitting phrase would be "I'll love you if you love me," or "I will act in certain ways with you if you reciprocate."

If such statements as "I will love you no matter what" were left to idle verbalizations, there would be little problem. When they are taken seriously, they pose a very serious problem, especially for the teacher. The teacher is led to believe that teachers should "love" everyone, and, if this were not damaging enough, the teacher actually may believe that one should continuously *act* as though one loves all students "no matter what."

One of the most important differentiations concerning teaching and learning concerns two simple yet powerful concepts: contingency and consistency. Most people do not have a problem understanding consistency. Consistency is a common word that most people understand even if they have difficulty in achieving it. *Contingent* is more difficult and refers to cause and effect relationships, or if____then____situations. Whether or not something is contingent is extremely consequential. For example, one contingent principle that we try to teach all youngsters is simple. "When you do nice things, nice things happen to you. When you do bad things, bad things happen to you." Even allowing for slight inconsistency, if we truly believed and taught in a manner conducive to this end, we would shortly have many "nice children" in that a contingency has been established. Yet, we violate this principle regularly by teaching a child the exact opposite. This simple principle has several perversions: (1) When you do *bad* things, *nice* things happen to you; (2) when you do *nice* things, *bad* things happen to you; (3) no matter what you do, *bad* things happen to you, and (4) no matter what you do, *nice* things happen to you (i.e., I'll love you non-contingently no matter what). Perhaps the saddest ramification of this last distortion is that while we treat the child, for a time, as though all behavior deserves nice consequences, we finally give up on the child at that precise point when the child has finally learned exactly what we have taught: No matter what the child does, nice things happen. Having established this non-contingent relationship, teachers sometimes state, "I've tried everything with that child and nothing works," or, "I just can't get through to that student."

Discipline is a process whereby certain relationships (cause–and–effect associations) are established. It is a way of behaving, conducive to productive ends. First, it must be taught; secondly, it must be learned (i.e., internalized). Love, if it is to transcend mere rhetoric, is a way of feeling and acting conducive to productive ends. Most teachers enter the teaching profession because they truly love children (care about students) and desire to help each child achieve his greatest potential. Sometimes people are paid to care about children, that is, to teach.

The most difficult aspect of human interaction based upon love is to develop the ability to withhold overt acts of love (ignore or disapprove) to help the child learn appropriate ways to behave. When love responses have been previously established, we can then respond in similar kind to the child's behavior. Thus, when a child demonstrates inappropriate responses and we actively withdraw our overt responses of love, we teach the child that certain behavior is not deserving of love responses from us. The most tragic mistakes of the teacher occur when the courage to act in this way is absent, and the teacher succumbs to "giving in." The child learns a perverted association: "When I do bad things, nice things happen to me." In the long run everyone suffers, but mostly the child. The authors call this teaching behavior "mistakes of love." More appropriately it might be classified as "naïveté" or "lack of courage." It is amazing, although apparent, that some people actually believe that all responses should be regarded with overt acts of love. The teacher who really loves a child will have the courage to teach the child proper associations. We discipline only those people we care about; others we leave alone.

Whom do we discipline? —We discipline those we love.

WHY DO WE DISCIPLINE?

Discipline is necessary if a child is to function properly. All teachers have had the unfortunate experience of observing either children or adults who are "undisciplined." We usually refer to such people as lacking motivation, apathetic, rowdy, or even mean, spiteful, or deceitful. But why are children so classified? How do they become this way? If self-discipline is to be internalized, then how is the child to achieve this attribute? The answer is obvious—*it must be learned.* Teachers often "beg the question" by stating that it must come from *within* the child. Yet, how does motivation or proper attitude get "in"? Even if some of it is "in," will it continue to serve in the future? These are questions with which the teacher must deal.

Particular patterns of responses are learned from the external world (external stimuli). If a student is "motivated," it is because the student has learned to associate certain behaviors with certain outcomes. Motivation does not exist in a vacuum; it is a way of behaving. If the teacher wants a student to behave in a certain way, the teacher must structure the student's external world (i.e., control the environment) to ensure that the desired behavior will be learned. The disciplined child is a child who (1) has learned to behave socially in appropriate ways, and (2) evidences proper patterns of responses to academic work. If either one of these two general categories of behaviors is absent, we usually say the child "has a problem."

We must be very careful, however, not to designate many behaviors into one or two artificial categories and believe that we have solved the problem because we have arbitrarily classified it or given it a name. People react differently to various situations (stimuli). It is very interesting to take a pencil and paper and write down one's own responses in different situations. How do we act in the classroom, in church, at a football game, in faculty meetings, swimming, buying shoes, driving a car, getting out of an invitation, giving a speech, eating dinner, listening to beautiful music, listening to an argument? Yes, we act differently, we dress differently, we talk differently, and we even smile differently in these diverse situations. *If we were brave enough to list our most secret behaviors, we would probably shock those very people who believe they know us the best.* It is unwise to classify behaviors into artificial categories that have to do with only a few situations. Perhaps some justification can be made for categorizing general attributes (e.g., apathetic, aggressive, boisterous, unmotivated), but such classification is extremely deceptive and, at best, provides only partial information.

When learning is defined as a change or modification of behavior, then three things are necessary: (1) experience, (2) discrimination, and (3) association. For instance, a child is presented with a color (*experience*). After a time the child *discriminates* the color from other colors or the absence of the color. Through repetition, an *association(s)* is made with the color (e.g., red). The child may then evidence in some behavior, most often previously learned, (e.g., pointing, matching, speaking, thinking) that the color has been learned. The preceding definition of learning based on reinforcement theory does not quarrel with the cognitive or mediational processes in learning or with the material to be learned. It proposes a method to promote or expedite this learning. In short, it asks, "How should we go about teaching the color red in the best possible manner to ensure correct association?" If the child responds favorably to teaching, we assume the external stimuli are associated in a way that functions as a reward for the child. But what if the child does not respond? Then we must restructure the external environment so that the child does receive proper motivation.

How then are we to get the student to learn the many behaviors that will provide the necessarily skills to achieve a productive life? Within the complexity of many responses to the external environment, we must structure the external world to provide proper relationships to be learned. We should not sit back and hope that motivation will somehow "get inside." We must structure the environment to provide the student with proper associations. Discipline must first be external; it must come from *without* before it can be from *within*.

If learned relationships to external stimuli are conducive to productive ends, the child will have a repertoire of responses that will serve the child well when meeting the constant challenges of life. If the child is capable of following rules, acting enthusiastically regarding new learning experiences, staying on task during work periods, relating well with other children, knowing when to be assertive and when to acquiesce, indeed, if the student has learned to respond appropriately to many specific situations, then we say the student is well disciplined.

Why do we discipline? —We discipline to provide for social order and individual productivity.

WHY DEVELOP TECHNIQUES FOR DISCIPLINE?

Mother has just finished teaching and expects her seventeen-year-old son to pick her up from school at approximately 4:00 P.M. Four arrives, and no son; the woman begins to pace a little and thinks about a hectic afternoon and a ruined supper. At 4:15 P.M. she becomes a little angry and thinks about her inconsiderate offspring. Four-thirty P.M. arrives, and, in spite of trying to do something else, she begins to worry about his whereabouts. Between 5:45 P.M. and 6:00 P.M. (while many transportation invitations are turned down) he is imagined dead in a car wreck, attacked by someone, unconscious in the hospital, picked up by the police, drunk in an alley, and sundry other things, all of which are negative (she has even lost her concern for transportation). Is it not strange that during these times most people do not imagine that the son happened to get involved with a classmate and forgot the time while having a wonderful talk, enjoying a pleasant stroll, meditating by himself while walking in the park, or perhaps shopping for a surprise gift for this mother?

What, in reality, is the problem in this case? The mother who is "fretting and worrying" about possible catastrophic events, or a seventeen-year-old-son who is late? One real problem is the worry. When pickup time arrived, if mother had waited a reasonable amount of time and then arranged other transportation, there probably would have been much less of a problem.

Unfortunately, what often happens is that people reinforce in themselves (substitute spouse for son and reread the above example) and others the very worst. We often train ourselves to worry unnecessarily about terrible things that only might happen, such as potential loss of loved ones or inability to succeed in the future, for example. The problem is actually the worry itself, especially when nothing is done to change behavior. Many people manage systematically to increase their worrying and, in addition, convince themselves that it is being done because of sincere concern for themselves or others.

It would seem that every person should be trained explicitly to prepare for foreseeable emergencies. We should teach ourselves and our students specific actions to deal with emergencies (what do you do when a stranger tries to pick you up, if the school is on fire and smoke is coming from somewhere, if you are hurt on the playground, if you are offered narcotics, etc.). Potential situations should be handled by these procedures with extensive role-playing. Correct responses may then be based on the values of teachers and should clarify just what "normal" routines ought to be in emergencies. When values *and* techniques are specified and practiced, then, if worry occurs, it is definitely not conducive to happiness. When we are waiting for errant progeny it is too late to do any teaching, and if some accident has occurred there is nothing to be done until we are notified.

Worry, or "depression," usually represents nothing more than statements to oneself or others indicating that we "feel sorry for ourselves" and, as such are definitely unproductive. Frequently, as we interact with each other and begin to spill our tale of "worry and woe," the "significant other" listens intently with nodding head, exhibits a "sad" face, and asks us questions. Generally, as one performs for us this disservice, we pretend that the one "understands," which further reinforces our "depression." Teachers might tell friends, each other, and especially their students that if one wants to feel sorry for oneself and waste precious time instead of *deciding* what to do and then working on the problem, that one should find someone else with whom to talk. Often those students who "forget" or refuse responsibilities just want to spend time complaining. The only negative or similar comments we might allow are comments that honestly report the facts of a situation and are followed by an attempt to give a statement about what behaviors are being planned to alleviate the problem. "Tell me what you intend to do; do not give me your problem." It is astounding to find how fast "depression" and "worry" are relieved in children (and even adults) when no one pays attention and the negative verbal behavior is either punished or ignored while positive solutions are praised. "Is that what you will do next time? That's excellent. Let's pretend that I'm the other person and you show me what you will do."

A teacher might also be careful not to reinforce young children for crying following refusals and thereby reinforce the self-fulfilling prophecy that if only the child would cry it out the child will feel better. The teacher might focus on delineating the problem without reinforcing emotional responses and, at the same time, take the responsibility of planning a program with the student that will lead to behaviors incompatible with feeling sorry for oneself (doing something about the problem when possible or engaging in a "fun" activity when it is not possible to structure other responses).

While *serious long-term depression should be handled by a professional*, worry, anger, and other responses are expected in human beings of all ages. These responses might be acknowledged immediately and then followed by behavioral techniques to change the emotion. They should not be reinforced or worried about. Young people should be trained to deal with a problem immediately, rather than receiving reinforcement for extended periods of worry. Hence, the focus becomes one of solving the problems that have produced the worry, anger, or crying (depression), and, thus, of acting one's way into a new way of thinking.

Why develop techniques for discipline? —To stop worrying and start acting.

WHAT DOES DISCIPLINE TAKE?

In his book *Profiles in Courage*, the late President Kennedy stated the problems of the politician in facing the demands of continued popularity as opposed to having the courage to act on his convictions. Politicians are not alone in this dilemma. Few people realize the pressures placed on the teacher for conformity and popularity. This pressure comes not only from community, administration, and parents, but also from colleagues and students. It is much easier to go along, to not rock the boat, and to reevaluate one's position, especially in relationship to touchy problems. It is difficult to discipline the principal's daughter, to face the disapproval of a colleague, or to face irate parents who insist their child has been dealt with unfairly. It is difficult to explain a simple behavioral approach that rests on direct immediate consequences and not on intriguing deceptions. It is difficult to explain to a parent that *the question of discipline is not one of strictness or permissiveness but one of cause-and-effect relationships*. It is difficult to help a child when the behavioral interactions required might be different from those the teacher and the child are used to, or to show parents how they can help their child when the teacher's instructions to them require opposite parent/child interactions than those previously established. It is difficult to live through the first day of a new program in discipline without "giving in." It is most difficult to lose, for a time, the favorable response of a child.

Every teacher is faced with the problem of wanting to be liked. In our society, being liked is an admirable goal. It is indeed easy to demand a little less, hoping to be liked. *Some people's desire to be liked is so great that they will suffer mild contempt for the privilege.* Furthermore, even though most adults do not hesitate to have a young child suffer momentarily for long-term gain (e.g., medical inoculations, drudgery of learning hard concepts, etc.), many teachers do not have the courage to initiate a program of discipline that might cause temporary disruptions in classroom routines, yet would benefit the child in the long run. In addition, most teachers come to realize that even the most sophisticated students often evaluate a teacher's worth in terms of entertainment: "Here I am; what do you have for me today?" The value of discipline is not likely to be cherished immediately. "Why didn't I have anything fun to do today?" Students may even respond negatively when entertainment is not forthcoming. Nevertheless, it should be remembered that the *teacher's approval* is probably more important to the student than vice versa. The teacher's personal approval is a most effective reward. *It should not be given indiscriminately.* Indeed, the teacher never does a student a favor by letting the student get away with anything, especially those things that the student does not like about his/her own behavior. If we really know what we believe, then we are much less likely to succumb and give in to pressures.

What does discipline take? —It takes courage.

WHAT IS EFFECTIVE TEACHING?

It has been suggested that so long as the teaching profession could not effectively demonstrate that it could ensure specific educational outcomes, few seemed to care a great deal about specific aspects concerning curriculum, who should teach, and so on. Now it would appear that advances in technology might renew interest concerning all aspects relating to teachers, students, and what educational experiences ought to be.

It seems apparent that no teaching technique can be effectively divorced from the person who uses it. This point, however, makes a case for more rigorous screening of prospective teachers and not for the abandonment of effective techniques. It is a curious argument that maintains that effective techniques must be kept from teachers because then teachers may actually teach more efficiently. Because of the effectiveness of certain procedures, it seems that the profession should address the truly important issues:

> What specifically should be learned? Or, more importantly, who will decide what is to be learned, both socially and academically? What values and accompanying behaviors evidencing selected values should be learned? When, where, and by whom?

> Who should be given the responsibility to interact purposefully in the learning process, that is, to teach?

> Should society require any objective evidence for this learning, that is, data from observation or other formal means?

> If continued research demonstrates the efficacy of empirical cause-and-effect relationships (data based on observation), ought derived principles to be systematically implemented within the schools?

> If so, then what should be the boundaries concerning choice and application?

It seems very unwise to mix the above value questions with questions relating to techniques. The choice of a particular teaching approach does not help the teacher decide why, what, and who is going to learn. These issues represent much more important value choices. However, after questions relating to these values have been answered, effective techniques may be used to enhance learning. Of course, the choice of a particular technique as opposed to another approach represents a value choice. In addition, if certain approaches are implemented, selection of specific procedures (e.g., discovery versus errorless discrimination) as well as choice of potential student/teacher interactions (e.g., approval versus punishment) represents another value issue.

It would seem that initially we should address the more important issues concerning learning rather than extol or condemn a technique by alluding to many ancillary values or detriments that we feel might ensue from its application.

Figure I should be useful in illustrating this point. Fill in three or four of the most important values you think should be learned by students (academic, social, or both). For example, academic values might be reading, writing, computation, etc. Social values might include consideration for others, respect for property, self-actualization—whatever you consider to be positive. Now list some things you consider to be negative (e.g., lying, stealing). It is obvious that many different techniques might be used to teach "negative" as well as "positive" values.

The purpose of this exercise is to indicate that effective methods, much like any human product (e.g., atomic energy, jet propulsion, governments), may be used either to the benefit or detriment of other human beings. Scientific techniques are characterized by definitions of behavior that can be observed (pinpointed) and then measured (recorded and counted). These techniques include the isolation of specific cause and effect relationships and thereby provide a scientific methodology for the evaluation of learning.

Non-observable techniques are much more difficult to explain or measure, but they may be extremely important in teaching/learning situations where "scientific techniques" seem inadequate. It should be remembered that there is no absolute agreement concerning almost any aspect of education. It might be wise to develop a tolerance for ambiguity while deciding which particular instructional procedure is appropriate for each situation, student, time, or place.

What is effective teaching? —That which implements selected values.

STUDY GUIDE FOR CHAPTER I

Questions:

1. What is suggested as an important variable in being an effective teacher?

* 2. State the behavioral principle that we try to teach children and the "perversions" of the principle. If you disagree with this, state why.

* 3. What does "discipline" involve?

4. State specifically to what discipline and motivation refer. What is the difference between intention and function?

5. What is a general attribute?

6. Paraphrase the gist of the paragraph beginning, "When learning is defined...." (See page 8).

7. How is self-control or self-discipline acquired?

* 8. Why is discipline neither "strictness" nor "permissiveness" but related to cause and effect?

* 9. What is one of the most effective rewards a teacher can use?

*10. How is worry (depression) reinforced?

* Using the preceding questions indicated by an asterisk (*), transfer the concept dealt with in the question to specific content area classroom teaching situations—in chorus, band, orchestra, art, physical education, social studies, language arts, special education, arithmetic, English, history, algebra, geometry, science, modern languages, forensics, dramatics, football, track, chemistry, literature.

LEARNING ACTIVITY I— VALUES-TECHNIQUES DICHOTOMY

Behavior modification represents the use of a series of techniques that have been scientifically verified in an attempt to promote more effective learning for both social and academic subject matter (see Part II). A behavioral approach does not help the teacher decide why, what, and who is going to learn. But behavioral principles may be used to enhance learning of appropriate behavior after questions relating to values have been decided.

Study the Values-Techniques Dichotomy Chart shown here and fill in three or four of the most important values—academic, social, or both—you think should be instilled in the students you are going to teach. Do the same for values that you feel should not be taught to your students under any circumstances. In addition, write a short paragraph on how behavioral techniques could be used to teach both negative as well as positive values.

The purpose of this exercise is to demonstrate that behavioral techniques, much like any human product, may be used either to the benefit or the detriment of other human beings. These techniques can be used to isolate specific cause-and-effect relationships by affecting the consequences of behavior and thereby providing a scientific methodology for the evaluation of learning.

POSITIVE VALUES

1. Pinpoint: Observable

2. Record: Measurable

1. Nonobservable

2. Nonmeasureable
   (inferential)

TECHNIQUES

Behavioral
Techniques _____|_____ Nonbehavioral
Techniques

3. Consequate: Cause-and-Effect
                Relationships

4. Evaluate: Isolate causes
                through specific
                addition and removal
                of consequences

3. Non-determined
   (random, chance, chaotic)

4. Non-explainable
   Complex Causes
   Unknown Consequences

NEGATIVE VALUES

Figure 1

LEARNING ACTIVITY 2— VALUES-TECHNIQUES DIFFERENTIATION

Many values (implicit or explicit) are reinforced by teachers without a clear understanding of the difference(s) between values and techniques. The following list of values is derived from actual observations of classroom teachers. Any values may be reinforced using either approval or disapproval techniques.

1. In the blanks provided, fill in specific consequences (see example) including both approval and disapproval techniques (See Chapter Seven for examples).
2. Circle all teacher values which you do not value (i.e., behavior inconsistent with your value system).
3. Go back and review your lists of consequences and change ten examples to consequences which you would prefer not to use (i.e., consequences inconsistent with your value system) that you have either observed or read about.

Teacher Values	Example of Specific Consequences Following Behavior	
1. Following classroom rules	A(pproval)	teacher's praise
	D(isapproval)	_____
2. Working (staying on-task)	A	_____
	D	_____
3. Academic achievement (learning to read)	A	academic grades
	D	_____
4. Working quietly	A	_____
	D	_____
5. Working well together (cooperation)	A	_____
	D	_____
6. Respect for teacher (not being sassy)	A	_____
	D	_____

7. Waiting quietly (patience)   A   _____

                                        D   _____

8. Doing extra work (industry)   A   _____

                                        D   _____

9. Effort   A   _____

                                        D   _____

10. Raising hand to get attention   A   _____

                                        D   _____

11. Completing assignments on time   A   _____

                                        D   _____

12. Staying in seat while working   A   _____

                                        D   _____

13. Following directions   A   _____

                                        D   _____

14. Walking inside building   A   _____

                                        D   _____

15. Taking responsibility for own materials A   _____

                                        D   _____

16. Liking school and school work   A   _____
    (positive attitude)   D   _____

CHAPTER 2

Discipline— The Way to Learning

WHAT DO STUDENTS BRING?

At any time in the chronological development of a child, we are prone to look back into the child's history to explain the child's present behavior. Thus, we have a never-ending spiral that assesses blame backward (behavioral antecedents). Colleges blame the public schools, public schools blame the home, and the parents blame each other or the child's progenitors, ad infinitum. If we must stop somewhere, let us stop at birth, although, some theoreticians would impute motives even before the child's first breath.

Let us consider three oversimplified, but rather characteristic, views of the child at birth: (1) the child is born good, (2) the child is born bad, and (3) the child is born neither good nor bad. If, as some believe, all children are born basically good, then the child's only impairment is the corruption of living. The teacher's goal would be not to corrupt the child's basic nature. This would not be difficult in a Utopian world. Perhaps it would not be difficult in the world in which we live if all behavioral responses were predestined to be ideal. A problem arises, however, when "good" is specifically defined; each person's idea of "good" does not always coincide with another's. A second problem arises for the teacher if the child has somehow been previously corrupted, for now the child evidences both "good" and "bad" behavior.

The second view proposes that children are born bad. In this case, the teacher's job would be to correct the basic "badness" so the child could be "good." Again we have a problem with the definition of "bad," especially without reference to specific overt behaviors. It is curious that many people who believe in this "badness" theory assume quite readily that children's good behavior is not learned, while insisting that all bad behavior (usually referring to moral transgressions) must be eliminated. Regardless, if the child has learned any "goodness" at all, the child will still present a mixture of both "good" and "bad."

The third position postulates neither good natures nor bad and, therefore, assumes that all behavior is learned. The teacher's job in this situation simply would be to teach the child correct responses. Nevertheless, in all probability the child will have picked up some "bad" behaviors. Therefore, the same situation will be evidenced as with the other two positions. The important question regarding the foregoing is "What should the teacher do?" Regardless of philosophical orientation, should the teacher's responses to the student be any different? Indeed, is it possible to start teaching at any other place than where the student is? Suzy, Sam, and Fred all cry out in class— Suzy because her sweet nature has become corrupted, Sam because he was born bad, and Fred because he learned some incorrect associations. Do their personal histories or the teacher's philosophy really matter? The important question would seem to be "What does the teacher do now?" Even if we could solve the philosophical problem or know the particular individual reinforcement history of the individual children, *they are still crying.*

All too often, we pretend that we have solved a problem because we can find some explanation for the behavior (e.g., high score on "problem child tests," family depravity, "bad seed," terrible first-grade teacher). Unfortunately, the children will continue to cry out in class until we do something to change their behavior. During the very first processes of interacting with the child, the teacher should be able to find out just *where the student is both socially and academically* and assess the extent of any specific problems. These first encounters with the student provide all that is needed to determine where the student is. The teacher then can begin to do something concerning the student's behavior. A long involved analysis of the child's "personality" is generally both unproductive and unnecessary.

What do students bring? —Does it really matter?

WHAT DO TEACHERS BRING?

Most individuals working in education seem convinced that the learning environment should be a relatively positive place where students learn "to be nice people and take joy from learning." In fact, many teachers, administrators, counselors, and others have been asked to respond to the question of whether or not they believe the classroom atmosphere should be predominantly positive (approving) or negative (disapproving). Responses overwhelmingly indicate that school personnel believe that teachers should be predominantly positive. Over 99 percent of respondents on questionnaires "strongly agree" or "agree" that teachers should have a positive classroom environment. Ninety-seven percent also agree that a strong indicator of a positive environment would be one where more approving than disapproving comments and non-verbal behaviors are directed by the teacher toward students. However, this human self-report data is in sharp contrast to results based on actual classroom observations.

Interaction patterns based on definitions of approval and disapproval between students and teachers observed by trained personnel show an entirely different distribution of results. Less than 10 percent of teachers (kindergarten through high school) actually dispensed more approval for appropriate than disapproval for inappropriate social behavior. This difference between verbally stated values and actual behavior seems even more disparate when it is realized that trained observers used the teachers' own definitions of appropriate and inappropriate student behaviors.

It is amazing that actual interaction patterns of teachers with students are so different from their intended outcomes (intention versus function.) Results clearly indicate that there are definite differences between the verbal reports of values and actual in-class overt behaviors. Computations indicate that the approval ratio is less than 50 percent in 92 percent of the cases. It should be noted that many teachers are not as negative in dealing with academic behavior (34 percent do give more approval to appropriate than disapproval to inappropriate academic behavior). The computation for the approval ratio is based upon the amount of approval dispersed relative to all reinforcing behavior and does not depend upon the absolute frequency of reinforcing behavior. Thus, the approval ratio is based upon the percentage of approval teachers give independent of the total frequency or amount of behavioral interaction. It has also been observed that the higher the grade level, the more time the teacher spends questioning, stimulating, or explaining rather than reinforcing appropriate social behavior.

The extent to which successes or failures occur in pupils' learning can probably be attributed to the degree of success the teacher achieves in arranging the total school environment. It is also assumed that successes or failures concerning teacher effects should be demonstrated in observable classroom results. Therefore, precise methods could be assessed as to effectiveness and durability. Specific effects should be demonstrated concerning environmental change as well as documented procedures used in the interaction between those who learn and those who teach. A systematic analysis of some of the variables within the learning situation that could bring teacher experiences in line with their own values appears to be needed. The premise is that through learning effective techniques teachers will be better at their jobs—better able to ensure academic and social improvement and better able to prevent potential problems that might interfere with learning.

What do teachers bring? —It really does matter.

WHO IS SPECIAL?

Teachers usually have a large variety of students, all different in many, many ways. Yet in every class there are several students who seem to be "gifted," as well as students who appear to have "problems." While the teacher almost immediately notices the children with "behavior" problems and the children who have physical limitations, the teacher also comes to realize that there are several students who seem to be very special in other ways. Some of these youngsters finish their work more quickly than do others. Often they delve more deeply into all school subjects or they have a very sophisticated knowledge of a specific subject area, or they have special hobbies and/or extraordinary talents. Many of them also seem to have much more "adult" and/or novel explanations of almost everything. With just a little interaction the teacher suspects that these children are "gifted" and recommends them for the *gifted program.*

Gifted programs are generally of two distinct types, conceived as either enrichment programs or accelerated programs. The enrichment programs are designed to let children experience additional material, subject matter, or environments that the "regular non-gifted" children do not get to experience. Accelerated programs allow the gifted child to advance in traditional subject matter, but in a faster and/or more comprehensive manner. Many college students were once youngsters eligible for gifted programs.

Another group of special youngsters is comprised of those who have physical and/or processing difficulties. During the past several decades most school systems have made outstanding progress in "including" these children, some of whom are also *gifted.* However, there are still teachers who do *not* make the necessary transfers for their inclusion, or claim not to have the resources that these children need. Actually some teachers do *not* have the extra help and resources that these children need. Regardless, much like other "problem" children, these youngsters still must remain in the system. More importantly they ought not to *get lost in the system.*

Generally, the teacher *refers* these children (i.e., sends these special students to be *tested*). The school/county psychologist is usually the person who administers the tests to students with problems as well as to those who are thought to be gifted. Most often the tests are standardized instruments selected by the psychologist who individually examines each referred child. The individual school or school district has previously determined just what "scores" a youngster needs in order to be labeled a "problem" or a "gifted" student. One might ask how it is that a teacher comes to recognize these *exceptional* students so quickly. Of course, it is the *behavior* of each individual (good, bad, or nothing) that commands the teacher's notice. These students are not "bad" or "good" because of their test results; it is their behavior that the teacher notices that gets them tested. After the children have been tested, they will come back to the classroom and behave either as "problem" students or as "gifted" students. *It is not the test that makes the behavior; it is the behavior that stimulates the testing.* The teacher knows little more about these children after they have been examined than before the teacher sent them for testing.

Many of the teacher's "problem" students also seem to have "problem" parents; "gifted" or "special" children seem to have "gifted" and/or "special" parents. These parents want to have a good deal of interaction and involvement with the school as well as with the teacher and sometimes assume expertise that they do not possess. For example, some of these parents are not pleased when they realize that criteria to be eligible for the district's "gifted program" or "college for kids" or any other "special program" may be somewhat different from school to school, county to county, or state to state. Actually, what counts as gifted or problematic is generally some arbitrary cut-off score representing the highest or lowest portion of scores when comparing a certain youngster with others of the same age. If the child "passes" the test (i.e., gets above/below the pre-selected cut-off score) then the child is said to either have a "problem" or to be "gifted." Many parents are extremely pleased when their child has been labeled with high test scores and express with great pride that their child is in the "gifted program." Usually, these parents justify advanced experiences as being necessary to engage their child, to keep the youngster from being bored, or to make sure that their child is getting the attention that the child's intellect and/or special talent requires. Some parents might even *shop* for the school or teacher that will recognize how special their child really is. Thus, the teacher has two different kinds of problems with parents—one group that wants too much control and another group that seemingly does not want any control or interaction whatsoever.

The teacher now has many sets of special youngsters, some of whom will probably participate in "pull out" programs. The students with problems will get extra attention; the students who are gifted will get extra attention; the children who have physical or processing difficulties will get extra attention. Many teachers who enjoy getting some extra help with (or reprieve from) their "problem students" resent the absence from class of their best students. They reason that regular students also benefit from interaction with these youngsters. Yet perhaps all students would benefit from interacting with one another. Sometimes schools "track" or assign students to different classes according to ability levels and/or disabling conditions. The issue of "tracking" receives ongoing debate and is extremely controversial. However, we are beginning to notice many "special" youngsters who have been included in all of the school's activities and learning environments, albeit with many unique modifications. Teachers who previously thought that they could not include these students are now finding ways to accommodate them.

It would seem that all children—the gifted, almost gifted, high normal, normal, low normal, slow, very slow, as well as children who are physically limited, or "problematic" in other ways probably need many of the same things—to achieve both socially and academically in every way possible. What the teacher needs to know is what to do with all of these "special" students.

Who is special? —Everyone.

WHO HAS THE RESPONSIBILITY?

Teacher X has an extremely difficult problem child, specifically a problem boy. No one seems to know why, but most problem students are boys. In almost every situation when this youngster should be acting one way, he is acting another. His behavior gets constantly worse in the classroom until the teacher can take it no longer. The teacher passes the point of feeling frustrated and, if honest, may even admit dislike toward this source of constant irritation. The teacher decides to find out just what the student's problem is. The student is sent to the school counselor and, after an extensive battery of tests, social reports, and time-consuming investigation, the teacher gets an answer: "Johnny is a problem child." On every one of the "problem child tests" (personality scales), he scored extremely high. Not only did all the tests indicate that he was indeed a problem child (exhibited deviant associations), but the report concerning his home life was even worse. Teacher X cannot help feeling pity when learning of his terrible home situation and begins to wonder how he survived as well as he did. Teacher X discusses his home situation with a close colleague, and both of them marvel anew at how bad life for some children can actually be. Johnny continues to be a problem child, but now his teachers *"know why"* (high test scores—bad home). He may not even finish school; he will probably grow, continually harassing society, and end up in other more stigmatized institutions. "How tragic, but what can a teacher do with a home situation like that?" Obviously nothing—the end?

Johnny is a complex organism. Among his many attributes is the ability for exceptional discrimination. All of his empirical senses provide a basis for remarkable differentiation. At an early age (approximately six months) he could even discriminate among people. He learned what to touch and what not to touch; he learned a complex language system; he learned auditory and visual discriminations; he learned to yell at playtime and not to sit quietly during individual study periods. He even learned to "put on" a teacher when he could get away with it.

Of course Johnny is a "problem child." That is precisely why he was sent to the counselor. And how unfortunate that there are many "diagnosticians" whose major purpose is merely to confirm the prognosis of the teacher—if their terminology can be understood. Johnny will continue to be a problem child until someone teaches him different responses. He has learned a repertoire of responses to deal with his world; the more antisocial his home environment, the more deviant his responses.

The truly pathetic situation is that no one will teach Johnny and change his behavior. The only place there is some hope for Johnny is in school. Yet many teachers quickly abdicate responsibility once his history is known. *Johnny can discriminate*. He can be taught new responses to deal with the other world outside the home. He can learn to read, write, and spell; he can learn new rules of social interaction and thereby break the cycle of his past. If cooperation with the home is not possible, he can even learn these responses *in spite of a bad home*.

It is not easy to deal with the Johnnys. They take time, energy, and a disciplined teacher. All the Johnnys do not change for the better or even survive, yet, for these children, *the school is their only hope*.

Who has the responsibility of discipline? —The teacher.

WHY DON'T THEY LEARN?

Many questions have been raised in relation to why children do not learn. Sometimes even if youngsters are "learning," invidious comparisons are made when parents read about higher test scores in other schools. Too often, criticism comes from proponents of this question who do not support their queries with long-term constructive encouragement or positive alternatives. Instead, scathing indictments are directed toward those very teachers who spend a great deal more time worrying about why some children do not learn than do most of their critics. In every aspect of learning, continued educational research is needed to ascertain and remediate learning difficulties. Yet, at present, the teacher must strive to do the best job possible.

Education is stressed in many ways in our culture. Quite naturally we often assume that everyone wants to learn. We even assume that they want to learn what we want them to learn. Some children do not want to learn. Others do not want to learn what we think they should learn. The reaction of the teacher should not be amazed bewilderment (the teacher's reinforcement history includes values established through sixteen years of learning), but a basic question: *Why should they want to learn?* Some children must be taught to be motivated, curious, or interested, that is, to establish their own goals. Other children are just too comfortable to learn. Why should one learn to speak, let alone properly, if all desires are met without this particular mode of verbal symbolization? Why should one learn a difficult mathematics system if gazing out the window passes the time better? Why should one practice spelling if one finds that more attention is received when one wanders around the room or writes a "special note" or plays at the pencil sharpener or does any number of things more fun than spelling?

Most children bring a natural curiosity to school. One of the greatest joys for teachers who choose to teach at the early childhood level is to interact with this wonderful naiveté. Other children have been systematically taught to love learning by their parents who have spent countless hours reading to, interacting with and explaining to their children. Some children once had a love for learning, but somehow experienced an untoward environment or maybe a punishing teacher who extinguished it. For these children *the desire to learn must be taught or re-taught.* Appropriate learning behaviors, such as good study habits, paying attention, or working for long periods, must be established that provide some reward for the child. No thinking adult wastes time in idle pursuits that are difficult and meaningless. How can the teacher expect everyone automatically to want to learn, especially when it may represent work?

Why don't they learn? —Because the rewards of learning have not been firmly established.

WHAT IF IT'S WORK?

Most people assume the responsibility of work. We speak often about work: working on a project, going to work, getting work, finishing our work, yet we have a burgeoning conspiracy to turn work into play. Most teachers realize the importance of making work as palatable as possible. If students get excited about work, they consider it play, and everyone is much happier. The ingenious teacher has striven for years to turn work tasks into play. The great teachers are those who are able to elicit a pleasurable response toward the most rigorous pursuits and make the most difficult tasks pleasant.

Unfortunately, our highly technological society has turned many work tasks into play without a corresponding discipline toward those tasks that entail "work-work" as opposed to "play-work." The young girl's delight in finally building her very own model airplane wanes appreciably when she is confronted with a common battery-propelled toy that flies instantly and can be purchased for a fraction of her allowance. The young boy's joy in actually learning how to read music quickly dissipates when given a computer game where he can play any tune he chooses with very little effort or personal creativity. Most adults will testify with pride to those endeavors that represented, for them, hard work and true discipline. Patience, repetition, and arduous industry are still required for long-term achievement and happiness in almost every activity of life. Yet we have more and more "instant avenues to success." The problem for today's teacher is not only in structuring "play-work" (technology is providing wonderful aids in this regard), but also in teaching the necessary discipline for long-term rewards as well (i.e., establishing maturity).

If behaviors conducive to long-term goals are not acquired early, it is much less likely that they will be acquired at all. If a child does not learn early in life to work hard and long for specific goals, then the child is not likely to change with age. Today's schools provide many extracurricular activities with almost as much turnover as there are activities. The possibilities for diverse activities become greater and greater for the growing child. Almost all one's time can be spent changing from one activity to another. Consider specialized fields, such as music, art, and creative writing. How many times have we said as adults, "I'd give anything to play like that, or to paint like that, or to write like that?" Of course, we would not. We know what it would take in time and effort. The irony is not that we do not often have such skills; it is that we do not have enough understanding concerning the importance of long-term skill acquisition to appreciate the skill evidenced in others and to ensure that our students stay with an activity or task long enough to master it.

This should not indicate that the teacher ought to take pride in being a punishing taskmaster. It is extremely unlikely that students will want to continue learning (past formal experiences) if their true "reward" for learning (working) has been merely to have the gruesome experience stop. The secret for developing the capacity for work is to stretch the length of time between rewards so that the student will strive through some misery to seek long-term goals: Goals that culminate in a college degree, creative writing skills, continued reading of great literature, ongoing enjoyment in listening to music masterpieces, or an insatiable desire for scientific precision.

Thus, the problem for the teacher is not only to make work tasks pleasurable but also to develop the capacity for work. *This constitutes a process of teaching for delayed rewards over an ever-increasing temporal span.*

What if it's work? —Then work it must be and the capacity for work must be developed.

WHO DECIDES WHO DECIDES?

Power, by whatever name, is one of the most problematic of all behavioral interactions. When referring to physical objects in motion, such as a moving automobile, few people question the power of the car to damage a person's body; only the intent, skill, or responsibility of the driver are questioned. Some people seem to assume power over other people; others manifest power that is thought to be given to them, such as the power of elected officials to enforce laws. Literary sources often portray individuals seeking power—others avoiding it. Most of us, however, choose either to re-label power (especially in this age of the euphemism) or to pretend that power actually does not exist. We prefer, instead, to talk about responsibility, duty, or rights, as in the discussion in this chapter. Perhaps most of us would like to believe that no one has power over us and that anything we say or do is only by choice. Often it frightens us to realize the power that does exist, especially the power we, as teachers, have over our students. Not only are teachers often bigger, at least for a little while, but most of us also think faster than youngsters and, therefore, are able to "snow" them. We work through a problem quickly, we know many important facts, we answer a difficult question—*the awe and respect of students is very reinforcing.*

Often we use our sophistication to "manipulate" students into doing something that they do not think about: "Would you like to put your materials away before lunch?" We do not ask them, "Do you choose to be messy?" It seems that most often we do about "everything in our power" in order to impose our value systems on them: "Choose any story you wish . . . then we will take a vote on it . . . you must take turns . . . now we do want our room to be clean don't we . . . of course you don't take money from another student without asking . . . etc." It would appear that most of what we just assume to be the correct thing to do represents the imposition of our value system on the student. Probably almost all of our "acculturating process" actually represents the imposition of values, whether these values come from home, school, community, church, or elsewhere. Who decides a child should read, write, spell, not steal, or finish school? Teachers who have not thought about these activities as an "imposition of their values" sometimes become extremely upset and state, "Well, how do you expect the child to live a happy life or get a decent job or anything else!" "I can't sit by and watch that child hurt himself." "Do you expect me to be silent when I know she's ruining her life by quitting school now?" At the same time, teachers may say, "I do want my students to think for themselves and I want them to establish their own values. . ."

Teachers who do not make clear differentiation in their own thinking about who decides who decides probably will have many problems. Teachers are charged legally with the imposition of certain values concerning students' behavior. Many would say that ethically teachers ought to be responsible for much of the student's behavior, and some would say that is precisely what being a teacher is all about: to instill within each child the selected best from the cultural heritage in order that, following school, the young adult will function productively. Regardless, *who decides* is not nearly as difficult a question as *who decides who decides,* for most teachers truly want their students to be able to make decisions for themselves. Teachers therefore decide to allow their students to decide certain innocuous things: *When* do you choose to clean up your materials? *Where* can you be reached in case we need you? *Which* assignment do you choose to do first? With *whom* will you be leaving? *Where* do you want to do your work?

Teachers who start early to teach students precise definitions and specific allocations of power will be better able to deal with apparent inequities as situations arise. Some teachers refer to this structuring as "defining limits" or specifying acceptable behavior regarding such aspects as social relationships, propriety, honesty, and so on. If a person is taught early that a teacher is not always right or an all-knowing genius, and that teachers do not always evidence perfect taste, heal all wounds, or even "understand" some of the latter ones, then the child might not have to be so disenchanted when discovering our feet of clay. If a teacher states precisely what power resides with the teacher and what decisions rest with the student, perhaps the student will continuously strive to earn more privileges rather than to feel sorry for him/herself by not being permitted to do something. Issues regarding power are not easy to think through, nor are their behavioral contingencies easy to establish. Much like issues concerning "fairness," problems relating to power rest on the values of all individuals concerned. Even some adults have not established who decides who decides in regard to major issues concerning themselves and their employees or even spouses. Also, in the upper grades teachers and students must often decide to *agree to disagree* if harmony is to prevail. Anger is not reinforced in relation to those decisions that we definitely believe are not ours—only with those decisions that we believe ought to be within our own control and not someone else's.

Who decides who decides? —As far as the student is concerned, the teacher.

STUDY GUIDE FOR CHAPTER 2

Questions:

1. What is suggested as an important variable in being an effective teacher?

* 2. List the three states in which children are considered to be born. Explain the teacher's role in each. What is your position?

3. Why is a traditional analysis of a child's problem behavior often unproductive?

* 4. Why do you think there is such a disparity in what teachers desire to do and what they actually do in classroom settings?

* 5. Why do teachers give more approval to academic behavior than they do to social behavior?

6. What is a "special" child? What is special about all children? What should the teacher do with these special children?

7. Describe why some children may not want to learn. Explain why they are not just "born that way." Provide an explanation of what can be done.

8. Where does this analysis put the notion of motivation? Since motivation is typically referred to as an "inner" state, explain why unmotivated behavior is not explained this way.

9. Why is the capacity for work necessary? How is the capacity for work developed? Some people are industrious and some are lazy; how is this difference analyzed?

*10. What is meant by "who decides who decides?"

*Answer these questions within your subject matter area (e.g., Language Arts, Social Studies, Physical Education, Advanced Mathematics).

LEARNING ACTIVITY 3 — HUMAN ECOLOGY AND REINFORCEMENT: POTENTIAL SPHERES OF BEHAVIORAL INFLUENCE

1. Write or discuss what the teacher can realistically expect to accomplish based upon the following diagram. Keep in mind the question "Who has the responsibility?" for specific behaviors, and that the student is subject to many potentially contradictory sources of reinforcement, but also possesses abilities to learn discrimination and therefore behave differently under different conditions. Discuss your ideas with other participants.

2. List different behaviors that adults exhibit under the following conditions: (a) sports events, (b) in church, (c) eating in a restaurant, (d) watching TV, and (e) playing tennis.

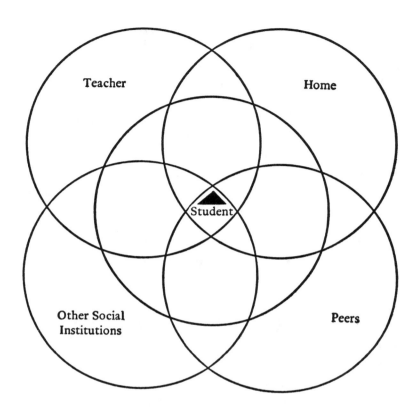

LEARNING ACTIVITY 4 —
DEVELOPING TECHNIQUES FOR SPECIAL LEARNERS

Many problems arise regarding "special" students. Often discussions center on "techniques" regarding what *to do* with certain youngsters without separating the values from the techniques used to effect the values. Sometimes determining values is a group decision made by a local school board. Often state and national governments determine the values (laws). Each person should have previously thought about what his/her teaching situation will be in relationship to special populations. The person who states "What am I supposed to do with those children who have special problems," often is confusing values with techniques (perhaps purposely) and not preparing the necessary specific techniques for the realities of today's schools.

This exercise is designed to assess specific values/techniques regarding the inclusion of all students. Only after individual and collective values are differentiated should techniques be developed to implement the value system. It is important that each student begin to "think through" these issues on a personal basis. Participants should first become aware of all local, state and national policies. Next students should write a one-page essay describing the approaches he/she might use, presupposing that every classroom will include every possible student grouping within a community, regardless of intellectual ability, level of learning, mental/physical challenges and so on.

As you write down specific techniques, assume that you can make a consequential and important difference with every child who has special problems and/or special needs. Some prospective professionals (therapists, special education teachers, etc.) must assume that their entire teaching environment will be filled with children who have special needs. Initially, a prospective high school teacher might think, "I am not interested in remedial work, I only want to teach those students who intend to go on to college" yet the realities of state and national legislation makes this assumption untenable and use of inclusive techniques required. Or a high school instrumental music teacher might think, "I want everyone in my bands, the entire school if they all wish, but I want to have at least one really good performing group, even it is a very small ensemble." This assumption may, or may not be tenable, if provisions are made to include all youngsters. Again, the instrumental music teacher needs an alternative approach.

In this exercise it is important to approach the topic as honestly as possible regarding the learning environment that will actually exist when one enters the teaching profession. Many times prospective teachers idealize anticipated settings. Other class members might not have thought through the issues and sincerely do not know how they actually might deal with aspects of inclusion. Nevertheless, it is important to begin preparation as soon as possible.

After each individual has written individual essays, the class should be separated into small groups of approximately four to six to discuss implementation techniques. The small group discussions should take place for 15-20 minutes after which the groups should be changed. This interaction will begin to stimulate ideas and strategies. It is important during these discussions that students not "fight" with each other (i.e., "How can you believe that! You want to just teach the best and shoot the rest?"). Class discussions might include several rules such as listening without interruption and agreeing to disagree. Sincere attempts to start building a repertory of instructional interventions will help each prospective teacher begin the necessary process for effective work in any setting.

CHAPTER **3**

Learning— The Modification of Behavior

WHAT IS BEHAVIOR MODIFICATION?

Behavior is a common word that is used casually in referring to many things. The term *behavior*, as used in this book, refers to *anything* a person does, says, or thinks that can be observed directly and/or indirectly. Besides referring to specific cause-and-effect relationships, behavior modification includes techniques for changing behavior. A well-behaved student is one who behaves in ways that the teacher and/or student thinks are appropriate to the situation. It should also be noted that every behavior modification program, when used with people, is actually a cognitive/behavioral program in that one is dealing with thinking, reasoning organisms.

Principles for teaching (shaping appropriate behaviors) should not be confused with other issues. It is important that techniques of behavior modification not be confused with the use of these same techniques to implement specific values. Many teachers regard the questions concerning *why, what,* and *for whom* as certainly more important than *how*. Therefore, after teachers have decided what is to be learned and why it is to be learned (i.e., chosen their values), a behavioral approach will help them go about teaching it. Also, teachers are encouraged to involve their students in these decisions whenever possible. There is a simple rationale to explain the efficacy of behavioral approaches. Simply stated, *behavioral change must be based on a reason:* People work for things that bring pleasure; people work for approval of loved ones; people change behaviors to satisfy desires they have been taught; people avoid behaviors they associate with unpleasantness; people act in similar ways to behaviors they have often repeated. The behavior modification approach actually comes from science and represents nothing more than simple (and sometimes complex) cause-and-effect relationships.

The scientific study of human behavior, or the study of cause-and-effect relationships, should not be confused with other value choices. As was stated in Chapter 1, it is generally useful to distinguish between values and techniques. For example, a positive value that many teachers hold is to teach youngsters to read (even if the desire to read is *not* present in the child). Once this value, and perhaps its imposition, have been determined, then the teacher may choose various techniques to effect the desired reading behavior. Application of a behavioral technique to establish this value would be concerned with the effects of academic feedback and/or other reinforcements on the youngster concerning shaping desired responses in relationship to the target goal (reading). It is important to realize that many values other than reading might be decided by the teacher, as well as other techniques to effect whatever values the teacher may choose to teach. Some teachers choose to have students raise hands for teacher attention, some do not. Some teachers specify "quiet time"; others prefer the "hum of industry." Some teachers choose "communication" as a value and spend a great deal of time in verbal interaction; others spend more time helping students interact with subject matter. Behavioral techniques can be used to implement any or all of these values. Students may be taught (reinforced) to raise hands, not to raise hands, or any combination depending upon the situation. The "hum of industry" can be implemented as can "quiet time" or any combination thereof depending on the circumstances and activity of the teacher. Students can be taught to communicate or to remain silent or to alternate during various time periods.

Techniques also can be used to implement what many teachers consider extremely negative values. Children can be effectively taught to cheat, lie, hit, steal, and even to "hate school." Of course, the selection of any technique represents a certain value choice; if one chooses a behavioral technique, then the determination of appropriate "reinforcers" represents an important value choice. However, basic social and academic values to be taught to students should not be confused with issues concerning techniques for implementation. It is assumed that Jesus, Socrates, and Moses were effective behaviorists. So was Hitler.

Some teachers might say, "Yes, but isn't that a cold approach?" Certainly not. Even though behavior modification is based on scientific principles verified in the laboratory, it is largely the nature of material to be learned that represents important value choices. Actually, because of its consistency and simplicity, behavior modification or cognitive/behavior modification effected and applied by means of contingent reinforcement (approval-disapproval) represents a very kind and understandable system to students of all ages. The behavioral scientist who observes a classroom activity can behaviorally classify almost everything that goes on, regardless of how well the teacher may understand principles of reinforcement. Cause-and-effect behaviors are always present. For example, some teachers do not realize the effects of their own behavior on their students. Others do not understand the effects of their own approval or disapproval and do not realize when they are being sarcastic: "Why don't you just stand up and tell the *whole class*, Jimmy?" Whereupon Jimmy does! In such a situation teachers may unwittingly reinforce a wrong behavior, and problems are created because the student is not really sure of the teacher's meaning. Being taken literally is the price one pays for using sarcasm. The applied behavior analyst could demonstrate how teachers might be more effective in the application of the teacher's own values through the judicious use of behavioral principles. Many teachers are actually surprised to learn how closely they approximate a fairly comprehensive behavioral approach, especially when giving academic feedback. After being apprised of behavioral principles, many teachers exclaim, "Why, that's what I've been doing all the time!"

What is behavior modification? —Techniques for implementing values.

IS BEHAVIOR BEING MODIFIED?

A high school teacher stops by a student working on math and checks correct/incorrect responses. This teacher has observed that most students learn more efficiently when they are given prompt *academic feedback*. He is using a principle of behavior modification to improve academic performance.

He goes back to his desk to correct assignments. It is important to him that he finish by the end of the day. He has discovered that, by randomly picking out a different day of the week for students to receive corrected papers, he can dramatically increase their academic performance. Again, behavior modification.

The same teacher seeks another student engrossed in his work assignment. He moves quickly to this student's seat, smiles, and whispers in his ear, "It's good to see you working on your assignment." He has noticed that if he can praise him while he does his work *without the other students noticing*, the student works much more. When the teacher recognized him while he was not working, this student used to be the "class clown." Both situations represent behavior modification, but achieved very different teacher goals.

An elementary school teacher goes to her desk to correct assignments. A little boy comes quickly to her desk and asks a question. She ignores him completely and calmly goes about correcting her papers. He stays about 15 seconds and then goes back to his work. The teacher smiles to herself as she checks a chart designed for this particular boy. She has almost extinguished his habit of running to her desk (only once this week; initially he did it 28 times a day and that was *after* she started recording it). The teacher sets her handkerchief on her desk as a reminder to go to this child after he has been in his seat for a few minutes. She hopes that his question was not a really important one, that it can wait two or three minutes.

She waits for a few minutes and then takes the time to check on the child who came to her desk—he wanted to know if he could get a book from the library—she returns to her seat. She hears Suzy starting to talk to her neighbor. The teacher immediately gets up, goes to Suzy, and firmly tells her that she should stop visiting until her work is done. The teacher notices that Suzy appears a little sad. She is a sensitive child, and the teacher has long since discovered that a bit of teacher disapproval will halt her inappropriate behavior. *Behavior modification.*

As two students fight instead of quietly visiting, the middle school teacher thinks about the token system the school counselor is trying to establish in some of the rooms. She has read many reports about "token economy" systems and understands that they represent an effective application of behavioral principles, but she does not choose the technique for her class. She has never liked material rewards for learning (except for herself) and prefers to use other things instead. Besides, she cannot imagine how her class could be much worse than it is. She really is discouraged. She knows also that the counselor sometimes uses very strong disapproval as well as a special "time-out room" for some students. The effects of his procedures are well documented and consistent with behavioral approaches, but she prefers not to use them. She tries to reason with her students, but actually ends up yelling nearly all day long. She uses disapproval (almost 80 percent of the time) in efforts to modify social behavior, but generally with little effect. Although she knows that this interaction is about the same for most teachers, she sincerely wants to be more positive. Principles of behavior modification are indeed operating within this classroom, but the teacher's behavior, regardless of her intent, is not producing the desired effect.

Across the hall, another teacher interacts quietly with her students. She also does not like the counselor's particular token system. She has decided to become more contingent with her own verbal behavior alone. At first it was difficult, not "natural." She had to learn to effectively use techniques of behavior modification in order to reinforce certain academic and social behaviors. Now, when she hears the loud adult voice in the adjoining classroom, she thinks about the discussion of honesty she had with a colleague. Should a teacher be honestly disapproving most of the time because it is a "natural" response? She has decided no.

She stands in front of her class. "Students, I would like your attention. Suzy's looking at me. Good, Sam. Now David's looking at me. Now I have everyone's attention. Thank you." (Again, behavior modification). "You may all stop your individual work now and visit until time for music. . . ." (When the students helped make class rules earlier in the year, they expressed a desire for individual talk time. Establishing rules with student help represents a value that has very little to do with behavior modification.)

The above paragraphs describe procedures whose efficacy or non-efficacy has been documented in behavioral research. In essence, this research shows that behavior is maintained and shaped by its consequences. It should be apparent from the above that behavior modification or cognitive/behavior modification represents the use of a series of scientifically verified techniques that may be used to promote more effective learning of both social and academic subject matter. A behavioral approach does not help the teacher decide why, what, and who is going to learn. These issues represent important value choices. However, after questions relating to these values have been answered, behavioral principles may be used to enhance learning of appropriate behavior.

Is behavior being modified? —Always, but not necessarily in the direction we choose.

IS SOCIAL BEHAVIOR IMPORTANT?

It should be obvious from the above that for learning purposes we must be able to specify *behaviors* that can in some manner measure what is being taught and learned. Much academic subject matter is made up of symbols that can be demonstrated and measured. Yet, teachers are also concerned with establishing correct *social* responses. Many teachers do not make a distinction between social and academic behavior and assume that everything must be learned. Indeed, this is a prevalent attitude among teachers of small children as well as teachers dealing with "special students." Teachers of older students, however, often make a major distinction when dealing with academic behavior as opposed to social behavior. This distinction expresses itself in various ways and deals with what teachers believe that they *must* teach (academic material) versus that which they believe the students should already know (appropriate social responses).

This distinction is perhaps best understood concerning assessment procedures when contrasting a *merit* approach versus a *demerit* approach. While almost everyone agrees that students must learn the academic material in order to earn their academic grades (merit approach), social behavior is often graded on a demerit system. A merit approach assumes that students start from nothing (or build on previously learned material) and earn their grades; it does not assume that students already know the material. A demerit approach assumes that a student starts from perfection (knows all of the responses and should continually exhibit them) and points or grades are "taken away" for misbehavior. Sometimes the demerit consists of a check mark, writing the student's name on the board, or a statement such as "not satisfactory" or "needs improvement" indicating a condition less than 100%.

Most report cards for older students evidence this same distinction. Students earn academic grades; students lose their social grades. Thus, a student may receive 2 A's, 3 B's, and a C for academic work, and receive no social *demerits*. Or perhaps this same student receives no demerits in four classes and a "needs improvement" in one class and an "unsatisfactory" in another. Generally, academic grades are received for learning something, and social grades are received for not being "perfect"; often the *best* social grade is nothing. While most teachers do not assume that their students already know all of the academic subject matter, all social behavior is thought to have been previously learned such that one can only receive a demerit for misbehaving and receive nothing for "being nice." Now consider an opposite situation. What if academic grades were given on a demerit system with everyone receiving straight A's after which students would lose some of their grades when they evidenced incorrect academic responses or gave wrong answers? What if social grades had to be earned? What if students had to earn their social grades starting from nothing? What if a student got 2 A's, 3 B's, and one C for exhibiting correct *social behavior*, and a "not satisfactory" or "needs improvement" for *academic* work.

It should be obvious that there are differences between merit and demerit approaches. These distinctions are prevalent throughout many schools as well as most of society, whereby most people believe that academic and job related material must be learned, and bad behavior must be punished. Correct academic behavior gets a lot of positive approval; incorrect social behavior receives a lot of disapproval, and "ignorance is no excuse for breaking the rules." Yet, *if all behavior must be learned* then correct social behavior needs the same kind of support (reinforcement) as do academic tasks.

For example, consider a positive program where "academic" and "social" are purposefully not differentiated, where all behaviors must be learned, and where ideas (values) concerning appropriate behavior are very specific. If one were to read the Scouting oath, one would find little guidance for meaningful action. A Scout is admonished to be *cheerful, obedient, kind, trustworthy*, and so on. Yet, if the young person is left with only those *words* it seems doubtful that the ideas could be acted upon or that they would provide much guidance. Fortunately, many extremely specific programs are promulgated, appropriately sequenced, and reinforced with a highly effective token system (merit badges), culminating in overt behaviors. For example, swimming, along with simulated life saving, is a specific behavior that is often necessary to progress through the ranks of Scouting. One can feel as *"helpful"* or *"prepared"* as one is able. But to *"be prepared"* is to have specific skills, to prepared to do something. Some young people might even quit Scouting because they never learn the overt act of swimming. It is unlikely that an action program, such as Scouting, would benefit from replacing the action preparation with an increased litany of verbal utterances, such as "trustworthy," "loyal," "helpful," "friendly," and so on.

Contrast the Scouting program and its highly organized and "hands on" approach with the vague and nebulous theoretical constructs sometimes found in education writing and research where what one does is not left to stand alone, but is renamed or, even worse, is used to justify elaborate theories that perhaps only exist in the conceptual reality of the investigator. In an attempt to give meaning to human behavior, we often give explanations that merely rename specific overt functions in different language or suggest other "reasons" for actions. This may not provide "greater understanding" and actually might obfuscate the important issues of assessing cause–and–effect relationships. This is especially important when dealing with social values.

Is social behavior important? —Important enough to be specified and taught.

HOW DO WE GET FROM IDEAS TO BEHAVIORS?

Problems concerning adequate teaching of social values as well as documenting this learning seem truly complicated. No matter what we measure, and regardless of how skillfully we use words (or other symbolic representations), we still must depend on language if effective communication is to take place. There are some that argue that we should use fewer words, use words more adroitly, or perhaps use many words to suggest our "meaning." Others contend that we must rely on greater meaning through the insight developed between the reader and writer, or the teacher and student as an interactive constructive process. Of course, the subtle nuances of "body language" and vocal inflection also make a great deal of difference. It has been said that all expression depends on only a very few interpretive attributes— loud/soft, short/long, and slow/fast. Yet, the precise arrangement of these attributes is extremely important. It appears that much more cognitive research needs to be done in this area, especially concerning the subtleties of words and expressions to sort out their various meanings.

Yet, while this may indeed be the case, teachers are still left with the task of telling students, or in some other way arranging the environment such that a student "discovers" what to do, in order to demonstrate understanding. Additionally, the teacher most often must document these "understandings." Each separate skill or understanding (behavior) that the teacher has a student do must be documented such that it can be measured—an obvious necessity when dealing with accountability issues and/or specifying classroom rules. The beginning step in this process is to structure commonly used words that represent "ideas" or abstractions into specific, overt, demonstrable behaviors. It should be noted that even though all "words" may merely be symbolic representations, some words seem specific in their elicitation and, therefore, are preferred in describing empirical relationships. Thus, "verbalizes facts" appears more quantifiable than does "honest."

Most teachers believe students ought to be kind, communicative, cooperative, and sensitive. Yet, for these ideas to be effectively taught, they must be described in greater specificity such that they can be counted, that is, *helps others, talks with others, looks into eyes, shares materials, asks for help,* and so on. This specificity is very important when dealing with "classroom rules." We must define our values (rules) so that the way a student acts provides some overt evidence as to whether the student is developing (or not developing) the particular patterns of responses that we desire. Every teacher usually demands this type of behavior in reference to academic responses (assessments, questioning, tests, etc.), yet does not specify as accurately concerning social behavior. *A specific behavior is anything a person does that can be observed and measured.* Ideas are generally made more and more behavioral as behaviors are specified in observable and measurable terms. This is obviously the first step in structuring any learning sequence: To define values so that the behavior of the student provides some indication that social/academic learning is taking place. This seems especially important when dealing with young children (or others) who have limited ability for abstract thought.

Yet, while very young children are generally not skilled at advanced academic quantification, they are quite good at describing social behavior. For example, if a child is asked what she/he does to make his/her mother happy, the child might say such things as "clean up my own mess" or "make my bed so my mother does not have to," or "come in from playing when my mother calls me." If a child is asked what the child does to make the teacher happy, the child might say, "do all of my work," or "let everyone be the boss and play on the bars one at a time," or "be quiet going to the lunch room," etc.

Alternately, when adults are asked to describe specific overt behaviors dealing with social values, they have a strong tendency to describe ideas with other ideas instead of with measurable *behaviors.* For example, an adult may say "empathetic" or "sensitive" when attempting to describe "communicative," or "explores" for "creativity," or "reads with understanding" for the idea of "comprehension." And while other adults might "understand" what these definitions mean, the definitions are not specific enough to be measured and counted. While it would be possible to observe "eye contact" when people communicate, it would be difficult to count the numbers of "sensitives" or "empathics" while observing people communicating. It might be that when adults state these ideas (as opposed to describing overt behavior), they actually may be "thinking" about some observable behavior. For example, a person might state a similar idea such as "improvises" for the *idea* of creativity, yet be thinking about an actual improvised musical performance (behavior).

The main point concerning the above is that, as teachers, we may well engage in a sort of pretend (some might say pretentious) game of "understanding" that actually might not exist, especially when describing what our students (especially our older students) learn as far as social values are concerned. That is, so long as we continue to use concepts and words that we do not—or cannot—adequately define and/or measure, we might not answer some of our most important questions: What are the specific ingredients of social interaction that elicit appropriate responses? Can these responses be measured? Can they be learned? Can they become more predictable?

When the teacher is successful in getting students to engage in specific overt behaviors, the teacher will probably come to realize that there are very few overt behaviors that can be described by many social ideas. For example, observable behaviors, such as "touches someone" or "engages in an activity together," can be subsumed under all of the following separate ideas: *Appreciative, Communicative, Kind, Cooperative, Sensitive, Empathetic,* etc. Indeed, there seem to be only a limited number of behavioral descriptors that can be observed, whereas there appear to be almost an infinite number of ideas that can be used to describe these behaviors. While this may seem surprising, completion of Learning Activity #5 will demonstrate this tendency.

Specificity is the key to behavioral analysis; the teacher must deal with each specific situation in order to teach proper associations. Differentiating in terms of one specific behavior that should occur in a particular situation is necessary for effective teaching. In academic work, most teachers would not begin to classify children into all-inclusive categories. Because Mary is excellent in spelling does not mean that she is exceptional in geography. Similarly, because she does not constantly disrupt the class does not necessarily indicate that she is "well-behaved." Is it not curious that when referring to the many social skills necessary for students, we tend toward greater classification with much less justification, considering the magnitude of individual responses to social stimuli? These classifications are even more undesirable if we consider that in our complex communication, we have developed a certain "shorthand" for descriptive purposes. Words such as "love," "motivation," and "discipline" are used as though these words had meaning apart from specific situations.

Of course, it would be extremely difficult "to communicate" without using such a "short-word system." We should remember, however, that each situation is different. Every particular word refers to many different behaviors, and each association merits specific consideration. We must remember to deal individually with each behavior. When speaking of the "value of discipline," we should specify both the nature of each situation and the response. We must specify exactly *what* happens as well as *when* it happens. We must specify the nature of the situation (antecedent), the response, and the consequences that follow. When we use the word "discipline" as an abstraction referring to many separate behaviors, we must realize that definitions of discipline must be specific to certain behaviors if the teaching of proper associations is to take place. Disciplining a student, therefore, means something different in each situation if procedures are to be effective.

How do we get from ideas to behaviors? —By specifying appropriate and inappropriate behavior for every situation.

IS SUBJECT MATTER DISCIPLINE?

The recent impetus for behavioral theory, or reinforcement theory, or whatever one chooses to call behavioral principles, substantially grew from the works of B. F. Skinner. Programmed instruction is the best-known result of this initial work, as are many other "systems" relating to teaching, treating mental illness, behavioral research, and clinical psychology. Indeed, the entire rationale concerning behavior modification is that behavior is *learned*. What behavior? *All behavior, including knowledge of subject matter.* Behavior thusly defined includes emotional responses, attitudes, reading, listening, talking, looking into the mirror, liking a person, wanting to talk out a problem, hitting, being frustrated, staying "on-task," getting "off-task," responding appropriately to the desires of a teacher, not responding to the desires of a teacher, all "good" behavior, all "bad" behavior, disturbing the class, being well behaved, being excited about learning, hating to learn, and so on—and so on—and so on.

The most basic reductions of reinforcement theory as an explanation to assess a person's responses at any given time are the following: (1) a person has *not learned*, (2) a person has learned correct associations, or (3) a person has learned *incorrect* associations. Exactly the same principles are used to teach subject matter as are used to teach appropriate social skills. If the teacher wishes that children have a real desire to learn a particular subject matter then the teacher must structure the external environment so that children will seek the structured contingent rewards for their academic work tasks. After initial manipulation, the rewards for learning will often come from the reinforcement of the learning material itself. Incidentally, this is precisely what most teachers do when they initially make a "game out of learning." The children become enthused concerning the game, *per se*, not realizing that it is a subtle hoax to stimulate effective learning. Curiously, some teachers who try desperately to make learning "fun" also say they reject any "manipulation techniques."

The teacher's job is to structure learning experiences. This structuring process involves manipulating the environment conducive to effective learning, whether the goal is simple word associations, complex problem solving, or concept formation. It would seem that the teacher should structure as wisely as possible. One should know the subparts necessary to any complex academic task (e.g., English, reading, algebra, history) and structure the situation in order that each child have a "rewarding learning experience." It can be seen that even in reference to our most cherished clichés, we allude to behavioral manipulation. It appears paradoxical for the teacher to reject manipulation when this is indeed the essence of the teacher's work.

Behavioral research demonstrates that if subject matter can be geared to the student at the student's own level and presented in logical sequences with appropriate feedback concerning correct/incorrect responses, then *learning will certainly take place.* In its most simple form, this includes teachers' (A) giving a student a specific instruction, (B) having the student respond, and (C) letting the student know whether the response was correct or incorrect. If correct learning does not take place then we must re-structure and sometimes use contingent rewards for successive approximations toward defined goals. The teacher's primary task is to ensure student learning.

Is subject matter discipline? —Yes.

ARE GOALS NECESSARY?

Traditionally, teachers have been instructed to prepare goals for the classroom. This usually represents, at best, a vague effort, often after the fact, to state formally toward what the learning experiences are aimed, that is, what should be the learning outcome. The major problem regarding goals is that they are usually stated in euphonious clichés: "To prepare for life in a democracy"; "To develop language skills"; "To understand the different cultures of the world"; "To develop an appreciation for music." What do such statements tell us? How will we know if we have achieved our "goals"? Some educators try to solve the problem by proposing even greater hierarchies, including overall philosophy, ideals, goals, instructional objectives, student objectives, formation of attitudes, and so on. While this may be important, problems still remain unless the teacher is much more specific. The problem is easily solved if the teacher states goals that represent overt behavior. How else, incidentally, will we know that a student "understands" or has "learned"?

The teacher must also decide whose goals are to be effected in the classroom—students', parents', administrators', and/or what combination. Often a beginning teacher does not realize that accepting a teaching position within a school carries with it the tacit acceptance of many pre-established values (goals). When a teacher agrees to teach within an established environment, the teacher is expected to enforce whatever "rules" and procedures exist. This may cause a conflict within the teacher; sometimes it causes a very troublesome conflict. A teacher might not have assumed when accepting a certain position that there might be many, many rules and previously agreed upon expectations that are to be enforced by the teacher. For example, the teacher may have very detailed procedures that she/he expects to use concerning "discipline" and find that the school has a completely different view of how all teachers should act. Or the teacher may have a certain expectation of what the specific "learning environment" should be and find that a supervisor has a very different expectation. A teacher may plan to have students earn certain privileges for learning and displaying appropriate social behavior and find that the entire school has previously established a demerit only system that progresses from small infractions to expulsion.

This represents a "who decides who decides" situation where the new teacher should be certain what procedures, expectations, and goals exist before accepting any teaching position. This is especially important when considering the large variety of schools that often exist within one city or school district. Specific goals for the teacher are as important as goals for the students, perhaps more so. All teacher expectations should be stated in behavioral terms: "Every teacher will physically supervise his/her students during lunch"; "All teachers will stay until all children have left the building"; "No teacher will contact any parent without checking with the assistant principal"; and so on. Goals stated in behavioral terms are important for the teacher because this is the only way that the teacher knows precisely how to act; the more specific the expectations, the less conflicts that will probably arise.

Goals stated in behavioral terms for students are not only manageable, they are also clear in defining the behaviors to be learned: "To be able to verbalize the Constitution, giving dictionary definitions to all words found therein"; "To recognize on a map the separate nations of the world"; "To differentiate between ten musical compositions"; or "To have a reading, writing, and spelling vocabulary of three hundred selected words." If concepts such as appreciation, understanding, or attitudes are to have meaning, these meanings should be defined in ways conducive to assessment. It is very easy to hide behind generalities. Sometimes such generalities generate many problems among students, teachers, parents, and administrators. If a teacher is to behave in certain ways then the teacher must know specifically what these expectations are. If children are to learn, then we must know precisely what it is they are to learn, how to teach it to them, and also how to determine if they have learned it.

Are goals necessary? —Certainly.

CAN BEHAVIOR BE MEASURED?

The most critical difference between a behavioral approach that pinpoints specific observable and measurable behaviors and other approaches to teaching is the keeping of behavioral records. Evaluation of any procedure instituted to induce learning (behavioral change) is virtually impossible without records. Formal and informal tests have always provided indications of academic behavioral change. Other indices of measurement, especially relating to social skills, have previously seemed to defy classification. It is possible, however, for the teacher to learn to assess social behaviors. Most individuals are not content to rely on a "feeling" concerning their bank balance, and the bank is even less likely to honor an overdrawn check because the depositor "feels" his balance is sufficient.

Is it not then curious that when we deal with the social behavior of human beings (who are more important than bank balances), we change rules, reinterpret contingencies, and fail to follow through because we "feel the behavior is really not that bad" or "feel" that the student really understands the regulations or perhaps "feel" that we may lose the student's respect? Measurement and specific records are crucial for accurate evaluation. The only difficulty regarding these classification procedures is that they take a little extra effort. Behavior always occurs in time intervals. If teachers are to know whether a particular social behavior is getting worse, better, or staying the same, the frequency of behavioral occurrences must be recorded *across time within specific time intervals.* Recording procedures are not difficult; one needs only paper, pencil, and some measure of time (clock).

For example, what if undesirable behavior in a particular classroom is defined as standing up? Instead of doing work at their desks, many students walk around the room. The first procedure would be to know precisely how much standing up is taking place (baseline). If this recording does not take place and the teacher first takes remedial steps then it will not be known if the undesired behavior is getting better, worse, or staying the same. It may seem that this procedure is not necessary. "Why not just tell them to sit down and see what happens?" The problem, however, arises *in time,* that is, some children will sit down immediately, but in the *long run* more children may stand. Even if the standing students do sit immediately, the problem may not be solved, it may continue with the other students across time. To conduct this type of recording, the teacher might assign a work task and then sit so as to see every student and count the number of children standing in a number of time intervals. After a few days of recording the number of such behavioral occurrences on one individual or on many, the teacher has some idea of the *frequency of the behavior.* A checklist at the students' desks also can be very effective.

The same basic procedure may be used for speaking out, talking, playing at desk, looking out the window, cheating, hitting, sharpening pencils, disturbing others, crying, or any other conceivable behavior (adaptive or deviant). It is important for the teacher to have a record for social behaviors as well as for academic behaviors. A general "all right" or "satisfactory" will not accurately assess a student's academic progress over a period of time; nor will it accurately assess a student's social behavior. The time these behaviors take to record does not compare to the time a teacher spends repeating instructions (nagging). It is interesting that one of the authors' experimental teachers who absolutely refused to "waste my time with all that book work" was recorded by experimental observers saying, "Now stop that talking," 143 times in one morning session. The teacher, with a minimum of effort, can develop checklists for assignments of any kind. This process represents nothing more than extending principles of record keeping across time within specific time intervals (for example, twenty minutes, A.M., P.M. during rest time, one day, one week, playtime, lunchtime, ten seconds, ninety seconds, or any other time period).

Can behavior be measured? —Easily.

STUDY GUIDE FOR CHAPTER 3

Questions:

* 1. What does the behavioral approach represent?

    2. Why is it possible to teach different values using identical techniques?

* 3. What types of behaviors are learned? Are any of these types amenable to change through behavior modification?

* 4. At any given time, a person's responses may be thought of as coming from one of three explanations. List these three explanations.

* 5. Why is it that some teachers do not realize that they are using principles of behavior modification?

* 6. What is specificity? State some specific academic values and some social values. How is it possible to specify values?

    7. What is the difference between a merit and a demerit system?

* 8. Be able to present the argument for specifying in detail the goals of education. Be able to analyze one of the generalities listed.

    9. Why is it necessary to record behavior?

   10. How might you record talking out, looking out the window, or a similar activity? (Remember, the first step is to define the behavior specifically, then to count it in some time interval such as the number of occurrences per 45 minutes, class period, hour, day.)

* Transfer the above questions to your subject area (e.g., Algebra, Art, Human Sciences).

LEARNING ACTIVITY 5 — TRANSLATING IDEAS (VALUES) INTO BEHAVIORS

The objective of Learning Activity 5 is to structure commonly used words that represent ideas (values) concerning social behavior into specific overt demonstrable behaviors. As has been previously stated, while all words may merely be symbolic representations, some words seem specific in their elicitation and, therefore, are preferred in describing empirical relationships. Thus "looks into eyes" appears much more quantifiable than "communicative."

Read the two examples under each idea and note How Observed and Counted Across. Next add two additional behaviors. Then fill in how they would be observed and the observational time intervals. Remember that the period of time a behavior might be measured across depends upon the urgency of dealing with the behavior, and the logical amount of time needed to determine whether or not the behavior is stable or infrequent (marriages are measured in years while eye contact would be recorded across seconds).

You may prefer to use actual behaviors that have been demonstrated in classrooms or to use behaviors you may wish students, or even yourself, to acquire.

Idea: Honesty

Behaviors	How Observed	Counted Across
1. Returns materials	visually	A.M./P.M.
2. Verbalizes facts	visually/aurally	days
3.		
4.		
5.		
6.		

Idea: Dishonesty

Behaviors	How Observed	Counted Across
1. Steals others' materials	visually	days, weeks
2. Fabricates experiences	aurally	days
3.		
4.		
5.		
6.		

Idea: Appreciation

Behaviors	*How Observed*	*Counted Across*
1. Says thank you	aurally	A.M./P.M.
2. Expresses positive facial expressions	visually	seconds
3.		
4.		
5.		
6.		

Idea: Democratic

Behaviors	*How Observed*	*Counted Across*
1. Votes	visually	months
2. Follows Rules	visually	minutes, A.M./P.M.
3.		
4.		
5.		
6.		

Idea: Kind

Behaviors	*How Observed*	*Counted Across*
1. Helps others with work tasks	visually	A.M./P.M., days
2. Brings a present	visually	days, weeks
3.		
4.		
5.		
6.		

Idea: Communication

Behaviors	*How Observed*	*Counted Across*
1. Talks with others	visually/aurally	minutes
2. Looks into eyes	visually	seconds
3.		
4.		
5.		
6.		

Idea: Good Human Relations

Behaviors	*How Observed*	*Counted Across*
1. Appropriate touching	visually	seconds
2. Interacts with everyone in class	visually	days, weeks
3.		
4.		
5.		
6.		

Idea: Cooperation

Behaviors	*How Observed*	*Counted Across*
1. Shares materials	visually	A.M./P.M., days
2. Asks for help	visually/aurally	A.M./P.M.
3.		
4.		
5.		
6.		

Idea: Sensitivity

Behaviors	*How Observed*	*Counted Across*
1. Appropriate talking	aurally	seconds, minutes
2. Picks up nonverbal motor cues	tactually	seconds
3.		
4.		
5.		
6.		

Idea: Creativity

Behaviors	*How Observed*	*Counted Across*
1. Writes using new word organization	visually	weeks, school term
2. Nonverbal expression in new media	visually	weeks
3. Divergent solutions to school, social, or building problems	aurally/visually	weeks
4.		
5.		
6.		

LEARNING ACTIVITY 6—YOUR BEHAVIOR CAN BE MEASURED

As stated previously the most critical difference between a behavioral approach that pinpoints specific observable behaviors and less systematic approaches to human interactions is the keeping of behavioral records. Evaluation of any procedure instituted to induce behavioral change is virtually impossible without records. Measurement and specific records are crucial for accurate evaluation. The difficulty regarding these classification procedures is that they take extra effort. Behavior always occurs in time intervals. If we are to know whether any particular behavior is getting worse, better, or staying the same, the frequency of behavioral occurrences must be recorded across time and in specific time intervals.

One important aspect of learning record keeping is for a person to develop the self-discipline necessary to keep individual records representing his/her own behavior. A good place to start is with the time spent on this course or workshop. Each participant is urged to maintain an individual time log indicating amounts of time spent engaged in learning activities. Each week one time log should be completed. (Academic instructors may require that the log be turned in weekly, workshop directors daily.) A model time log is provided.

The time log is divided into four mutually exclusive categories—Reading, Discussion, Writing, and Other—since two or more behaviors cannot occur at precisely the same time (although discussion and/or writing and reading may be closely interspersed). Any class preparation or learning time that is not covered in the Reading, Discussion, and Writing categories may be recorded under the category of Other. This category includes classroom observations, supervision behaviors, or any activity assigned but for which no category exists. These should also be listed on the back of your log.

Keep accurate records and, each time you engage in an activity, log the amount of time in the upper half of each square which is diagonal (round up or down to fifteen-minute time periods). The number of hours are important in order to ascertain how much time one is spending on the course or workshop. It is critical to record time spent as immediately as possible. Few people have a good enough memory to record time spent after even a one-day interlude. After recording time spent, record a subjective rating in the lower half.

TIME LOG

RATING KEY

1 = Time in Minutes
2 = Rating

A = Very Worthwhile
B = Some Value
C = Little Value
D = Wasted Time

Class _____
Name _____
Week No. _____
Dates _____

Days									Wkly. Total	Last Cum. Total	New Cum. Total
A - Readings											
Texts											
Behavioral Articles											
Others Related											
B Discussion											
Class Attendance											
Class Members											
Other (Specify)											
C - Writing											
Learning Activities											
Summaries (Behavioral Articles or Texts)											
Other Assignments											
D- Other											
Observing											
Supervising Practicing Mini - Teaching											
Course - Related Thinking											

Comments on Back   Grand Totals _____ _____ _____

Behavior— The Contingent Result of Life

CAN WE CONTROL OUR ENVIRONMENT?

One of the most important issues in understanding a behavioral approach is to consider the total *environment* and how we are influenced by it. The affects of environmental control (or lack of control) have both very large and extremely small influences on our lives continuously. Many influences of the environment are so prevalent that it is difficult to appreciate the many separate and collective effects that the environment has upon us. *Environment* is defined here to mean everything and anything that provides any feedback or altered perception that influences us in any way—and of course that includes almost everything. We have become "conditioned" by so many aspects of our environment that it is difficult to realize all of the influences that the environment has upon us. Following is a series of questions that will help in understanding the magnitude of environmental influence.

Isolate for a moment some of the *physical* aspects of your current environment. Start with the weather. Obviously, we cannot control the weather, yet we can do some things to prepare for it. Is the weather outside pleasant, not so pleasant? Think about your living environment. Is your home or apartment too cold or too hot? Does it have comfortable air conditioning and/or heat? How did you dress this morning? Did you dress especially for the anticipated weather, or did you wear something that would make you feel good, or look good? What is the weather like right now? Do you want it to change or stay the same?

What did you do when you last changed something in your immediate living environment? Did you hang a picture, change some furniture, or buy a plant? Did you organize anything concerning your clothes or your food in any way? Where is the place you wash and dry your clothes? Is it convenient? Is there any activity that you engage in just to relax? Do you read for pleasure? Do you ever play certain music to influence your mood? Do you ever go to a special place—any place just to relax? What comes to mind when you think about "peaceful?"

Obviously there are both "safe" and "unsafe" environments and these environments have very different influences on us. Think for a moment of a place in which you feel very peaceful, safe, and secure. What first comes to mind? Did a physical place come to mind? Or were you in the presence of a person? If a certain place came to mind, was it an indoor or outdoor environment? Was this place a certain room, did your memory contain a special object, a special group of friends, or was it a combination of things? Now think of a place where you would be extremely *uncomfortable*. Where are you? What are you doing? Are any people there? What seems to be the most salient aspect within this environment? How does thinking about this make your body feel right now?

Now think about your home, going home, or returning home after being away. What comes to mind? What physical objects are there? If you have been away for some time, how does your "hometown" appear to you now? How did it make you feel the last time that you approached your hometown in a car? Did you notice any physical changes? What things do you remember from your childhood that were important to you at that time? Do they include a favorite book, a special toy, a special object, clothing, or a blanket? Do you have a pet? Did you ever have a pet? What comes to mind when you think of your pet?

Think about several of the people in your life. How do you feel the instant that each person comes to mind? Is it a warm nice feeling, or a feeling of anxiety or apprehension? Does the thought of a special person make you feel physically excited? Does the thought of a certain person make you feel angry? Think about your family. What person first comes to mind? Why? How do you feel when thinking about each individual family member? Do you have exactly the same feeling for each individual?

Consider now any personal problem that you have—large or small. It does not matter what the problem is. Now think about the various environmental settings that help to either make this specific problem better or worse. Think about where you are when the problem is worse. Where is it better? *When* is it better? What is happening in the immediate environment that makes it better or worse? When do you think about it? What are the cues that make you think about it? When was the last time that you thought about it besides when reading these words? Just a little thought should make you realize that there are many, many aspects concerning the environment that influence us in many different ways.

Now imagine different *learning environments*. Think about a class in which you felt excited about learning. What first comes to mind? Is it a teacher? Is it an activity? What does the room look like? Are there any special decorations or equipment in it? Are other people there? What do you think are the most important aspects of a good learning environment? How should the learning environment appear physically? How should it be characterized concerning teacher/student and student/student interpersonal interactions? What constitutes the cues for learning, or not learning? Do you believe that the learning environment should be primarily a positive environment? Are there things about an academic environment that can have negative influences on students?

One of the most important aspects of teaching concerns controlling the learning environment. As teachers, we have the responsibility of providing the "best learning environment" possible. Indeed, it is the teacher who "sets the stage" for learning. Sometimes inadequate physical aspects work against this learning. The size and shape of the room, the color of the walls, the necessary equipment including adequate learning materials—all of these matter, and they matter a great deal as far as the student is concerned. A teacher must be aware of these environmental influences in order to structure the environment in whatever manner possible toward increased learning. Perhaps the most important aspect of controlling this learning environment is to structure our own personal interaction patterns. This is particularly necessary when dealing with "problem students."

Can we control the environment? — We control the environment that in turn controls us.

WHO HAS THE PROBLEM?

Perhaps one of the most challenging tasks for today's teacher is to know what literature to believe and what to reject, which authority to respect and which to discount. In our multimedia world, we seem to have experts by the score with almost as many admonitions as we have experts. Presumably, many teachers are saying, "Why don't they get together; one says that what is right today was wrong five years ago; what we got when we were growing up was wrong, or another says right, depending on whom you read." The authors are sympathetic to this situation, especially since we are constantly dealing with children's problems. It is our strong belief, however, that many problems may be "caused" by reading and acting on some of the pronouncements of these articles. Teachers come to us constantly with "students' problems" that did not exist before an article was read. We are reminded of the man who worried for twenty years about latent fear until the day he decided he didn't have to worry about it as long as it was latent.

It would be less than honest for the authors to presume that we are not admonishing; we certainly are. Foremost, *severe problems should be referred to a professional.* It is our hope, however, that teachers will rely on their own honest assessments concerning most teaching. Honesty, we believe, is the key to behavioral assessment by teachers, even if students are being advised by professionals. If teachers are honest, they will not *give their problems away and absolve responsibility.* A graduate student in psychology who was presenting to a graduate seminar the case of his first interview with a client perhaps best illustrates the attitude of giving a problem away. He was apologizing to the other members of the seminar, "I guess I fouled up; about the only thing that I established was that the client had a studying problem." One of the older supervisory clinicians rose to his feet, smiled at the young man, and addressed the group, "As some of you know, I was an obstetrician before I changed to clinical work and I didn't learn much from my previous medical specialty that had immediate transfer. I did learn one thing, however, and that concerns *who's pregnant!* You know, the very first time a patient came to me, the one thing I tried to firmly establish was who's pregnant. 'No *we're* not going to have a baby, your *husband's* not going to have a baby, your *mother's* not going to have a baby, your *family's* not going to have a baby—you, *you're* the one who is going to have a baby.' It was always amusing to me to see some of the expectant mothers trying to give their problem away. Of course, it was the mother who had to eat properly, receive supplements when needed, go through the entire pregnancy, and so on. Son, if within that first session with your client you established *who* had the problem, you succeeded. If your client left realizing that her studying difficulty was not her roommate's problem or her professor's problem or her mother's problem or her counselor's problem, then you are well on your way."

Assessing who has the problem requires a teacher to decide if the problem really belongs to the student or to the teacher. Often, both have a problem: the child, an inappropriate behavior that needs to be changed; the teacher, the responsibility to do something about changing it. Many times, however, problems are not real. The only problem extant is in the head of the teacher. After reading some article, the teacher begins to worry about a potential problem, sometimes to the extent that interaction with the student actually creates the very problem suspected. Certainly, these self-fulfilling prophesies should be avoided, especially when the suspected problem cannot be specified as a behavior(s), but refers only to an idea such as inferiority, lack of love, need for expression, need for individual achievement, or other non-specified ideas.

Even though the teacher is advised to be self-reliant in behavioral assessment of children's problems, the teacher also should be careful not to believe that deviant behavior is *just a stage* the youngster is going through. If, by "stage," we mean precisely the length of time that a child exhibits incorrect responses until something is done to ensure improved behavior, or, if by "stage," we mean those behaviors quite proper for one age but not for another, then there is no cause for concern—no reason for alarm. If, however, we refer to "stage" in an attempt to *give away our problem* hoping that in some mysterious manner, a day will come (perhaps next year) when the problem magically goes away, then perhaps we should reevaluate. The very young child's occasional "disrobing" should not be equated with an occasional "lie." The social contingencies operating within the environment will probably modify the clothes wearing behavior, but probably not the lying. The student who occasionally "has severe temper tantrums" should not be equated with the student who occasionally "forgets to clean the desk." The youngster who occasionally "refuses to share" is not comparable to one "who plots to enhance personal gain by secretly bringing physical harm to another child." Classifying problems into "normal stages of development" should be done with great care.

Teachers should realize that even seemingly innocuous behaviors probably change because something or someone in the student's *environment* interacts to modify specific responses, that is, some problems will extinguish when the older students' environment sets up different expectations; other problems will intensify. The extent to which these problem behaviors change is determined by the cause-and-effect relationships interacting within the student's environmental influence, not by magic or by just growing older. There are many old liars, adults who constantly lose their temper, and teachers who scheme in putting down other colleagues, workers, or even friends to get ahead. Being honest, there also are adults who are exhibitionists, extremely messy, and even stingy.

Who has the problem? —You decide.

WHAT IS THE PAYOFF?

A traditional viewpoint prevalent in education is to focus on many antecedent events (reinforcement history) leading toward a particular goal, rather than to focus on the manipulation and control of the present environment. This procedure of looking backward is both unproductive and unnecessary, especially when it absolves the responsibility of solving the current problem. When the teacher wants to change a specific inappropriate behavior, the teacher must first *find the payoff* and eliminate it if possible. *Behavior that goes unrewarded will extinguish.* The teacher must watch the student carefully to determine the payoff. The teacher must also recognize individual differences; the payoff is often different for each person. For example, a high school teacher has three young men, A, B, and C, who constantly talk in class. After many warnings, the teacher finally sends them to the principal's office. This is just exactly what student A wanted; he finally managed to goad the teacher into "punishing" him. Student B just liked to make the teacher angry. Every time she got stern it just "broke him up." He knew he was bothering her, and he enjoyed her distress: "Wow! She gives me such *stern* looks." Student C does not care about the teacher or the principal. He does care a great deal about students A and B. Every time he talks, they listen. On the way to the principal's office, student A fills the others in. "Listen, the principal sits you down and comes on with all this 'You've got to be a good boy' stuff. Man, the last time I was in there, I really had him snowed. Besides, he never checks to see if you go back to the class, so we're out for the day." When students A, B, and C return to class, they will continue to talk—even more.

Teachers who have simple monolithic explanations for all maladaptive behaviors will be generally ineffective. "All those children need is a little love." "The thing they need is a good, hard paddling." "Get them out in the world; then you'll see how they do." "They need a decent place to live." "They need someone who truly understands them." The problem with this type of analysis is that it is neither differentiated nor individualized. There are some children who may fit one, none, or all of the above categories, plus countless others. The one thing that children exhibiting inappropriate responses *do* need is a teacher who can find the payoff. What is maintaining the problem, keeping the behavior alive? If the payoff can be found and completely eliminated then the behavior will gradually extinguish—*if consistency is maintained.*

A word of caution is important. One significant result of eliminating the payoff is that the undesired behavior will get initially *worse before it gets better.* The teacher must remember that the student has learned a behavior to get what the student wants. When the "reward" is abolished, the student tries even harder (i.e., the inappropriate behavior increases) before coming to realize that there is no payoff. After this initial surge, the behavior will extinguish. The initial rise is extremely important to remember. Many people give up during the storm before the calm, "Oh, I've tried ignoring, but the baby cried even louder."—Of course.

Finding the payoff can be difficult, and sometimes the payoff comes from a source that the teacher cannot control (e.g., parents, peers, physiological reactions, internal imagery, etc.). Nevertheless, cutting out the "reward" can solve many problems.

What is the payoff? —That which keeps the behavior alive.

P.S.: Give student A a task much less desirable than talking in class, preferably where he cannot talk to anyone (i.e., in isolation). Smile at student B when he is not talking; absolutely ignore him when he is. Move student C to the other side of the room away from students A and B.

WHAT CONSTITUTES REWARD?

After a teacher determines the payoff for a particular behavior and eliminates it, the teacher will soon observe a decrease in undesirable behavior. Sometimes this alone is all that is needed. Yet, more often, other things in the students' environment (stimuli) must be controlled, that is, other contingencies must be structured in order to discipline. It is better to start with just one behavior and not try to eliminate everything simultaneously, unless the teacher has a great deal of help and can initially devote available time just to social behavioral problems. If many undesired behaviors are prevalent throughout the classroom, the teacher is advised to establish a priority and start with the inappropriate behavior that most interferes with learning. As has been previously noted, it is important that teachers deal with overt behaviors, not ideas (for example, "getting to work on time" as opposed to "a bad attitude about math").

It is also advisable to make up a set of easily understood rules for each activity. In making up the contingencies (i.e., structuring the rewards), the new payoff for *desirable* behavior (following the rules) must be known, tangible, and close enough to the student's own behavioral responses to motivate the student to seek it. Initially, it is far better to give too much reward than not enough. The idea is to get the student "winning" as soon as possible. In the initial stages of control it is important to have the student achieve success quickly, after which the time between behavior and reward can be stretched for longer periods while continuing to pair appropriate personal responses from the teacher (e.g., words of praise, expressions such as smiling, and closeness such as positive touching). In time, the personal approval of the teacher, and later the student's own personal approval will probably be all that is needed for proper motivation. This is certainly what most teachers desire, but in order to achieve this level of sophistication, one must start where the child is. Some children enter school with response expectations amenable to smiling, pleasing teachers, being obedient, etc. Others have to learn appropriate responses through more tangible rewards.

Another important factor that many teachers do not fully realize is that all approval/disapproval must be *age appropriate*. Some of the most ineffective teaching is caused because the teacher is not sensitive to the sophistication level of the students—the teacher must discriminate. Those things that constitute a reward for very small children will probably be very punishing to an older student. For general control in the early elementary years, words, contact, and expressions are highly effective; group activities and peer group approval provide powerful rewards for the adolescent years (middle school, junior high, and high school); material things and individual activities are useful for young adults (junior high, high school, college).

Various "token systems" are generally effective and come closest to representing our own monetary system. Token systems may be set up at all levels of sophistication in preparation for eventual adult employment. For very young children, a token (or sticker) actually might function as its own reward and does not have to be redeemed. For other students, correct responses can earn "tokens" that can be exchanged for tangible goods (e.g., most young children enjoy things such as toys, trips, or food). Tokens may be chips, papers, check marks, stickers or anything convenient. Rewards earned for tokens should have specified values (i.e., colored paper equals five points, a ruler equals eight points, a commercial game equals ten points) so that students can receive tangible credit for exhibiting appropriate behaviors, such as following specific rules (written on chalkboard). Each student can have a small notebook marked by the teacher, another student, or both. At appropriate intervals (after study, before lunch, following discussion, etc.), the teacher marks the students' points.

The teacher may begin a program by displaying rewards and asking students toward which reward they are working. Then, the teacher may go over the rules. The rules should be written down in a conspicuous place and explained daily— at a time other than when they have been violated: "We sit quietly during individual study." "We raise our hand before we interrupt to talk." "We stay at our own desk during study time unless given permission to leave." "We respect others' rights, and property, etc." At opportune times, the teacher circulates and writes down the points. The very act of recording may be used as an effective control. It is critical for the teacher to try very hard to *catch the child being good* and reward the child with points paired with words and expressions of praise instantaneously.

One effective technique for small children is the use of food (candy, juice, and flavored cereal) as contingent reinforcement. The teacher may start the very first day of the new program with a "goodie" party. The teacher gives the students a treat, and while the students are eating, the teacher says, "We will have another "goodie" party if you are quiet while I count to ten." (The teacher then counts aloud quickly making certain they win.) After giving the treat, the teacher says, "If everyone is quiet for five minutes we will have another party, but if someone talks we will not get to have one." Now the teacher sits back and waits; in all probability, someone will talk, whereupon the teacher says, "Oh, I'm *very sorry*. Kaitlin talked before our time was up; now we will not get to have a party. Maybe tomorrow we may have one if everyone is quiet." (Some children will think this is not "fair.") *Because the teacher does not get angry with Kaitlin, Kaitlin cannot give her problem to the teacher.* Kaitlin receives the disapproval of the group, so there is no payoff from the other children. Instead of interacting directly with Kaitlin, it may be better to use *vicarious reinforcement* and modeling. To use this technique the teacher chooses one of the most well behaved children and says, "I surely like the way Sheila is sitting so quietly. If everyone behaved like Sheila, we could have our party." Sometimes the teacher may wish to give rewards to those children who were quiet and not give anything to those who were not. (Kaitlin may not think this is fair.)

The use of group approval/disapproval is very effective, particularly with older students. When activities are given or denied contingent on the behavior of all concerned, the children themselves will take the responsibility for discipline, and discipline will start to evolve from within the group. *Peer approval is* extremely important to teenagers. This is precisely the reason for such high "esprit de corps" in many group organizations such as band, athletics, social clubs, and street gangs. When teachers, as well as the other students, are taught to cut out the payoff for a particular individual's inappropriate behavior, the undesirable behavior will generally decrease. Of course, students may indeed be embarrassed after receiving such responses from their peers—so be it. It is precisely this contingent embarrassment that solves the problem. If students do not care what others think of them then withholding approval or verbal disapproval will not be effective.

One extremely important issue concerning all of the above is for teachers to be aware of potential hazards when starting any new program. It is always wise to think ahead and ask oneself "If what I do does *not* work the way that I intend it to, then what might happen?" "And afterward, when it didn't work the way I intended, then I would have to do something else, and then what might happen?" "And then what might happen after that?" If a teacher can anticipate students' reactions, then the desired effects of any new program are generally assured. Accurate assessment occurs when the teacher fully understands behavioral principles and has observed enough student behavior to have a good idea of what will work in each specific case—or at least has a high probability of working in each case. *If the teacher institutes a program that fails, then the teacher must live with the failed results.* It is the residual effects of many failed programs that constitute the greatest challenges for today's teachers. Sometimes this residual accumulation seems to be solidly entrenched in certain youngsters. The very best teachers are those who generally "know" what the effects of their interactions will be; others are constantly "trying something," desperately hoping that "it will work." The teacher's value system combined with the reinforcement history of the students determines what contingencies ought to be used. Contingencies, in both approving and disapproving ways, that the teacher can use include:

1. *Words* (spoken and written)

2. *Expressions* (facial-bodily)

3. *Closeness* (nearness-touching)

4. *Activities and privileges* (social-individual)

5. *Things* (tokens, materials, food, playthings, money)

Other than the rewards of the activity itself (sometimes there are none), these categories constitute the *entire resources* that the teacher has for structuring. Teaching should develop them well. (Study the examples and lists in Parts II and III.)

What constitutes reward? —That toward which the student will work.

IS THE WORLD FAIR?

For years, teachers have been advocating the uniqueness of every student. "All children are not alike," they say. "Each child has had many different experiences." "Children come from many different backgrounds." "They need individual attention." One would assume from this dedication to individual differences that teachers would teach differently and meet the discipline problems of each student in a unique manner, but this does not seem to be the case. Most teachers also seem preoccupied with an *undifferentiated* concept of "fairness."

Children do not have a problem with undifferentiated "fairness" until someone teaches it to them. Usually, children's parents, who manifest the same thinking as some teachers, are the ones who teach it first. With little hesitation, parents will talk at length about how different their children are. Equally without hesitation, they try as hard as possible to be "fair." Fred and Jane are different in many, many ways. They like different things, they respond differently, and one child is almost always older. Yet, when Fred gets to go, Jane gets to go; when Jane gets candy, Fred must have candy; if Fred receives a toy, Jane must, also. Fred and Jane learn quickly. "Why can't I stay up late?" "Why don't I get to go?" "How come I don't get a present?" "Why does she always get the biggest apple?" Thus, Mother and Dad spend a great deal of time and energy trying to be "fair." They also create much anxiety for themselves by not admitting that they do treat the children differently and, from time to time, may actually even like one child more than the other. These are all unnecessary attempts designed to solve the problem of undifferentiated fairness they have created for themselves. "But Fred, your birthday will come next month." "Jane, you see Fred is older than you; that's why he stays up later." "OK, if you're going to fight over who gets the bigger apple, neither one of you can have one."

People *are* different. Some are extremely different, particularly if they have physical or mental handicaps. It would seem that the kindest teaching behavior would be to instruct students in this regard—let them know that the world is not always "fair." Prepare them for the suffering they will endure because of others' mistakes. Let them realize from the beginning that their efforts are not always evaluated fairly. Help them understand that in a democracy the group often suffers from the actions of a few. Let them realize that occasionally they will be punished for things that they do not do. Teach them to understand that justice is an ideal, less often a reality. *Yes, and also instruct them to be just in their own personal behaviors, but not always to expect it from others.* Some of the gravest problems encountered by students come from an undifferentiated concept of "fairness."

Fairness is not a simple matter. People have labored for centuries to ascertain "what's fair" in relationship to many different situations (laws). Within the academic realm, the teacher also works hard at differential assessment. Grades are assigned differentially, as are special projects, reports, reading groups, and so on. Thus, *the teacher* establishes rules of academic discriminations (fairness?). How naïve, then, to equip the students with one special response the teacher knows will cause the child problems as the child matures. The teacher also loses a most effective technique (group approval/disapproval) when refusing to use the group in "shaping up" individuals, for to punish the group because of the actions of one individual or vice versa does not seem "fair." Ideally, proper interaction patterns will eventually evolve from within the group. Students will help discipline each other, not by punishing or tattling, but by ignoring, attending to what is proper, not talking or listening to each other when they should not be, and generally *staying on task.* Discipline, however, will not evolve from the group unless the teacher uses the group to bring particular individuals "in line."

No one wishes to be punished for another's actions. In cooperative societies, however, this goes on continuously. If elected officials in a representative government decide to enter a war, they do not ask the individual student. If a student in the bud of maturity fights, and subsequently dies in battle, then who suffers? Why not prepare students for the world in which they live, where everyone's life is affected by the acts of others? Let them realize early that if we are to function socially then we must take the responsibility and the results of interacting with others—we do not stand alone. Help students understand that "what's fair" is a big question relating differentially to almost all aspects of life. Do not prepare them for certain disillusionment with one undifferentiated response. Help them discriminate between the many issues of fairness and be prepared to deal realistically with this discernment. Students may then come to accept life's inequities while doing something to change many of them, rather than feeling sorry for themselves because they find some aspects of interaction "unfair." When the teacher deals with fairness, optimism need not suffer—only naïveté.

Is the world fair? —Sometimes.

CAN CONTINGENCES BE STRUCTURED?

The basic premise of reinforcement teaching is to arrange the stimuli of the external world to shape the behavior of the students—to *structure the environment* so that the student receives approval/disapproval reinforcements contingent on appropriate/inappropriate behavior. Therefore, *reinforcement teaching is the structure of approval and disapproval reinforcers, across time in precise intervals, to shape desired behavior toward specific goals.* Experimentation in learning demonstrates that: (a) If students know specifically what is expected and (b) they want to do it then (c) they probably will. The necessity for specific measurable goals (expectations for students) has already been mentioned. The crux of the problem rests with (b), arranging the contingencies of reinforcement so that a student will want to do what the teacher expects.

Five techniques used in structuring contingencies are:

1. *Approval* (rewards)

2. *Withholding of approval* (withholding rewards—hope)

3. *Disapproval* (punishment)

4. *Threat of disapproval* (fear)

5. *Ignoring* (not attending in any manner, verbal or nonverbal)

Approval is easily understood. Approval is anything that is generally thought to be related to "happiness": words used as praise; *expressions,* such as smiling; *closeness,* such as embracing or touching; *activities* that are enjoyable; *things,* such as games, badges, food, trinkets, stickers etc. Teachers must be sure, however, that what they believe is functioning as positive reinforcement is truly positive (some children don't like ice cream).

Withholding of approval (withholding rewards) is used when the positive reinforcer functions to produce "hope" for the attainment of a reward the next time when the behavior is improved. In a way, this procedure functions as "punishment" (disapproval), although with potentially greater effect for improvement and less wear and tear on everyone concerned. Teachers may also place the responsibility for improvement on the student and perhaps avoid negative emotional reactions directed toward the teacher following punishment. "I'm sorry you didn't finish on time. Now you cannot go out to play. Perhaps tomorrow you will finish on time. Then you may play."

Disapproval is also easily understood. Disapproval is generally synonymous with what most persons term *unhappiness.* Disapproval comes in such forms as *words,* when one is getting yelled at; *expressions,* such as frowning; *closeness,* when one is being hit or placed in isolation; *activities,* as when one is deprived of something one wants or made to do an unpleasant task; and *things,* such as feared objects.

The teacher must also be careful not to conclude too easily what constitutes disapproval. Students may often exhibit many inappropriate, maladaptive, and perverted associations. "I like to get spanked." "I enjoy making my teacher angry." Extreme disapproval (corporal punishment) should be used very sparingly, if at all. Perhaps the most important thing to be remembered about physical punishment is that if teachers decide to use it, *it should be strong enough to stop the behavior immediately and eliminate the problem at once.* Otherwise, teachers may only ensure that the student will engage in similar behavior in the future and, therefore, punishment will probably intensify, especially if teachers become angry and do not realize that they themselves are contributing to the problem. Many children have been gradually conditioned to endure severe beatings, usually *without* a decrease in maladaptive responses.

Threat of disapproval (fear) should be used rarely, yet it is profoundly effective once the knowledge of disapproval is established. Individuals learn how to behave in order to avoid disapproval (unpleasant consequences): "I am careful when crossing the road to avoid getting killed." "I don't play with guns because I could get shot." "I study so I won't fail." Even though fear is an extremely effective suppressant of many inappropriate behaviors, it does little to establish the joy of learning and living. Children (or adults) who are completely negatively motivated are usually tense, unenthusiastic, quiet, shy, passive, and generally fearful. Some of these children do eventually succeed, although this negatively motivated "success" usually comes at the high price of guilt, compulsivity, generalized anxiety, and, perhaps later, stress related medical problems.

An additional aspect relating to *disapproval* and *threat of disapproval* concerns classroom rules that are set up using only a *demerit* system. While these are not recommended, they are somewhat typical (especially regarding social behavior) and represent situations where there is no reward for positive behavior, yet there are negative consequences for misbehavior. In these situations, the teacher must remember that *the rule* does not exist as *threat of disapproval* only; it becomes a rule only when someone breaks it and is punished. This situation is very similar to traffic rules concerning speeding. Everyone realizes that regardless of posted speed signs many drivers will repeatedly break the speed limit if no one ever receives a speeding ticket. It is recommended that every rule have both positive and negative consequences. In this manner students will eventually learn to seek the positive and avoid the negative. Also, when following the rules receives positive, there is the possibility that many students will obey the rules for the positive reinforcement that they receive from the teacher, never (or infrequently) needing to be punished.

Ignore—just that—Ignore.

The formula in Table 4-1 represents interactions for behavioral shaping. The teacher is advised, if at all possible, to use primarily approval, withholding of approval, and ignoring in controlling behavior. There is some indication that these "positive approaches" can be more effective, but more importantly, *they are much less damaging than using extreme disapproval (punishment).* This does not mean the teacher should be permissive. It indicates that as teachers structure the students' environment contingent on appropriate behaviors (i.e., produce appropriate cause-and-effect relationships), they should diligently try to do so through the use of "positive" techniques and structuring incompatible responses. Withholding an overt love response seems much kinder than introducing corporal punishment. Alternately, there are times when disapproval (punishment) might need to be used. Some maladaptive behaviors of children are much worse than the punishment it could take to eliminate them.

Can contingencies be structured? —They must.

Table 4-1

		Teacher Behavior			
		Approval	Withholding of Approval	Disapproval	Threat of Disapproval	Ignore
Student Behavior	Appropriate	Yes	No	No	No	No
	Inappropriate	No	Yes	Yes*	Yes	Yes**

*Unless payoff

**Unless dangerous

ARE THOUGHTS BEHAVIOR?

Laura was in her third year of teaching high school English. She had just returned from Thanksgiving vacation and discovered that she was pregnant. Having tried repeatedly to achieve this state, she was extremely happy, yet she "worried constantly" concerning how she was going to finish the school year. She was concerned about her classes, she worried about finances, and she did not know just how she was going to tell her principal.

Laura's classes were near perfect, as far as she was concerned. It had not always been that way. During the beginning of the school year she had had the normal kinds of problems until such time as she was able to develop her own *style* in a manner whereby her students responded to her as she wanted them to. At the beginning of the year she had noticed that her oral disapproval (even when she used it sparingly) was actually functioning as "nagging," whereupon she had determined to use only oral *approval* and had set up other consequences for student misbehavior. After several weeks in achieving consistency, she had settled down into a pleasant year.

Yet, as the holiday season approached, the problem of her pregnancy continued to bother her. Sometimes the ambivalence seemed to be unbearable. Even during the nicest parts of the school day when students were not just doing good work, but were actually being tender to each other, she felt preoccupied and distant. One day when she had students sincerely applauding the accomplishments of each other, her mind suddenly wandered to the yet dormant life within her and she felt that same old pang of uneasiness.

Laura decided that she definitely must do something about this problem, as it seemed to be getting worse daily. She finally discussed it with a close friend who was also a teacher, but became upset because her friend had suggested that she use one of those "behavioral programs" to deal with it. "How absolutely insensitive," she thought. How could any of the techniques that she was using in her classroom apply to her problem? She remembered asking sarcastically, "Am I supposed to give myself a token every time I don't think about it?" Her friend had answered, "Yes."

Laura thought about that conversation for some time. Then she decided to do exactly what her friend had suggested—not give herself a token, but to engage in an incompatible behavior (a thought-stopping process) every time she found that she was thinking (actually worrying) about her problem. She also decided to apply some of the instructive advice she had been giving her class all year in settling their problems by taking an action step. She told her principal—and wished that she had done so earlier because her principal was so supportive. She then told her students who were even more receptive. More importantly, she taught herself to stop worrying about her condition unnecessarily by writing down on a small card several sentences: "I don't want to waste my time worrying about this; this worrying is completely unproductive; I am going to put this card in my purse and stop worrying NOW!"

Like many others, Laura was very capable of applying principles of behavior modification to help students within her classroom, but she was not initially capable of applying those same principles to remedy her own problems. While it is always difficult to see one's own problems as being as simple as other people seem to think they are, it is still necessary to have some plan of action. It is also important to act in a positive manner conducive to effecting resolution of one's problems. Sometimes it is advisable to seek professional help; more often, it is advisable to apply the same external reinforcements to control thought processes just as one would do to decrease or increase more "observable" behavior.

Most sophisticated people live in a "world of ideas." Sometimes these ideas are productive and pleasant; sometimes these ideas are destructive, even to the point of complete debilitation. A burgeoning field relating to "cognitive behavior modification" is attempting to sort out the variables, schedules of reinforcement, and the positive/aversive histories of people in order to help them to live more productively. While this area seems extremely complicated, it is beginning to demonstrate that thoughts can also be modified.

Are thoughts behavior? —Think about it.

STUDY GUIDE FOR CHAPTER 4

Questions:

1. Name at least 25 aspects of "environmental control" that have influenced you since getting up this morning.

2. What point is made with the example of students A, B, and C? Explain why teachers should understand the analysis of students A, B, and C.

* 3. How does one decide just who has the problem? How is the choice made about what competing or inappropriate behavior is to be eliminated first?

* 4. What is vicarious reinforcement and modeling? Give an example. When might it be used? When might it be counterproductive?

* 5. What is meant by age appropriate? What makes group approval-disapproval work effectively? Why should a teacher think ahead "and then what might happen, and then what might happen after that, and then what might happen after that?"

* 6. How can you tell what will be rewarding? Can you predict in advance what may work? In what circumstances is a rule not a rule until it has been broken and punished?

* 7. Should a teacher treat all children the same in academic and social situations? Explain.

8. Should a child be taught that the world is unfair? Why or why not?

* 9. Which three techniques should be employed most in structuring contingencies by teachers? Why?

10. Are thoughts behavior? List some thoughts that you might change with principles of behavior modification.

* Transfer these questions to your specific situation (e.g., Vocational/ Technical Education, English).

LEARNING ACTIVITY 7—CONCEPTUAL BEHAVIORAL ANALYSIS

Instructions:

1. Experienced teachers

A)   Choose from your experience a personal example that you consider an unqualified success. Pinpoint the behaviors involved and analyze your solution in terms of consequences applied. Include some indication of the frequency of the behavior prior to your intervention (Record) and also following (Evaluate).

B)   Choose an example from your prior teaching experience that you consider a failure. Pinpoint the behaviors which were part of the problem, indicate the frequency of the behavior (Record), analyze your consequence(s) in behavioral terms, and discuss the reasons for the failure and what procedures you would now apply to the same case.

2. Prospective teachers

A)   Pinpoint the following problems in behavioral terms.

B)   Indicate potential strategies for short-term and long-term intervention (Consequates).

    (1)   Shy, withdrawn girl, non-communicative, dresses in a manner considered weird by her peers.

    (2)   Twelve-year-old boy recently returned from a state detention center for delinquent youths, fights with others, has "chip on shoulder," and lives with foster parents who say they "just don't care."

    (3)   Six-year-old who dominates entire house by screaming, yelling, throwing severe tantrums; parents are at "wits end."

    (4)   Sixteen-year-old, tenth-grade boy who states he wants to get out of school, failed all classes preceding term.

    (5)   Active "hyperactive" student who is continually engaged in minor and major motor behavior as well as humming, whistling, cracking joints, tapping feet.

    (6)   Student who tests high on achievement scores but fails to complete any assignments to be turned in within the class.

LEARNING ACTIVITY 8—INTERPERSONAL EXTENSIONS

1. Pinpoint 15 specific problem behaviors discussed in class, small group sessions, or from your own experiences that relate to interpersonal behaviors. Develop and outline sequential consequences based upon behavioral principles that would alleviate, remediate, or prevent additional or similar problems in the future.

2. Discuss solutions in small groups with continued recording and reporting of positive and negative comments made by each participant during the discussion of related problems.

Life—
The Structure of Activities
in Time

IS TIME IMPORTANT?

Thank you, reader. Thank you for what? Thank you for reading the next paragraph. You have not read it yet? Oh.

Why is the preceding rather absurd? It is because the "thank you" comes before the fact. Therefore, it has little meaning and even less significance in modifying your behavior (except perhaps in creating confusion). In all research concerned with behavior, no one has ever been able to teach anything through the use of antecedent rewards. *Rewards must come after the fact.* Thus, we enter the most elusive aspect of teaching—time. All events take place in time. Benjamin Franklin has this maxim: "Dost thou love life? Then do not squander time, for that is the stuff life is made of."

One of the most basic differentiations of the growing child comes in the progressive sophistication regarding time. Even adults cannot really tell time, as evidenced by the chronoscopes we strap to our arms. Our temporal span is exceedingly short, and our assessment of ongoing time becomes humorous (try to estimate a minute without counting to yourself)! Even with a minute you must "fill it up with something" in order to approximate the passage of time. Now consider these foolish temporal contingencies: One-year-old: "baby knows I'll pick her up after I finish my work." Three-year-old: "Tomorrow we will go out to play." Six-year-old: "Be good, next week is party time." Nine-year-old: "When you get to eleven, you may join the Scouts." Thirteen-year-old: "If you pass all your classes, you may have a car when you're sixteen." Sixteen-year-old: "You must graduate from high school if you expect to have a good life." College freshman: "Study diligently and you will be a good teacher." If these sequences sound long, try a few out on yourself just to see how close in time a contingent reward or punishment must be to motivate you. "One more drink and tomorrow morning, wow!" "You don't have the money, why not just charge it?" "Better stop this late discussion—8:00 A.M. comes early." "Better start studying—final exams are in just two weeks." As you can see, your temporal motivation is not long at all. Of course, you realize the necessity of working toward or avoiding all those things, but they are up there in time somewhere—not now—not close enough in time really to motivate you.

If contingent rewards/punishments for behavior are to be most effective, they should take place immediately, and *the teacher must always know, before the fact, just what the contingencies are to be.* With small children this is tremendously important. "Daddy's going to spank you when he gets home" is a typical example of a ridiculous contingency.

It is also important to correct any inappropriate behavior before it becomes full-blown—to "nip it in the bud." The teacher who believes that a small disturbance "will get better" is right. It will get better and better and *better* and BETTER! Full-blown disorder is usually encouraged by hesitation and caused by self-deception. *Initial stages of control are the most important.* As the child matures, the child's temporal span will increase if the child is taught proper behaviors while progressively lengthening the time between action and consequence. If the bag of oats is too close to the horse, he eats the oats; if the bag is too far away, he does not move.

An additional aspect of timing concerns "setting the student up for success." In order to set the student up for success, the student might initially need to be *prompted* or *cued* in order to elicit the correct response. Even after being cued, it is still important for the teacher to reinforce the correct response. Effective prompting (combined with effective reinforcement) is one of the most important aspects of teaching. The effective teacher always structures to provide success for students as opposed to setting them up for failure.

Time and the control of reinforcement schedules across time are imperative. Reinforcers can be delivered on many different schedules depending on the circumstances (fixed time, fixed interval, variable time, variable interval, or mixed). Also, a distinction should be made between a reinforcer and a reward, in that a reinforcer is intended to increase behavior, while a reward might come too far after the fact to exert much of a contingency. When the distinction between reinforcer versus reward is made, it is made on the basis of time.

The job of the teacher is to meet the student where the student is and then progressively take the student to the point where the student will be content to wait for longer and longer rewards while still exhibiting proper behavior (e.g., structuring progressive work tasks toward final grades). Actually, many people guard time more jealously than anything over which they have control. *The art of living evolves from the structure of meaningful activities in time.*

Is time important? —Time is life.

HOW SHOULD WE SCHEDULE ACROSS TIME?

Schedules of reinforcement concern events across time. Understanding aspects of "scheduling" provides extremely important information when analyzing human behavior and is vital if teachers are to function effectively—*timing is everything*. Schedules are generally either *fixed* or *variable*, and an analysis of these schedules provides the understanding one needs in order to determine teaching/learning contingencies. For example, if one desires to increase work productivity, it is possible to structure externally schedules such that a person will work much harder than previously thought possible because of efficient external structuring of reinforcement schedules. However, differentiating between our own internal structuring as opposed to *having structure imposed upon us* remains a troublesome aspect concerning reinforcement schedules.

This issue not only relates to temporal differentiation, but also relates to "who decides who decides." Therefore, these issues are often difficult to grasp and sometimes people react negatively to them because of an aversive schedule to which someone else has previously subjected them. A good example of this point concerns financial remuneration. It has been repeatedly demonstrated that one's pay functions as a stronger contingency when one is put on some kind of *variable* or piecework schedule, as opposed to an *intervallic* rate-per-hour schedule. Most of us do not like to receive pay based on a variable schedule because it takes away our "security," that is, pay becomes more contingent on work and less related to the passage of time. The issue of "control" must be understood if one is to gain a clear understanding concerning schedules of reinforcement. Since this text is written for teachers who are given the responsibility for structuring learning experiences, including giving feedback to students (feedback is always given on some schedule of reinforcement), the information is presented as though the teacher is the one "who decides."

Reinforcement can be given on the basis of a *work product* (i.e., on a ratio schedule that is either fixed or variable) or on an *intervallic* (time) schedule that is also either fixed or variable. *Ratio* schedules are best conceptualized as feedback or payoff directly following certain responses. *Interval* or temporal scheduling relates to delivering reinforcement for behaviors after a specified period of time has passed since the last time reinforcement was received. Both ratio and interval types of reinforcement can be delivered on either a fixed or a variable schedule. In a *fixed* schedule, reinforcement is delivered either after a set number of appropriate occurrences of a behavior (fixed-ratio), or after the behavior occurs following a fixed time period since the last reinforcement was delivered (fixed-interval). In a *variable* schedule, reinforcement is delivered after a predetermined number of appropriate behaviors (variable-ratio), or after predetermined time periods have passed (variable-interval), but the predetermined events or time periods may change after each event.

Fixed-interval schedules, for the most part, concern seconds, minutes, hours, days, weeks, months, years, and so on. Humankind has developed a tremendous sophistication in the measurement of time, and most of life is structured around certain fixed-interval schedules. In a fixed-interval schedule, a behavior is reinforced upon its occurrence and then not reinforced again until a fixed period of time has elapsed, regardless of how often the behavior might recur in the interim. After this set period of time has expired, the next time the behavior occurs, the individual is again reinforced. An example of a fixed-interval schedule might be when an algebra teacher collects homework every day in class, but only grades and returns every seventh assignment. This same schedule might also exist in a different manner with report cards. One knows that a grade report is produced at the end of the term, and this term grade is usually the only formal feedback parents receive from the school system, regardless of their child's daily progress throughout the term.

Fixed-ratio schedules refer to reinforcement given after every two times, every five times, six times, or any other aspect that would refer to fixed feedback after certain occurrences of behavior. An example of a fixed-ratio schedule would be payment for piecework or reinforcement for every correct problem or finished assignment. It is obvious that this represents a stronger contingency because it has to do directly with quantities of production as opposed to set time intervals (i.e., fixed-interval schedules above). Most aspects of life that are considered routine, and about which we rarely think, are structured within fixed schedules. While a fixed schedule provides the most security, it also provides the least motivation in modifying or changing (student) behavior when contrasted to a variable schedule. Additionally, those behaviors that are maintained on a fixed schedule are probably the easiest to extinguish.

In the *variable-ratio* schedule, certain behaviors are paid off or reinforced over random time intervals. The most easily understood *variable-ratio* schedule concerns gambling. Obviously, if one knows that one is going to lose every time, one will not gamble. If one were to win every time, someone else would have to pay the price of the gambler's winning. Therefore, as far as the "manipulator" is concerned, the idea is to have the gambler win enough in the short run in order to lose money in the long run. This is not a difficult thing to do if the manipulator is keenly aware of the effectiveness of certain schedules of reinforcement. Initially, the notion is to get the gambler winning, or to get the gambler "hooked on gambling" as it were, such that a pattern of expectancies would keep the gambling frequency high. In this manner the gambler gradually loses money to the one in control. The particular behavior under question can be maintained for longer and longer periods of time in anticipation of reinforcement that is never quite "fixed."

A *variable-interval* schedule concerns reinforcement happening after some erratic or randomly determined temporal period. A common example of a variable interval schedule might concern receiving mail, where one is not really sure what day (or if) a response will come and eagerly waits for correspondence. It should be noted, however, that bills also arrive by mail, although a simple distinction is made by most people concerning bill receipt as opposed to happier correspondence. Furthermore, bills are generally considered aversive. Regardless of how many bills are received, they are most often saved until some fixed-interval, whereby they are paid or manipulated in some other way. Receipt of happy mail including electronic mail is generally on a variable schedule, but the mail is generally dealt with more immediately on a fixed-ratio schedule (response for each event). Of course, the above example does not represent the case when people receive mail every day. In this case, receipt of mail every day would again represent a fixed as opposed to a variable schedule. Receipt of mail precisely at the same time every day or every week would also represent a fixed schedule. Other common examples concerning variable intervals have to do with receipt of company, good and bad news over periods of time, and many other events that keep us in anticipation of further happenings. Obviously, this anticipation can be defined as both good and bad. It can provide some variety, but it may be too costly in relationship to other issues.

Variable schedules are generally thought to provide much less security and, therefore, be much more effective than fixed schedules in modifying behavior. Variable schedules are used in many ways to increase or decrease certain behaviors. The effect of these schedules is to teach one to go for longer and longer periods of time before receiving a payoff. When the teacher is dealing with appropriate behavior and wants to build perseverance so that a student will go for longer and longer periods of time without needing reinforcement, this schedule is extremely effective. However, this variable schedule is also what keeps some people going for long periods of time exhibiting inappropriate behavior. Remember that the definition of what is appropriate or inappropriate depends on value issues, not on the schedule of reinforcement. A student may have been "inadvertently taught" to go for longer and longer periods of time exhibiting inappropriate behavior just to get the teacher angry.

While variable schedules are very effective, they can also create the most anxiety. Think of a young child who goes for long periods of time doing things she/he hopes will please a parent, yet gets little or no attention. Think of this same child interacting with an alcoholic parent who is very erratic (variable) in giving attention when intoxicated. In laboratory experiments it has been shown that it is possible to get lower animal forms to exhibit many behaviors of "mental illness" by carefully controlling schedules of reinforcement. Therefore, it is suspected that in certain cases *variable-schedules* might also be a common aspect that contribute to depression and other aspects of mental health.

The final concept that must be understood when considering schedules of reinforcement is *thinning*. Thinning is where reinforcement is initially scheduled to be quite frequent, (i.e., a fixed ratio of 1:1, where every occurrence of a behavior is reinforced), and then the ratio of reinforcements to behaviors is gradually extended to where the reinforcement occurs less often (i.e., a ratio of 1:8). This usually progresses to the point where reinforcement is then put on a variable schedule. Eventually, a naturally occurring reinforcer will take the place of the societal agent's need to supply the reinforcement. When a person achieves this state, the person is usually described as being "self-motivated." Yet, some people go for such long time periods without extrinsic reinforcement from their environment that they actually become impervious to this very environment—even when reinforcement eventually comes. These people are not described as self-motivated; they are often described as asocial or even mentally ill.

It should be noted, as with other principles of reinforcement, that the entire issue of *establishing values* needs to be predetermined so that we can teach or structure consistently with a previously determined value hierarchy. If we wish to act responsibly as teachers, it is essential that we understand the subtle and sometimes not so subtle reinforcement schedules that are operating within the learning environment. Schedules of reinforcement are always evident regardless of whether or not they are understood by the teacher. This understanding is especially important in order to modify those detrimental aspects of a student's life that we desire to bring under control.

How should we schedule across time? —Very carefully.

IS CONSISTENCY DIFFICULT?

If one were to take the principle *"Behavior that is partially reinforced is the most difficult to extinguish,"* and asked to devise a system whereby one could make a million dollars through its use, one might come up with gambling. As has been previously stated, gambling is an activity that represents partial reinforcement at its best. If a person knows for certain that winning is absolutely impossible then the person will not gamble. Obviously one cannot always win, so the trick is to structure the environment so that the gambler *wins* often enough to *lose* money in the long run.

Such is the case with other behavior, for many students have been taught to gamble. The young boy does not remember the 1,321 times he went to bed at 8:00 P.M. He remembers the two times he got to stay up. The third grader does not really believe that the teacher will send her to "the time-out room (isolation) for five minutes." This is already the sixth time the teacher has threatened and nothing has happened yet. The ninth grader cheated before and didn't get caught, so he probably won't get caught this time. The college student has turned in late papers before; why should this professor be such a "hard nose?"

To illustrate how variable scheduling inadvertently is responsible for inappropriate behavior, consider a small child's crying for attention. Suppose that a newborn baby receives little or no attention unless the baby cries. In the earliest stages of care the caregiver may have become quickly "conditioned" by the baby and goes to the baby every time the baby cries. This arrangement works out well because the baby receives its needed care by "communicating" with the caregiver—when the baby cries, the caregiver attends. However, in some cases when the baby cries, the caregiver might be busy or preoccupied or perhaps asleep (as babies are not on adults' schedules). The baby must then cry longer and perhaps louder for needed attention. Additionally, after a period of time the caregiver may decide that the caregiver's schedule is more important than the baby's schedule and "changes the rules." The caregiver now determines to put the baby on the caregiver's schedule. The baby becomes understandably upset. Over time the baby would probably adapt to this new schedule, yet because of unmet needs and previous learning, the baby will continue to cry from time to time. The caregiver may "know" that the baby's needs are being met but probably does not adhere to a regular schedule. Also, the caregiver may "feel guilty" and sometimes attend to the baby at times when the baby cries, thereby creating confusion for the baby. Because of the caregiver's previous conditioning of going to the baby only when the baby cries, it is difficult to not do it; therefore, the caregiver becomes even more inconsistent in responding.

Now the baby is gradually learning to cry louder and longer and has been inadvertently put on a variable schedule. The caregiver does not fully understand this (nor does the baby) and begins to respond only to the baby's crying when the crying becomes intense. Of course, this teaches persistence from the baby as it is learning exactly what it has been taught—cry louder and longer—get attention. Also, the caregiver is usually not the only adult in the baby's environment as there are other adults (perhaps day-care personnel who are on their own schedule) that want to "pick up the baby when it cries." Many times the baby will stop crying when picked up which reinforces the adult who smilingly says, "the baby stopped crying for me." If thoughtful, this adult might realize that if the baby stops crying when picked up then perhaps the baby was not in great need of much vital physical "attention."

Or perhaps the baby has come to realize that whenever picked up, nice things are shortly forthcoming and stops crying—for a time. Regardless, since this inadvertent reinforcement teaches persistence, the baby begins learning to cry louder and longer and louder and longer and louder and longer. At any given point in time if *all* adults in the child's environment did not attend to the child except on fixed schedules when attending to the baby's physical and emotional needs, the child would eventually extinguish crying. Yet, because the baby's crying intensifies, the adults usually "give in" at the precise point of highest crying magnitude thus creating even greater persistence. Sometimes the baby cries for such long periods of time that its entire nervous system seems to get unbalanced and crying takes on a life of its own. Tragically, in some cases adults get to the point where they "cannot cope" with the distressed child, and they retaliate. To these adults, it seems so "unfair" that no matter what they do the baby still cries louder and longer and louder and longer . . . .

Inconsistency teaches just that—inconsistency. At best, it produces gambling children, at worst large-scale mental illness. *The most difficult task for a teacher is consistency!* The teacher should plan how contingencies are to be structured, make the rules, and *follow through.* The only thing that we teach a child when we break the rules is just that—to break the rules. How pathetic it is to observe children who have many severe maladaptive behaviors that have been paid off and, therefore, allowed to fester for longer and longer periods because of partial reinforcement. It is much like *favorable responses;* we stretch the temporal spans between reinforcement to provide longer periods of productive activity. The reinforcement history of some children's maladaptive responses contains so much partial reinforcement that they will fight for weeks and months before giving up their learned behaviors.

Is consistency difficult? —*It is the most difficult aspect of discipline.*

SHOULDN'T WE ESTABLISH GOOD HABITS?

Over time and because of a good deal of repetition, all humans develop habits. We develop many, many habits, both *good* and *bad.* Parents and teachers attempt to develop "good habits" with their children/students; they also attempt to get rid of "bad habits." *A habit is something that we do which we do not think about.* Remember for a moment when you were first learning how to drive a car. There were many aspects of driving that you needed to "think about" before driving became automatic. Now, as an adult, you probably do not think much about these skills because most aspects of driving have become "habitual." Now think about other physical tasks such as playing a sport or a musical instrument, or a game involving perfecting neuromuscular skills. Now think about small children learning how to open a book, hold a pencil, stack toys, put on shoes, or any other task involving skill development.

It should be obvious that in the initial stages of development, learning how to coordinate takes a great deal of concentration and time. Initial skill development takes "the entire core of our concentration" and we are not capable of doing or even thinking about much else at the same time. Afterward, these skills become perfected—sometimes so much so that we have to "concentrate on something to keep ourselves on task," such as when driving a car or operating dangerous equipment. And even if certain skills have not become "perfected," they generally become habits (i.e., bad habits) because of repetition. After developing such skills we generally "coast on automatic." We have developed many patterns of responses that seem to serve us well as we navigate throughout life.

The amount and strength of these habits can be awesome if we start to think about them or, more particularly, if we attempt to do things differently, contrary to our previously developed patterns. Put your watch on the other wrist for a few hours and see how it feels. Attempt to open a door with your other hand; see how long you remember to use your other hand. Attempt to get dressed in a different way. Start by putting on your shoes beginning with the "other one;" put on an article of clothing starting in a different way, brush your teeth with/without looking in the mirror, learn to pronounce an old word with a different pronunciation, hold your fork in a different position, and so on.

It does not take too much of this "changing" to realize that we are indeed *creatures of habit*. The importance of this for teachers is to realize that the strength of a habit is extremely "locked in" and very difficult to change once it has been established. We all know this because of the "bad" habits that we attempt to change: biting nails, popping our knuckles, scratching ourselves, needlessly putting our hands to our face, adjusting our glasses, adjusting our clothing, playing with or combing our hair with our hands, putting the snooze alarm on every morning, and so on, and so on.

Now think of patterned responses that should be "neutral" in that these habits do not really matter because they are really neither good nor bad, they are just different. For example, do you put your money in your wallet or purse in exactly the same way each time? Does everyone? Are your dishes arranged in a certain order? Are everyone's? Do you wash your face in a certain pattern/manner? Does it have to be this way? Do you get ready for bed in a certain way? Is this way necessary? Does it really matter? If thoughtful, we will probably admit to two things: Yes, we always do these things in a certain way, and yes, we believe that it really should be that way. The problem with this type of habit is that we begin to believe that everyone should behave in the same way. It "feels so good" to "have it right," especially with important things. Of course, the importance has been determined by our own repetition. On a clear day we realize that these habits are idiosyncratic and it really does not matter which way one does them. Yet, they have now taken on a certain *morality* because of long-term repetition. We become extremely irritated with those who have different habits. "How can you mix all your food up in one bunch like that?" "Yuck, you don't put catsup on those, do you?" "How can you stand to have your books all messed up and not in order?" "Can't you hang it up *this* way?" "The pencil *must* be held like this." "Yes, we *absolutely have to* clean our desks before we go to lunch." Many times needless conflicts occur not because of major issues, but because of issues that we believe to be major. THE TOILET PAPER SHOULD ALWAYS HANG FROM THE TOP!

Shouldn't we establish good habits? —Yes, especially when we are sure what habits are important.

IF AT FIRST YOU DON'T SUCCEED?

If behaviors can be learned, they can also be unlearned or relearned. Sometimes in our zeal to get through to our students, we make mistakes. Sometimes regardless of zeal we make mistakes. The effectiveness of behavioral techniques with severe problem behaviors within mental hospitals and institutions for persons who are retarded or handicapped should give us the courage to move forward. Behavioral techniques have demonstrated that even severely handicapped children can learn much faster and a great deal more than we previously believed possible.

Since it is impossible for the student to maintain two contradictory responses at the same time, the skillful teacher will program to elicit responses *incompatible* with inappropriate behavior. "Count to ten before you get angry; think before you begin your work; raise your hand before you talk; take three big breaths before you cry; speak softly so we can have a soft argument; now we are practicing good grammar; let's take a break so we can begin with freshness; I'll close the curtain so the outside will not distract us; let's put our other materials away before we begin the new activity," and so on. Severe disapproval (punishment) alone may stop inappropriate behavior, but it will not necessarily teach a correct association. The child who is hit with his spoon because he cannot use it properly will not necessarily learn proper etiquette. Similarly, the student who is punished for his faulty reading will not necessarily learn to read efficiently. The one child might shun the spoon; the other student may stop reading. Teaching incompatible responses is perhaps the most effective behavioral technique because it constitutes a double-edged approach. Not only is the inappropriate behavior eliminated, but it is replaced by a correct response as well. Thus, the student unlearns and relearns at the same time. It should be obvious that, in this case, appropriate responses are directly proportional to decreases in inappropriate responses. This procedure eliminates the need for much disapproval (punishment) and, at the same time, teaches correct associations. However, the teacher must deal with overt behaviors. *It is much easier to act your way into a new way of thinking than to think your way into a new way of acting.*

Four principles for the teacher follow:

1. *Pinpoint:* It is necessary to pinpoint explicitly the behavior that is to be eliminated or established. This takes place at many different levels relating to many differentiated behaviors. It leads to a hierarchical arrangement of skills and behaviors based on expected specific behavioral goals. Do not deal with intangibles or ideas. If the behavior cannot in some way be both observed and measured then you can never know if it has been either established or unlearned.

2. *Record:* List the specified behaviors in time intervals (seconds, minutes, hours, etc.) and thereby establish a precise record from which to proceed. Keep the record accurate. Do not guess; be scientific. As maladaptive responses are eliminated, or decreased, more time can be devoted to more productive learning.

3. *Consequate:* Set up the external environmental contingencies (including primarily your own personal responses), and proceed with the program. Contingencies include *approval, withholding of approval, disapproval, threat of disapproval,* and *ignoring.* Reinforcement techniques can be words (spoken or written), expressions (facial or bodily), closeness (nearness or touching), activities (social or individual), and things (materials, food, playthings, and awards). Remember that when you ignore, behaviors often initially increase (sometimes for long periods) before they are eliminated.

4. *Evaluate:* Be prepared to stay with a program long enough to ascertain its effectiveness. Compare records after consequating with records taken before. Is the behavior increasing, decreasing, or remaining the same? Learn from your mistakes. And:
   "If at first you don't succeed. . ."—Well, you know.

WHEN WILL STRUCTURE END?

It is clear that the final goal of the education process is to provide the student with behaviors necessary for self-discipline. Indeed, persons whom we as teachers have the privilege to instruct and teach at some future time must be able to be independent. This is, perhaps, the end for which the beginning was made. The goal is achieved less often than most teachers would desire. Students sometimes graduate in ignorance, or because of age, or to find a job, or to get out, but generally not because they have developed sufficient "love" for themselves and others to achieve a state of "independence." We hope that when they must leave for other reasons, they will be independent. It seems important to ensure that this goal is achieved, for when other conditions impinge on the youngsters' environment, they must be prepared.

When an individual has learned from past reinforcement history to arrange values hierarchically, to work productively over long periods of time, to delay gratification, to be content when alone and refrain from haphazardly seeking other individuals, and to modify and control the environment that, in turn, provides personal control, then the individual has achieved an appropriate level of independence. Many problems arise in interpersonal relationships because one or more of the individuals are unable to exhibit any independent behavior. Additionally, some teachers are concerned with vague concepts of "togetherness" that somehow are supposed to develop positive values automatically. Like many ideas (as opposed to overt behaviors), these concepts are highly elusive. When teachers sincerely believe that children will turn out all right if only the child graduates or spends time with "good" companions, this can be devastating.

It is necessary to specify both the overt behaviors that an individual values in terms of "independence" and the precise amount of time necessary to effect goals (e.g., honesty, kindness, creativity, sensitivity, communication, and spontaneity). Before training for independence, teachers should (1) assess specific values and arrange these values in a hierarchical order from the most to the least important. The next step is to (2) define specific behaviors that relate to each of the abstract values, and then (3) teach these behaviors (values) following the behavioral model. The amount of time to be devoted to teaching as well as the time important to spend with certain individuals (alone or in groups) should be outlined.

"Independence," or lack of it, becomes a problem when individuals are unable to be happy when alone or sometimes even when with others. It would seem that everyone should learn to be happy under each condition, as both situations are considered important. Therefore, structuring specified temporal intervals is important. Individual students should be helped with programs that increase both independent activity and joint activity. Truly happy people seem to be those who are happy to be alone, perhaps even for extended periods of time when necessary (vacations, military service, etc.), and also very happy when with others. This condition is not accomplished by students becoming dependent on others to provide a little more life into an otherwise dull existence. Regular routines to occupy one's time can be developed in advance and be readily available when a person needs to be self-reliant.

When will structure end? —With independence.

TEACHING—ART OR SCIENCE?

The question will continue to be asked: "What makes a good teacher?" We have all known some great teachers as well as others who wane by comparison. Analyzing teaching behavior is really no different from analyzing student behavior. Earlier it was stated that students must know what is expected of them and want to do it. Most teachers have at least a general idea of what is expected of them and also want to be good teachers. However, if they do not structure the behaviors to be learned, practice techniques of effective classroom control and subject matter presentation, and maintain consistency, then they fail. Every principle relating to student behavior throughout the preceding chapters also applies to the teacher. It is more important, however, for the teacher to realize that *it is the teacher's responsibility* to ensure that proper learning actually takes place—not the student's. How easy it is for some teachers to give *their* problem to the students. "They don't want to learn." "I can't wait to get out of this chalkboard jungle." "Why should I care if the students don't?" Perhaps the extreme of this attitude is manifested by some college teachers who judge their academic prowess by how many students they fail. The teacher who really cares will persevere. Through trial and error, the teacher will find better ways to stimulate students toward their optimum potentials. With or without a full understanding of behavioral principles, the teacher will come to find better methods of behavioral control and subject matter presentation.

The ability to recognize individual differences and to structure a class environment with meaningful contingencies relevant to specific situations represents an outstanding accomplishment. However, good taste is also of major importance. The authors know of one seventh-grade teacher who controlled her class by having the most deviant children "participate in a mock wedding ceremony if they were very bad." When the children evidenced proper behaviors, they were then allowed to "get divorced." This disciplinary procedure was tremendously effective and used behavioral principles. However, it raises serious questions regarding the teaching of other associations.

Another teacher told of a technique she used with second-grade boys. "When a boy misbehaves, I make him wear a girls ribbon in his hair." Does it work? Very well, but again we question the advisability of such insensitivity. It is ironic that this same teacher thought it "terrible" that parents were asked to send some children to school without breakfast occasionally in order to effect proper behaviors through *rewards* of cereal and milk.

It is readily apparent that regardless of how many "behavioral recipes" are available, the insensitive teacher will still be found wanting. The art of being a good teacher seems directly contingent on the behaviors of the teacher as a person. Modeling effects assimilated through the influence of an outstanding individual are still some of the most powerful and far-reaching. Most teachers will allude to a special teacher in their past who influenced them tremendously, even to the point of going into the profession. The truly effective teacher will combine the science of behavior with the art of living to create that exceptionally rare atmosphere—an environment in which children not only take excitement from discovery, but also learn to be nice people.

Teaching— Art or science?

SUMMARY

Teaching—The Art of Discipline

Most teachers have wonderful intentions when they first enter the teaching profession. Yet, many teachers leave the teaching profession because they have not developed effective functional techniques of classroom control and subject matter presentation. Even though some teachers believe that discipline refers to a continuum from permissiveness through strictness, it is easily observed that this is not the case. Effective discipline ensues from direct cause-and-effect relationships. Therefore, concepts such as spanking versus loving, classroom freedom versus dictatorship, and expression versus subjugation are extremely deceptive. Indeed, we discipline only those we love, social freedom can exist only within defined parameters, and self-expression, much like everything else, must be *learned*. The reason we discipline is to provide each child with behaviors necessary for individual productivity. Realizing that decisions determining what constitutes these basic behaviors (curriculum) are our responsibility, we should structure wisely and not deceive ourselves by stating that children are deciding all things for themselves. When we teach children to think (i.e., establish values, decide), we should do so with the express purpose of ensuring logical mediation sequencing and not use the euphemism "thinking" as a rationalization to eschew the responsibility of our job. Every teacher should initially realize that the teacher's primary responsibility is to acculturate the child. Teaching a child to spell, read, and write, as well as to be well behaved, represents the *imposition* of social and educational values that do not originate with the student. The teacher who states, "Oh, but that's not what I mean," obviously needs some personal remediation in thought processes to differentiate between those aspects of life that are definitely mutually exclusive and those that are not. Every teacher should know precisely what decisions are to be the student's and what decisions are to be the teacher's. If a teacher accepts this responsibility and does not try to "give the problem away" then children will acquire the basic learning necessary to develop their own values. Regardless, one should realize that it takes a tremendous amount of courage to act on the basis of one's value orientation, whether student or teacher.

Discipline—The Way to Learning

Learning necessitates experience, discrimination, and association. Since many children are either exceptionally gifted or exceptionally problematic, the first aspect of learning, both socially and academically, is to determine just *where each student is*; that is, to determine what behaviors currently are present and, therefore, to know precisely where to start. *Academic learning* involves structuring subject matter in easily attainable sequential steps beginning at the student's own level. In assessing *maladaptive responses,* the deviant behavior itself is the foremost concern. An involved history of how the student got that way is both unproductive and unnecessary. Academic assessment should take several days, social assessment several minutes. All too often, knowledge concerning a terrible home life, bizarre past experiences or personality test scores provides the opportunity for some teachers to give up on the child because the teacher discovers a "reason" for the deviant behavior. If students are not "motivated to learn" then motivation must be taught before the teacher should expect it to be internalized; it must come from without before it can be from within. Desire for learning (motivation) is taught by establishing *rewards* for learning, first extrinsically, later intrinsically. Realizing that at some point learning usually represents work, the teacher must stretch the ratio of previously established rewards to motivate students through the difficult times. This represents a process of partial reinforcement to teach for long-term goals, that is, establish maturity. The teacher also defines limits of acceptable behavior by initially deciding which decisions are to rest with the student and which decisions rest with the teacher.

Learning—The Modification of Behavior

Behavior modification is a process for structuring both social and academic learning experiences to provide both fine discriminations and correct associations. It seems amazing that there are some teachers who cannot imagine students being able to learn *academic* behavior without receiving feedback (e.g., math) and yet cannot imagine why they should give any feedback for *social* behavior. The process of structuring social feedback necessitates moving from ideas to behaviors. The teacher must deal with specified overtly demonstrable behaviors if the teacher expects to know what has been learned. It has been demonstrated that if students know precisely what is expected of them and they want to do it, they probably will. Preparing expectancies for students necessitates structuring goals. Instructional goals should represent definable overt responses that are realistic, manageable, and, above all, measurable. The teacher should be careful in differentiating between merit versus demerit approaches, and insure that all behaviors are capable of being recognized with approval as well as disapproval. All of these behaviors, both social and academic, must be measured *in time intervals*. Precise and accurate records must be kept.

Behavior—The Contingent Result of Life

Behaviors are learned in time through contingent reinforcement. Therefore, the teacher must structure the student's life experiences if effective learning is to take place. This structure involves controlling as much of the total school environment as possible in order to help the student learn. How much control is to be exercised depends on the values of the teacher (deciding who has the problem). *Reinforcement teaching is the structure of approval and disapproval responses, in time, to shape desired behavior toward specific goals.* Cutting out the payoff often eliminates deviant behavior; wholesome learning is established by instituting a payoff. The teacher must observe the student closely—paying particular attention to what happens immediately before and after a specified behavior—to become proficient in behavioral analysis.

It should be remembered that when the teacher begins to structure or restructure environmental contingencies, problems of "fairness" arise. The teacher then must discriminate between many separate and related social and/or academic issues to decide what is to be done, that is, what's fair. Approval/disapproval techniques for shaping desired behavior include every available personal response as well as all objects at the teacher's disposal: subject matter, words, expressions, closeness, activities, and things. Personal responses should be overtly practiced. Merely reading, discussing, and thinking about responses is not enough to develop these tools effectively.

Life—The Structure of Activities in Time

Everything happens in time; indeed, *life is time*. Temporal aspects of life are not only extremely important, but highly elusive as well. Therefore, in order to be effective the teacher must structure everything, especially the teacher's personal feedback, across temporal schedules that will result in appropriate student behavior. Precise timing in delivering responses cannot be overemphasized. While temporal consistency is the single most important aspect of discipline, it is also the most difficult. Since repetition across time will develop both "good" and "bad" habits, the teacher should be careful concerning this structure and make sure that the habits being established are beneficial for all students and not idiosyncratic to the teacher. Structural manipulation of the external environment is based on four steps: (1) *Pinpoint*—defining the *problem* behavior to be eliminated, the *new behavior* to be learned, or both (teaching incompatible responses). Pinpointing regarding *subject matter* is accomplished by structuring specific measurable goals; pinpointing *maladaptive social responses* necessitates defining deviant responses, specifically in overt categories, and observing the student carefully. These observations not only establish what stimuli are presently reinforcing undesired behavior, but also provide clues for selecting effective reinforcers that can be used to establish other responses. (2) *Record*—assessing behavior quantitatively. It is imperative that accurate records be kept. Otherwise, the teacher can never ascertain the relationship between the frequency and magnitude of the *old* social/academic, adaptive/deviant behaviors and the new. Records must be precise and recordings must be done in *time intervals*. (3) *Consequate*—controlling the external environment through the use of approval/disapproval reinforcers delivered contingently on time schedules to teach desired behaviors. (4) *Evaluate*—measuring the frequency of behavior to see if the behavior gets better or worse. Most often, thoughtfully prescribed contingencies decrease objectionable behaviors from the original recorded level and/or increase desirable responses. If selected reinforcers are not effective, a new structure may be required and other contingencies established. Indeed, restructuring regarding all aspects of instruction should represent a continuous process toward greater refinement and increased teaching effectiveness aimed toward student independence.

Effective teaching takes much practice. Similar to other pursuits in life, the rewards of teaching seem both proportional to, and contingent on, thoughtful involvement, structured action, and continuous learning and evaluation. The end product of this teaching will be a person who is informed, who is individually productive and socially responsible, who has the ability to analyze, criticize, and choose alternatives, and who has a compelling system of values, whereby life may actualize in a manner consistent with ever-increasing knowledge—in a word, a person who evidences *discipline*.

STUDY GUIDE FOR CHAPTER 5

Questions:

1. Explain how time is important in relating to life.

2. What is meant by the statement that rewards must come after the fact if they are to be effective?

* 3. Explain the various fixed and variable schedules using your own examples.

* 4. What is meant by the statement, "Partial reinforcement is the most difficult to extinguish"?

* 5. Why do you think consistency is the most difficult task for a teacher? Give an example.

6. Explain why it is much easier to act your way into a new way of thinking than to think your way into a new way of acting.

7. List and describe the four steps teachers can use in modifying classroom behavior.

8. What elements contribute to habit strength? List some of your own "good," "bad," and "neutral" habits. Do you believe that you do not have any "neutral" habits, that all of your habits are good? Why might others not agree with you?

9. How would you teach independence behaviorally?

*10. Why is teaching an art as well as a science?

* Transfer these questions to your own teaching situation (e.g., Music, Preschool).

LEARNING ACTIVITY 9—TIME AND BEHAVIOR MODIFICATION

1. Write an essay on: How is time important in modifying behavior? Make certain you concern yourself with the issues of (a) when the reinforcement is delivered, (b) increases in the success rate of material learned, (c) partial reinforcement effects, and (d) the learning of a reinforcement schedule.
2. Discuss, in small groups or in writing, how gambling is an illustration of the effects of partial reinforcement.
3. Using the pinpoint model, indicate: (a) How you would reinforce someone in order that the person becomes a constant gambler. (b) How you would reinforce someone such that the person would never gamble. (c) How you would teach an adult illiterate to learn to read, using the same consequences in (a) and (b) above.
4. Read and discuss other participants' essays and indicate how you would apply the same principle to academic responses (reading, mathematics, obeying classroom rules) by substituting actual academic behaviors for the gambling activity.

LEARNING ACTIVITY 10—ROLE-PLAYING ESSAYS FROM PART I

Participants work in groups of four to six and produce a skit to be presented to other participants that demonstrates principles covered in a single essay from Chapters 1 through 5. Each group is assigned one essay, such as "Is the World Fair?" pages 60–61, or "Who has the Responsibility?" pages 23–24, and other participants are not told which essay was assigned to another group. Thirty minutes preparation time should be sufficient to outline the skit, assign responsibility for props, decide who is going to play what roles, and practice.

Groups present skits and the others, those not presenting, use the following form, recording the name, date, and presentation number, and rate the presentation on all categories. Following the presentation, they attempt to determine which essay was being presented.

Following all presentations, the results of ratings should be given to participants and several aspects of the presentation discussed: What was the level of the role-playing situation? Was the approval/disapproval representative of the classroom level? Did the approval/disapproval "fit" the situation? Did it seem unnecessarily contrived? Was the skit creative?

INDIVIDUAL PRESENTATION RATING

Observer Name_____

Date_____

Group_____

Presenter No._____

Essay_____

	1 Fair	2 Below Average	3 Aver- age	4 Above Aver- age	5 Excel- lent
A. Model					
Specificity of behavior (pinpoint)					
Recording possibilities					
Consequences (logical?)					
Evaluation possibilities					
B. How points got across					
Communication of principles					
Organization					
Presentation (gestures, voice)					
C. Potential for consequences in classroom extensions					
Approval					
Disapproval					
D. Overall rating					

E. Comments _____

_____

_____

PART **II**

BEHAVIORAL PRINCIPLES APPLIED

Changing Wrong Associations

ESTABLISHING YOUR VALUE ORIENTATION

The preceding essays comprising Part I were not presented to express maverick points of view. These issues were developed to prepare the teacher to deal with human behavior more objectively. It is extremely easy to make-believe, to pretend that behavior is mystical or that somehow children learn the opposite of what they are taught. Are the fine, gifted students direct products of our inspired teaching, whereas the slow, mischievous, or dull students products of someone else? If we are honest, we must take our share of the grief as well as the joy. Perhaps the most frightening aspect of teaching is that behavior is most certainly learned, and, for this, we as teachers must take full responsibility. Pretending is easier, for discipline is an awesome challenge. We prefer to believe that the deviant child will somehow change—that the bad behavior is just a stage, or if only the student could work it out of his/her system, everything would be all right. We hope, but hope wears thin without positive signs of improvement. We struggle, we wait, we often become discouraged, and finally we realize that it is indeed a cause-and-effect world—in the long run we do "reap what we sow." After myths are laid aside, after the teacher stops worrying and starts acting, after personal beliefs, consistency, and individual responsibility are all in harmony, the teacher begins to teach. Subsequently, behavior becomes more predictable and effects of specific actions assured. As behavioral principles are practiced and applied, the teacher becomes confident that *wrong associations can indeed be changed.*

The following examples represent selected scientific and professional applications of behavioral changing. These excerpts are presented in a format that should be easily understood by teachers. *Scientific Applications* are summaries of scientific studies that have been published in journals or presented by researchers at scientific conventions. Sources for these reports are noted in the reference section with the example number preceding the reference. *Professional Applications* represent the attempts of "ordinary" teachers, parents, counselors, and others to deal with specific problems systematically. These examples are selected from the authors' files.

This format does not begin to do justice to the original reports. The thoughtful reader will not only seek other professional examples directly applicable to the specific teaching situation, but will also begin to read original scientific literature while trying to study carefully the cause-and-effect relationships obviously evidenced in behavioral research. The Introduction to Behavioral Designs/Terminology, pp. 303-330, is designed to help in this transition. It is important for the teacher to understand the principles underlying discipline before choosing specific techniques.

AND THEN WHAT? AND THEN WHAT? AND THEN WHAT?

The following examples are structured to start with simple applications and progress to more difficult and complex issues and procedures with some deviation for variety. When studying these examples it is important to remember that they are not intended to represent a cookbook approach. Subtleties concerning human behavior necessitate that each individual aspect concerning a person's environmental interaction needs to be studied very carefully. An approach that starts with looking up what someone else did hoping that "this will work for me" will probably be unsuccessful. Often teachers and parents "just try something" hoping that "it will work." Most of the time "just trying something" is not the right thing to do *especially* if the "it" does not "work." The problem comes in time. When a behavioral intervention does not solve the problem, then the teacher has to deal with even more negative learning acquired by the student and anything that the teacher now attempts must include the "reinforcement history" of these previous failures. The research literature is replete with well-intended interventions that not only did not work, but also created additional negative contingencies and thus more negative behavior.

One of the best ways to understand this issue is to consider the aspect of punishment. In our school systems and in our society there are many conflicting views regarding punishment. Some people believe (value) that every punishment should "fit the crime." This retributive view (which is consistent with our social punishment systems) suggests that every punishment be commensurate with the crime or transgression committed. Thus for a small crime there ought to be a small punishment; a larger crime *deserves* a larger punishment. In this manner the growing child is punished from time to time being given "what the child deserves."

The problem with this view is that it does not consider the long-term effects of inadvertently teaching the child to continue escalating his/her inappropriate behavior. The punishment may indeed "fit the crime" but not *solve the problem*. This happens because the child learns to gamble (because the child is not always caught) and to endure greater and greater levels of the punishment because the initial punishment was not severe enough to *stop* the behavior. If the goal of the teacher is to stop a student's behavior, then the level of punishment should *not* be commensurate with the crime; it needs to be strong enough to stop the misbehavior. Many children have been systematically taught to endure higher and higher levels of punishment without a reduction in their maladaptive behavior. We then have a situation whereby more and more punishment is given to these "problematic students" across time and yet, their misbehavior does not ever get any better, it gets continuously worse and worse. Every teacher should consider the strong possibility that measuring out "justice" for each transgression actually may inadvertently teach the student only to adapt to increasing levels of punishment. This is the precisely the case with many "hardened criminals." They do not start out this way, they learn by successive approximations to endure ever-greater levels of punishment while continuing to escalate their maladaptive behavior. Indeed, the inadvertent learning derived from punishment constitutes one of the strongest arguments for *a positive approach.*

Therefore, before the teacher starts any program, it is imperative not only to pinpoint the student's behavior and record its frequency, the teacher also needs to think ahead—and predict how the student will respond by asking oneself the question—if I do this, then what will the child do? And if I change to something else, what will probably happen with the student? And then what? And then what? If a teacher can accurately predict what will happen when applying an intervention strategy, then success is greatly enhanced. If the teacher has no idea of where to start, the teacher should probably not start at all. This is not a case where the teacher should *just do something.* Careful *observation* of the individual student combined with continuing study concerning differential effects of various intervention strategies (the effects of setting-up various contingencies) will help the teacher's intervention programs result in more predictable behavior.

WARNING: As you progress through the following examples you must make the discriminations necessary for implementing an effective program in relationship to your own values and the prescribed values of your societal setting. There are several examples that, while effective in changing behavior, are not within the value system of the authors and are included to teach discrimination. *Each person must discriminate.* Some of the pinpointed behaviors may seem very "wrong" to you. Additionally, some of the procedures used to effect change may appear extremely questionable. Indeed, some of the following examples are "home" and/or "adult" procedures not appropriate in most other settings and whose use are highly questionable (e.g., the use of physical punishment or contingencies concerning food.) It is mandatory that you differentiate among the many examples in order to select both behaviors and procedures that are not only legal but also appropriate to your own value system, personal teaching style, and within the policies of your societal agency. As has been stressed repeatedly, just because something has been demonstrated as behaviorally effective does not indicate that it ought to be done. Also, the following examples include many different behaviors and procedures that are not school-related. These are intended to stimulate thought toward greater understanding, sensitivity and discrimination. Processes and principles are of much greater consequence than is the choice of reinforcers. When processes of education are fully understood, fanciful gimmicks become sound pedagogy.

PINPOINT REFERENCE GUIDE

Preschool Examples

Example number	Pinpoint
1	Fear in young children
2	Fighting over toys
3	Crying when parents leave child at nursery
4	Low-frequency talking
5	Crawling during school
6	Discriminating rules for visiting children
7	Assessing truth
8	Physical aggression
9	Aggressive hitting
10	Isolate behavior
11	Walking in street
12	Repeated crying
13	Sex-role behavior
14	Mistreatment of animals
15	Screaming, yelling, fighting between siblings
16	Temper outbursts
17	Determining effective rewards to increase learning
18	Breaking household rules
19	Self-help behaviors
20	"Disobedience" and "aggression"
21	Children manipulating parents
22	Developing positive computer skill
23	Self-protection against abduction

Lower Primary Examples

Example number	Pinpoint
24	Show-off
25	Fear of going to school
26	Increases in speaking about oneself
27	Talking, standing, blurting out, noisy inattention, turning around
28	Child asks about sex
29	"Off-task" during individual seatwork
30	Striking children with objects
31	Following instructions
32	Inappropriate behaviors
33	Failure to eat "nourishing" foods
34	Hyperactivity
35	Writing vulgar words
36	Standing up, walking around
37	Using subject matter to reinforce low-level subject matter
38	Arson
39	Rest time disruptions
40	Teaching beginning reading
41	"Bad attitude"
42	Thumb-sucking
43	Unfinished assignments, bothering neighbors, playing
44	"On-task" attention, academic accuracy
45	Spelling accuracy
46	Stuttering

Upper Primary Examples

Example number	Pinpoint
47	Bothering teacher at desk
48	Teasing other children
49	Child interfering with other child's play
50	Overactivity
51	Littering
52	Homework completion accuracy
53	Disruptive classroom behavior
54	Positive piano practice
55	Failure to pass "Key Skills"
56	Disruptive noise
57	Reading "bad" literature

58	High noise level-lunchroom
59	Arithmetic achievement
60	Excessive dawdling
61	Teaching lying behavior
62	Inappropriate oral hygiene
63	Classroom "out of control"
64	Negative comments and high intensity "screaming" among family members prior to evening meal
65	Volunteering answers
66	Bed-wetting (enuresis)
67	Academic under achievement
68	Talking out, standing
69	Tardiness following recess
70	Remediation of mutually aversive interactions between a problem student and four teachers

Middle School/Junior High School Examples

Example number	Pinpoint
71	Homework study time
72	Low-level skill achievement
73	Noisy transition changing classes
74	Chewing-gum vandalism
75	High level off-task
76	Off-task individual study
77	Constant talking out and disturbing others during study time
78	Fighting during recess
79	Vandalism
80	Disruptive behaviors-talking, fighting, out of seat, throwing objects, noisy
81	"Joy riding"
82	Disruptive social talking
83	Juvenile offender
84	Disruptive school bus behavior
85	Teaching contractual agreements
86	Academic failure
87	Rebelliousness, disagreements, and refusal to talk to parents
88	Increasing math responses
89	Low arithmetic achievement
90	Obesity
91	Negative verbalizations
92	Physical abuse of mother
93	"Off-task," low-achieving students

High School/Adult Examples

Example number	Pinpoint
94	School failure
95	"Love-note" passing-boy-girl talking
96	Homework study
97	Boredom
98	Loud disruptive laughing
99	Positive verbalizations about oneself and positive social interactions
100	Noncooperation
101	Use of illegal drugs
102	Cocaine and marijuana dependence
103	Fear of failure, worrying
104	Increasing salad purchase at fast-food restaurants
105	Rehearsal effectiveness
106	Using adoption to control adults
107	Pedestrian cross-walk safety
108	Garbage removal from kitchen
109	Embarrassment
110	Inappropriate sexual advances
111	Illegal parking in handicapped spaces
112	Lawbreaking
113	Excessive local directory-assistance telephone calls
114	Low-level English achievement
115	Increasing athletic performance
116	Decreasing vascular headaches
117	Academic "apathy"
118	"On-task" versus cluttered communication
119	Developing a study routine
120	Dishonesty

PRESCHOOL EXAMPLES

Example 1

Pinpoint: *Fear in young children* (separate studies concerning 600 children, infants and school age)

Record: Overt signs of fear exhibited whenever children confronted fearful situations. Procedures reported from parent interviews and classified according to effectiveness.

Consequate: Following procedures reported effective by parents: (1) *Incompatible response.* Feared object or situation gradually introduced into child's presence while child engaged in fun activity; (2) *Gradual approach.* Child led by degrees (over a number of days) to come closer and closer to feared object or participate in feared activity; (3) *Modeling.* Feared activity or object made readily accessible to child while other children participated enjoyably.

Evaluate: *Incompatible responses, gradual approach,* and *modeling* eliminated about 85% of children's fears, according to parents.

Note: The following procedures were *not* successful: disapproval, social ridicule, scolding, verbal appeals, punishment, forcing child to participate, or changing the child's activity whenever he was afraid. When any fearful situation is forced on a child, fear may be *increased.*

Scientific Application (p. 331)

Example 2

Pinpoint: *Fighting over toys* (2- and 6-year-old boys)

Record: Children fought as to who owned particular toy (four times in A.M.); mother admonished children to share.

Consequate: Program instituted to teach children: (1) ownership and (2) sharing. Children told "ownership is when a toy belongs to you, and you can do anything you want with it," and "sharing is when you let somebody else use something that belongs to you." Children given separate toys (some for John, some for Marc, some for both), again admonished to share, and praised when they did.

Evaluate: Children initially hoarded their own toys (two weeks), then began to trade (three occurrences, two days), then to share (sixteen instances over four days). Fighting over toys diminished to an average of less than once per day.

Professional Application

Example 3

Pinpoint: *Crying when parents leave child at nursery* (18 children, infants through 6 years old)

Record: Parents recorded children crying and clinging an average of 9 to 12 times and also commented on "general upsetness" when parents ready to leave child (15 minutes prior to leaving, two to six observations).

Consequate: Parents "proved" to child they always come back (building hope in the child by successive approximations). Parents kissed child good-bye, ignored clinging, left immediately, walked around nursery, came back in the door. (Parents instructed to always wait until crying ceased before reentering.) Parents again left following same routine (hug and kiss), promising to return shortly. (Any hesitation at door reinforces crying; it is even worse to comfort child after he begins to cry, which teaches him that if he is upset enough he can delay parents' exit.) This same procedure followed for varying lengths of time (ten seconds, two minutes, thirty seconds, four minutes, one minute, six minutes, etc.; the technique is then expanded to longer periods of time). About every third time a special little treat is given to the child for being nice when parents arrive.

Evaluate: Goodbyes became happy times as children anticipate parents sometimes coming back with special small toys or treats.

Note: It is suggested to parents that when they begin this program for the first time, they begin at least one hour prior to normal departure time.

Professional Application

Example 4

Pinpoint: *Low-frequency talking* (4-year-old girl)

Record: Verbalization occurred only during 11% of all 10-second intervals observed (trained observers).

Consequate: Teacher attention to child contingent on talking; when child did not talk, she was ignored by teacher. Child also required to answer questions when requesting materials before receiving them (materials contingent on question answering).

Evaluate: Talking increased to average 75%.

What would happen if . . .

Consequate II: Teacher attention to child contingent on non-verbalization; when child talked, child ignored by teacher. (Reversal of contingencies.)

Evaluate II: Talking decreased to 6%.

Consequate III: Again teacher gave attention for verbalizations, but stopped requiring talking before providing requested materials.

Evaluate III: Child's talking increased to 61%, dropped to 28% when questioning and further talking eliminated.

Note: Authors indicate that since talking dropped when teacher discontinued the questioning as requirement for receiving materials, it is clear that it was not the teacher's social approval alone that was responsible for the high rate of talking. They report that questioning the child and requiring several responses before allowing access to materials is crucial.

Scientific Application (p. 331)

Example 5

Pinpoint: *Crawling during school* (nursery school, girl 3.4 years)

Record: Girl spent 75% of time (observed two weeks) in off-feet position. Also avoided contacts with other children and adults.

Consequate: Nursery school teachers *ignored* girl when not standing; approached, praised, displayed interest when girl on feet. Disapproval techniques such as anger, shame, disgust, or disappointment not used.

Evaluate: Girl stood 75% of time during first week. During second week, up as much as other children.

Consequate II: Contingencies reversed. Teachers approved off-feet behavior.

Evaluate II: First day of reversal, girl off-feet 75% of time; second day 81.9%.

Consequate III: Return to praise for standing.

Evaluate III: First hour of first day, on-feet 75.9%; first hour of second day, 62.7%; by second hour, 100%. *No relapses observed.*

Scientific Application (p. 331)

Example 6

Pinpoint: *Discriminating rules for visiting children* (13 children, 2 to 9 years old)

Record: "Total bedlam" (three visits from other children) reported by one parent who said, "If I have to put up with those neighbor's children again,

I'll even stop letting their parents visit." Another parent, "I can't do anything with that child after she comes from Grandmother's."

Consequate: *Difficult* program to teach parents to have enough courage to enforce their own rules with other children and also with visits to grandparents. Simple program to teach visiting children discriminations. "In this house you must follow (different) rules." Visiting children told when entered house about expectations and consequences: "If you play nicely, you may have a treat, and if you break our rules (carefully explained), you must leave." Own children told "when we are home from grandparents' we have different rules."

Evaluate: Children learned to discriminate (rowdy, undisciplined, only in situations where allowed) and followed rules in orderly house after being sent home twice (average) first week. Own children took average of one day to "shape up" after visit to grandparents.

Note: Only adults' behavior presents problems in these situations. However, an initial strong positive approach with other parents, especially one's own, usually solves the problem. When adults do set strong limits with neighbor's children (especially if they pay off, from time to time, children's good behavior), their house will usually be the one all the children "love to visit." When grandparents visit, it is wise to give them a set of the child's rules when they arrive, making sure to correct grandparents' deviations immediately and gently. Children also learn different rules in different classrooms.

Professional Application

Example 7

Pinpoint: *Assessing truth* (12 children, all under 6 years old)

Record: Children suspected of wrongdoing, that is, in this particular case parent entered room of two children after younger brother started to cry (parent's self-report).

Consequate: "Annabelle story" (or masculine counterpart name) instituted. Child given story paradigm that initially described a little boy or girl with all aspects of child's own physical features, home environment, and so on. After this initial programming, the suspected wrong is then recounted vicariously. For example, "Cherrie, you have such nice blue eyes, and you are such a big four-year-old with nice toys and a little brother. I am going to tell you a story. There once was a girl named Annabelle. She had pretty blue eyes and she was a big four-year-old. Annabelle also had a little brother. One day Annabelle was playing with her little brother, and Annabelle's mother heard the little brother crying. Why do you think Annabelle's brother was crying?"

Evaluate: Cherrie, "Because he took Annabelle's toy, and Annabelle hit him."

Note: This procedure works almost always with young children because children of this age do not have the power to think abstractly. It is often extremely difficult for parents to believe that children do not realize they are describing themselves. This procedure is *not* recommended except in those situations where physical harm is either given to or received by a child.

Professional Application

Example 8

Pinpoint: *Physical aggression* (nursery school, 27 boys, 3 to 4 years old)

Record: Physical aggression frequency during observation period totaled 41.2 incidents, verbal aggression 22.8, with total 64.0 incidents (one-week observation).

Consequate: Teachers ignored aggression and rewarded cooperative and peaceful behaviors (interfered only when bodily harm was likely). Approval techniques replaced reprimands.

Evaluate: Total aggressive behaviors decreased—64 incidents to 43.4. (Physical aggression 41.2 to 26.0; verbal aggression 22.8 to 17.4.)

Consequate II: Following initial consequate, researchers told teachers experiment completed. However, observations again recorded three weeks later.

Evaluate II: After experimenters left, teachers not as consistent. Total number aggressive responses increased 43.4 to 51.6. Physical aggression increased 26.0 to 37.8. However, verbal aggression decreased 16.4 to 13.8. Teachers found it harder to ignore fighting than to ignore verbal threats.)

Consequate III: Consequate I reinstated.

Evaluate III: Total aggression decreased 51.6 to 25.6. Physical aggression decreased 37.8 to 21.0; verbal aggression 13.8 to 4.6.

Note: This study substantiates the necessity of *absolute consistency.*

Scientific Application (p. 331)

Example 9

Pinpoint: *Aggressive hitting* (preschool boys, private kindergarten)

Record: Teacher complained boys went "out of control" during outside play periods (five children hurt in one week).

Consequate: Large punching bag dummy with red nose installed on playground.

Evaluate: No noticeable decrease in human hitting—six children hurt during week.   Dummy punched frequently, especially in nose. (Actually, boys fought each other to take turns at dummy.)

Consequate II: Punching dummy removed.   Individual boys isolated for duration of play period when observed hitting another child.

Evaluate II: After five days (seventeen isolations), hitting completely eliminated.

Note: Hitting, like other behavior, is most probably *learned*. The more children are reinforced for hitting, the more they will hit. Some people even develop a curious "self-fulfilling prophecy" in this regard. They sincerely believe that if they could just hit something they would feel much better. Thus, when frustrated, they hit something and, sure enough, they feel better.

Professional Application

Example 10

Pinpoint: *Isolate behavior* (girl, age 4.3 years)

Record: Varied repertory of well-developed skills pleased adults, but did not gain child-child interactions.   Observations during entire mornings by trained observers (one week) indicated: 10% child interaction, 40% adult interaction, 50% isolate.

Consequate: Maximum adult attention for child interaction. *No* attention for isolate behavior or adult interaction.

Evaluate: Over six days, child interaction increased to 60%, adult interaction decreased to 20%, time spent alone decreased to 20%.

Consequate II: Contingencies withdrawn.

Evaluate II: Child interaction *decreased* to 20%, adult *increased* to 40%, isolate *increased* to 40%.

Consequate III: Contingencies reestablished. Attention for interaction with children. Child interaction increased to 60%, adult decreased to 25%, isolate decreased to 15%.

Note: Follow-up observation showed girl to be maintaining the increased ratio of child interaction.

Scientific Application (p. 331)

Example 11

Pinpoint: *Walking in the street* (1.5 to 4-year-old boys and girls)

Record: Various occurrences (parent's self-report).

Consequate: Children spanked, yelled at for going into street, given approval for verbalizing comments concerning "not going into street"; taken to edge of pavement and taught discrimination if preverbal, that is, child put on grass, given approval, taken barely onto pavement spanked, yelled at. Child taught that when they hold parents' hand then and only then may they walk in or across streets, parking lots, and so on.

Evaluate: ?

Note: The strength of reinforcement required for teaching should be in direct proportion to the danger involved. Extremely strong contingencies are generally referred to as "doomsday contingencies" i.e., the results of what we do or don't do are so extreme that we cannot afford to miscalculate. (It seems unwise to put both dirty hands and potential death into the same "no-no" basket.) Sometimes complete supervision or instilling fear is the only alternative to potential danger; sometimes teaching for discrimination is advisable (i.e., concerning knives, hot stoves, scissors, electricity, poisons, water). *The adult must decide what is important.*

Professional Application

Example 12

Pinpoint: *Repeated crying* (4-year-old boy, preschool)

Record: Eight crying periods each morning following mild frustrations. Whenever boy cried, teachers comforted him (picked up, talked softly, held on lap, etc.).

Consequate: Boy ignored unless "real grounds" for crying; given approval for self-help attempts.

Evaluate: One crying spell in five days after initial decrease.

Consequate II: Teachers again paid attention to crying (10 days).

Evaluate II: Crying almost reached original level during record phase.

Consequate III: Boy ignored when crying; given approval for self-help (10 days).

Evaluate III: Crying decreased to zero and low level maintained.

Note: The cause-and-effect relationship between adult approval and child behaviors is clearly demonstrated in this case. The reader may be wondering why one would deliberately produce inappropriate behavior in a student. In a research study, the experimenter must determine that a particular reinforcer is really causing a specific effect. In this case the reinforcer was attention—the effect, not crying. When a teacher is "sure" what produces a desired change in the classroom, this may be enough. However, the scientist must be certain. The reversal technique will be noted repeatedly in scientific investigations. See chapter 10.

Scientific Application (p. 331)

Example 13

Pinpoint: *Sex-role behavior* (175 boys, 85 girls; ages 5 years, 10 months to 6 years, 8 months)

Record: Series of experimental studies recorded amount of play with toys that have been traditionally considered as sex-typed, as well as neutral toys. ("Girls' " toys included doll, pearl beads, high-heeled shoes, a mirror, play make-up materials, cups and dishes, and a baby carriage with a doll; "boys' " toys consisted of boxing gloves, a tank, a racing car, a sword, a gun, a catcher's mitt, and a baseball; neutral toys included a pegboard, three old blocks, and three pieces of tinker toys. The neutral toys were deliberately less inviting for purposes of the experiments.)

Consequate: Children observed peer and adult models playing with either "sex-inappropriate" or "sex-appropriate" toys. Some models gave approving or disapproving comments; that is, "I don't want to play with those; they are girls' toys." Some models said nothing while playing with toys and others gave verbal cues as well as playing. (Five separate experimental studies were completed with excellent control groups.)

Evaluate: Even with little total time exposure to models (less than 10 minutes), when children saw peer and adults playing with toys, they increased the time spent with toys. Children who saw models receive approval after playing with certain toys played more with these toys themselves (even when no approval was given to children). Children who observed others receive disapproval for playing with certain toys tended to avoid the same toys themselves. Children who observed someone giving themselves reasons for not playing with certain toys and who did not engage in play themselves were better able to gain similar control over their own behavior.

Note: These studies are extremely important for those who desire to increase or decrease the sex-role behavior of children. Society has changed very dramatically in past decades, and it becomes more and more difficult to draw distinctions between masculine and feminine roles—some would say that this is good. However, adults who are concerned should label verbally and reinforce whatever they consider to be appropriate behavior from a very young age that fit within the value system of the adults. These studies clearly demonstrate the cause-and-effect relationship between: (1) supplying a child with the label, (2) modeling "appropriate behaviors," and (3) producing same. It appears obvious that in the above study the "boys' " and "girls' " toys could have been reversed or mixed with similar results.

Scientific Application (p. 331)

Example 14

Pinpoint: *Mistreatment of animals* (5-year-old boy)

Record: Neighborhood adults reported to parents that they had seen boy striking their dog with sticks. Child also observed attempting to put cats under water (four occurrences in six weeks).

Consequate: Parents purchased small dog, made son completely responsible for care and feeding, including exercise. Boy paid small allowance per day when pet was fed and exercised. When boy forgot, he fed dog before he was allowed to eat himself. No payment was made when he forgot.

Evaluate: No incidents of animal abuse during next two weeks.

Note: After the boy had cared for his pet for six weeks he stated that he did not want any money for doing it anymore because now he really "loved Rags." It seems we learn to love by doing—perhaps this helps explain why parents love their children. However, this is yet another behavior that might need careful adult attention. Usually cruelty to animals constitutes a strong warning sign to societal agents. The boy in the above case learned correct associations; this same behavior in others might be an indication of extreme psychological problems.

Professional Application

Example 15

Pinpoint: *Screaming, yelling, fighting between siblings* (two boys, 3 and 6 years old)

Record: Boys fought whenever alone, damaged toys and furniture, older boy had recently broken neighbor's window. Observers (trained) watched when mother was not present (60 to 90 minutes daily). Inappropriate behaviors (kicking, hitting, pushing, name-calling, throwing objects at each other) and cooperative behaviors (asking for something, requesting help, pleasant talking, playing close), combined, produced a cooperative behavior ratio of 46% (cooperative behavior divided by cooperative behavior plus inappropriate behavior). Six-year-old boy professionally diagnosed as "immature and brain-damaged" as he was hyperactive, aggressive, and destructive. Observations indicated mother paid attention only after high-intensity inappropriate responses.

Consequate: Cooperative responses given approval by placing small candies in mouth and saying "good" every time a cooperative response occurred during *first two days*. Approval (things and words) given every second to fourth cooperative behavior next two days. Mother's helper (professional) told boys they would receive approval if they asked for things saying please and thank you, answered questions, and played nicely together. Instructions repeated each day. On the fifth day a token check mark system plus instructions instituted. Both boys' names written on chalkboard in playroom. Checks earned for cooperative behaviors were removed for inappropriate behaviors. Checks exchanged for candy bars, bubble gum, caps, kites, comic books, puzzles, small toys. The "price" boys paid for goodies was continually increased. Candies discontinued on twelfth day; a check system only for last four days.

Evaluate: Cooperative play averaged 85% (16 consequate days). Gradual rise in cooperative behavior prevailed (last day 100%) even though prices increased throughout program.

Consequate II: Check system removed for five days (observers recorded behavior but did not dispense approval).

Evaluate II: Cooperative behavior declined when no approval given (average 50%).

Consequate III: Check system reinstated with mother taking over management second day. Cooperative behavior increased but since some intense fighting occurred periodically, mother added disapproval contingency. When either child kicked, hit, pushed, name-called, or threw object, mother placed boy in bathroom (interesting items removed, closed door, and left him) for five minutes (last three minutes had to be quiet time for boy to rejoin group). Isolation used once per day for each child during first three days, only once overall during last four. Mother also increased amount of checks necessary for approval rewards (raised prices). Children cooperated for three days before purchase possible. Mother also given help in knowing when to use contact and words in approving manner.

Evaluate III: Combination of procedures, administered by mother, resulted in cooperative play ratio of 90%. Experiment in effect for an hour and a half during day, but as study concluded, both parents practiced using behavioral principles throughout day. Teacher of older boy reported school behaviors improved.

Note: Authors of this scientific study reported parents had probably extinguished many behaviors of the older boy for lack of attention except for very high-intensity behaviors, which received much verbal and physical attention (many spankings). Following study, parents started to change, that is, they reported using more approval to initiate and maintain appropriate behavior and established token systems for some household chores. Authors reported parents surprised that a "brain-damaged" child could respond. It would appear that placing these kinds of labels on children solves few if any problems and may even generate feelings of futility within the parents rather than determination to do the best job possible. Some parents give the problem away (abdicate responsibility) because child is brain-damaged, retarded, autistic, neurotic, emotionally disturbed, or any number of labels that may lead to resignation rather than a behavioral analysis of what is possible. *Every* child is "normal" in many ways, and *every* child is abnormal in others.

Scientific Application (p. 331)

Example 16

Pinpoint: *Temper outbursts.* (4-year-old boy—IQ recorded 72 and 80—possible brain damage)

Record: Frequency of objectionable behaviors varied from 18 to 112 during 16 one-hour periods (sticking out tongue, kicking, yelling, threatening to remove clothing, calling people names, throwing objects, biting, and hitting self).

Consequate: Consequences applied by mother in home two to three times per week for six one-hour sessions. Researchers helped mother by giving signals indicating: (1) she should tell her son to stop what he was doing, (2) place him in isolation for five minutes, or (3) give attention, praise, and affection.

Evaluate: Rate of objectionable behavior decreased (range one to eight per session). Isolation used four times; special attention given ten times.

Consequate II: No signals given; mother told to *"act as before."*

Evaluate II: Objectionable behaviors increased, but ranged well below original recordings (two to twenty-four per session). It appeared mother "learned." She reported more self-assurance, increased attention, delivered firm commands, and did not give in after denying a request.

Consequate III: Consequate I reinstated, except special attention for desirable play excluded.

Evaluate III: Objectionable behavior again *decreased* (almost identical to Consequate I, ranging from two to eight per session).

Note: No contact was maintained with the mother for twenty-four days after the experiment. She was given no instructions as to how to act and was given complete freedom to use any technique she desired. Later, a three-session post-contact check was made. Even after this long delay, the behaviors considered objectionable were still very low. The mother reported that her child was well behaved and less demanding. Isolation was used on the average of once per week. The mother's attitude toward her son was also considered to be more approving.

Scientific Application (p. 331)

Example 17

Pinpoint: *Determining effective rewards to increase learning* (kindergarten classes, 88 children)

Record: Low-level discrimination on auditory discrimination test.

Consequate: Contingent rewards for meeting daily criterion on auditory tasks. Reward groups consisted of (1) TV music lessons, (2) free play, (3) choice of TV *or* free play, (4) no-contact control group.

Evaluate: All those reward groups improved significantly on tested auditory discrimination.

Note: The children who were assigned to the TV reward improved as much as the group who were assigned the free play contingency. Since the educational television also produced academic learning, it would seem advisable to use educational rewards as much as possible.

Scientific Application (p. 332)

Example 18

Pinpoint: *Breaking household rules* (3- and 4-year-old boys)

Record: From 9 A.M. to 12 noon, mother's recording (six days) indicated an average of 29 rule violations—playing in toilet, pulling dog's tail, climbing in kitchen, breakable items removed from cupboards, toys left out, changing TV and stereo knobs, taking telephone off hook, throwing artificial fruit, that is, "doing the don'ts." Mother "caught the boys" about 22 times daily and (1) told them "why" what they were doing was wrong (reasoning), (2) scolded them, and (3) either slapped their hands or bottoms.

Consequate: Mother instructed to (1) ignore minor deviations unless some-one could be hurt; (2) give great deal of praise for good behavior, that is, "catch each child being good" and verbally praise at least five times per hour each day, at same time pass out chips, let boys "spend" them later on good-ies; (3) use approval for one child when the other is inappropriate; for instance, "you're playing nicely, you didn't turn the TV dials" (after brother has turned dials); (4) when disapproval is warranted punish immediately with no talking or warning, generally by complete isolation, for a period of not more than two minutes, and (5) go over household rules each morning plus three or four times per day when boys *are following* rules, *not* when they are disobedient.

Evaluate: Mother praised each child on an average of 13 times per morning. She also stated other instructions were followed. Disapproval averaged 34 during first three days with 27 isolations. Mother called consultant to report records and said behavior "hadn't changed" but had increased. Conversation indicated behavior change had indeed taken place (an increase in misbehavior). Mother instructed to maintain contingencies for 10 days. Next day (fourth) misbehavior decreased (23) with further daily decreases to average of three per day (ninth day).

Note: Disapproval (corporal punishment) was used in this case to stop inap-propriate behavior as well as isolation. When removing the child from a positive surrounding, one must be certain that isolation is not more reward-ing (e.g., playroom) than the closeness and verbal approval of the mother. Parents should also realize when starting new routines, as in this case, pay-offs have been received for a long time by "doing the don'ts."

Professional Application

Example 19

Pinpoint: *Self-help behaviors* (4.5-year-old boy)

Record: Nothing. Boy born blind, severe hearing problem, could not walk, braces on legs, not toilet trained, said no words, could not feed self. (Tested IQ of 22.) Mother waiting to admit boy to large custodial hospital for men-tally retarded.

Consequate: Pediatrician assured mother that boy was in good health and that food deprivation would not be harmful for up to 36 hours; mother instructed to not use spoon, but to place Rob in high chair, put his fingers in food, and lift food to his mouth on his own fingers, three meals daily for two weeks. Following this procedure, his mother prepared Rob's favorite food, sat him in high chair, put his fingers in food, lifted them to within two inches of his mouth, then dropped her hand (this repeated until Rob fed himself or until it had been done 120 times at which time he was taken out of chair and not placed back for period of two hours).

Evaluate: Rob cried when mother dropped her hands, threw his food, and made what mother called "his angry noises." Rob did not eat until deprived of food for 34 hours, and mother left house twice because of his "terrible crying and whimpering."

Note: Most very young children have learned thousands of cause-and-effect relationships regarding consequences of their own behavior, but in this case this young boy had not learned even the very first (i.e., put food in mouth, swallow, pleasant sensation). He had only learned the latter part of the sequence with no causal relationship between his internal behavior and the behavior of the outside environment, that is, getting food into his mouth. Starvation was used to maximize the effect of pleasure derived from the food. This boy, through elaborate series of shaping procedures, learned how to find his own way around the house (rolling to his food from ever greater distances as he couldn't walk), toilet training (using liquid juice as a reward), verbalizations (pairing feel and words starting with body parts), play skills (through the use of contingent music), and then progressed to more normal activities of childhood. These procedures allowed this child first to be placed in a private school (behaviorally oriented) and later to enroll in a normal kindergarten. After three years follow-up the child has progressed normally into and through the public schools. Extremely strong contingencies were necessary in this program that started *where the boy was*. It sometimes must be remembered that there is an infinite distance between zero and one.

Professional Application

Example 20

Pinpoint: *"Disobedience" and "aggression"* (4-year, 8 month-old boy)

Record: Trained observers recorded occurrence or nonoccurrence one hour per day (percent of time intervals behavior occurred). Aggression-defined as hitting, pushing, kicking, throwing, biting, and scratching—occurred 7.7% of the time and disobedience—defined as not following instructions by mother, which included name and a command to do or stop doing something specific—occurred 70.0% of the time (average for ten-day observation period). Observers noted that mother gave approval to undesirable behavior and was inconsistent in techniques of reinforcement.

Consequate: Appropriate behavior received praise and "goodies." Whenever mother noted aggressive or disobedient behavior she would tell boy, "You may not stay here (yard or playroom, etc.) if you do not do as you are told," and rapidly take him to time-out (isolation) room and leave him for two minutes. All items of child interest had been removed from the room. Boy remained two minutes *after* he stopped crying, screaming, noise-making.

Evaluate: Aggression decreased to 1.2% and disobedience decreased to 22.0% (average for 10 days of consequences with generally better behavior each day).

Consequate II: Mother returned to original routines, refrained from using "time-out" room.

Evaluate II: Aggression increased to 4.0%, disobedience increased to 57% (average for six days, however, disobedience was 80% on last day).

Consequate III: Mother used "time-out" (isolation) room and comments again as well as praise and "goodies" for appropriate obedience.

Evaluate III: Aggression decreased to 0.3% and disobedience to 22% (four days).

Note: Consistency in following a routine until behavior is changed is demonstrated by the mother applying consequences, removing consequences, and applying them again (reversals). Some children may take an extended period of time to "change wrong associations" and even longer to become "self-motivated." Any new program should have as much consistency as possible for two weeks before something new is attempted.

Scientific Application (p. 332)

Example 21

Pinpoint: *Children manipulating parents* (three children and mothers trained in Child Development Clinic—a 6-year-old boy attempted to force parents to comply with his wishes; a 4-year-old boy considered excessively dependent at home, aggressive in nursery school; another 4-year-old extremely stubborn in presence of mother but not with other adults)

Record: Each mother observed while interacting with son.

Consequate: Mothers instructed: (1) in delivery of approval techniques, (2) to ignore inappropriate behavior, and (3) to respond with praise and affection for appropriate behavior. Mother A responded positively to child *only* when he did not attempt to force compliance. Mother B ignored child's dependency, responded approvingly to independent behavior. Mother C ignored opposition behavior, responded to cooperative behavior. Later, Mother C was instructed to isolate son in empty room for at least five minutes immediately following opposition responses.

Evaluate: First two boys' behavior improved markedly through mothers' attention to appropriate behavior and ignoring inappropriate responses. The third boy improved only after isolation.

Note: This is a good example of differential treatment. The teacher should always remember that it is necessary to structure for each student. It should be noted that the use of disapproval (isolation) was necessary for one child before improvement took place.

Scientific Application (p. 332)

Example 22

Pinpoint: *Developing positive computer skills* (2-year, 4 month-old girl)

Record: New behavior. No instances of child interacting with "adult computer."

Consequate: Privilege of "playing with computer" approached as "having fun with grandma." Child provided the opportunity to sit on grandma's lap and play with "adult" computer. Educational software package for pre-school children selected to teach reinforcing computer interaction. In good educational software packages, very young child only move the entire mouse to activate "sites" (like/different, counting to three, turning off/on various musical voices, making animals pop out of a box, etc.) before moving on to "click" the mouse and more advanced eye-hand coordination.

Evaluate: Child asks to "have fun with grandma" each time in Grandma's presence. Time spent with computer gradually increases to 20-25 minutes per session across five weeks.

Note: Most children enjoy playing with toys as well as "playing" with computers, especially when they can interact and make things happen. Many children have various toys having computer chips that provide interaction, yet the advantage of establishing more sophisticated child/computer interactions appears obvious for today's youngsters. Young children's beginning computer skills are deemed too important by most parents to allow these first interactions to be perceived by the child as being negative. It is important, therefore, that when any new activity is instituted with a young child, that the adult supervises the activity completely (i.e., actively participates) and ensures that the experience is positive. Of course, as in the above example, the child must first perceive the association with grandma (or other adult) as positive.

Professional Application

Example 23

Pinpoint: *Self-protection against abduction* (74 children: 33 girls, 41 boys, aged 5 to 7 years)

Record: New behavior

Consequate I: Twenty children received no safety training.

Evaluate I: 25% of children verbally resisted staged abduction 1 to 2 days later. No children ran away from potential abductor.

Consequate II: Sixteen children received standard safety presentation including discussion of possible abduction scenarios and solutions, and short film warning children not to trust strangers.

Evaluate II: 37.5% of children verbally resisted staged abduction 1 to 2 days later. 12.5% ran away from potential abductor.

Consequate III: Nineteen children viewed a 20-minute color video, including scenes with abductors approaching children and children displaying appropriate responses. The videotape attempted to be interactive. That is, after each scene, the narrator on the tape asked viewers if the children in the film said and did the right things. Pauses were provided for viewers' replies. The narrator then praised appropriate responses and corrected inappropriate ones in this manner. "If you said _____, you're right, good listening! If you said _____, then I've fooled you. Watch again . . .

Evaluate III: 68.5% of children verbally resisted staged abduction 1 to 2 days later, 52.6% used the criterion responses viewed on the video. 47.4% ran away from potential abductor.

Consequate IV: Nineteen children viewed same video and practiced resisting possible abduction scenarios.

Evaluate IV: 84.2% of children verbally resisted staged abduction 1 to 2 days later, 63.2% used the video criterion verbal responses, 73.7% ran away from potential abductor.

Note: A one-month follow-up revealed that the videotape program with behavioral rehearsal was still highly effective in teaching children safe responses to potential abductors. Of greater concern in this study was that the standard safety program was effective with fewer than half of the children and three-fourths of the children who received no training immediately agreed to go with the confederate suspects.

Scientific Application (p. 332)

LOWER PRIMARY EXAMPLES

Example 24

Pinpoint: *Show-off* (8-year, 8-month-old boy)

Record: Three specific behaviors approved by peers. Out of seat 20 times per day, talking without permission 18 times per day, five incomplete assignments (one week).

Consequate: Program initiated retaining approval from peers. Instead of receiving laughter for getting out of seat and talking, child allowed to tell jokes; instead of receiving attention for misbehaving, child received praise for proper behavior. Boy stayed after school as reward rather than punishment.

Evaluate: First week, talking decreased to two occurrences, left seat only once. Second through fourth week, *no* rules broken. Only one inappropriate behavior in fifth week.

Note: A great deal of "show-off" behavior is maintained by peer attention. If one child is removed from the group this often solves the problem.

Scientific Application (p. 332)

Example 25

Pinpoint: *Fear of going to school* (50 children, ages 4 to 16)

Record: All children frightened of going to school were referred to University Human Development Clinic over eight-year period. They had at least 7 of the following 10 behaviors: (1) first episode of school fear, (2) begun on Monday following an illness previous Thursday or Friday, (3) had begun with no warning, (4) more prevalent in lower grades (40 of 50 children were age 12 or under), (5) mother ill or presumed so by child, (6) child expressed concern about death, (7) parents communicate well, (8) mother and father happy and adjusted in most areas, (9) father shows interest in household management and problems, (10) parents easy to work with (school, church, clinic, etc.).

Consequate: Parents ignored bodily complaints (did not reinforce child's talk about feeling sick), merely made appointment with pediatrician for a time *not* during school hours or, if necessary, a quick examination on way to school. Child was taken to school usually by father, with school personnel instructed to keep child in room when parents left. Parents were told that child's difficulty transient and informed that Monday would be difficult,

Tuesday better, and by Wednesday, problem generally absent. Parents told not to discuss school attendance over weekend (most referrals late in week). Sunday night parent stated, "Tomorrow you go back to school," and discussion attempts were ignored. Monday morning child was dressed and given a light breakfast (nausea generally existed). No questions were asked about fear (parents therefore did not reinforce fear). Monday evening parents gave approval for going to school and staying at school (no matter how many times child cried, vomited, or tried to leave). Child also often seen briefly and explained advantages of going on in face of fear (getting right back on a horse after a fall, etc.).

Evaluate: All 50 cases responded with complete elimination of school fear. All cases followed for at least two years with no recurrences of fear.

Note: Any inappropriate behavior of recent duration with an acute onset is probably best handled immediately. Talking about the problem merely serves to intensify and prolong the behavior by giving a great deal of approval as well as reinforcing procrastination. The time to talk is after something has been done to change. *Talk should not take the place of action.* Of course, where any medical problems may be indicated, careful examination is mandatory, but should be handled by parents matter-of-factly.

Scientific Application (p. 332)

Example 26

Pinpoint: *Increases in speaking about oneself* (third-grade boys, 30; third-grade girls, 28; sixth-grade boys, 21; sixth-grade girls, 20; tenth grade boys, 20; tenth-grade girls, 30)

Record: Each child verbalized 60 sentences during individual session.

Consequate: Students instructed to begin 60 sentences with pronoun of choice. Researcher commented "good" *only* after sentences starting with the pronoun "I." No comment after any others.

Evaluate: Number of sentences beginning with "I" increased significantly.

Note: This study demonstrated effectiveness of simple approval. However, the study also indicated that the sex of a teacher may also be a factor in effectiveness of approval. *Adolescent* girls responded to praise from the male researcher (first-year medical student) to a greater extent than did adolescent males. With *younger* students, the *boys* began more sentences with "I," indicating a same-sex preference for younger children.

Scientific Application (p. 332)

Example 27

Pinpoint: *Talking, standing, blurting out, noisy inattention, turning around* (10 children—five different classrooms; ages 6 years, 8 months to 10 years, 6 months; teachers recommended most severe problem children in class)

Record: Trained observers recorded inappropriate social behavior for six weeks. Average inappropriate behavior was 72%.

Consequate: Teachers: (1) made classroom rules explicit, (2) ignored behaviors that interfered with learning or teaching unless dangerous; (3) used withdrawal of approval as punishment; (4) gave praise and attention to behaviors that facilitated learning; and (5) attempted to reinforce pro-social behaviors *incompatible* with inappropriate social behaviors.

Evaluate: Average inappropriate behavior decreased from 72% to 19.5% over an eight-week period.

Note: The consequate used in this study represents the recommended procedure for most classroom inappropriate behavior. Participating teachers were given a workshop in behavior modification during the experiment. Opportunities for each teacher to see daily observation graphs probably helped to increase effectiveness of the procedures.

Scientific Application (p. 332)

Example 28

Pinpoint: *Child asks about sex* (18 children, 5 to 9 years old)

Record: Children exhibited no factual information—a few "inappropriate" responses when questioned.

Consequate: Program instituted to teach: (1) physiological functions with appropriate pictures from encyclopedia and other appropriate sources; (2) appropriate scientific terminology from same; (3) "improper terminology," that is, language used in different settings and by various subgroups to describe similar processes; (4) value indoctrination, that is, placing all the above within the value orientation of parents.

Evaluate: Factual information concerning sex verbalized; identification and discrimination concerning use of various words within proper context (at least four occurrences for each child over two week periods).

Professional Application

Example 29

Pinpoint: *"Off-task" during individual seatwork* (six elementary students, one first grader, two third-grade classmates, three other classmates)

Record: Observers recorded 40% study time (percentage of on-task 10-second intervals) during 30 minutes of seatwork. (Number of observations varied from 7 to 15 days.)

Consequate: Observers helped teachers by holding up small colored papers when children were studying (catching the children being good). Teachers would go to the student and use verbal, facial, and contact approval.

Evaluate: Study behavior increased to average 75% for the six students.

What would happen if . . .

Consequate II: Teachers *stopped* giving approval to study behavior.

Evaluate II: Average study behavior dropped to 34%.

Consequate III: Teachers again gave approval when observers signaled.

Evaluate III: Study behavior increased to 73%.

Note: Most teachers' attention to problem children was for non-study behavior during Record phase. It was also reported that classrooms were initially well controlled with a few students who did not stay on-task. Teacher approval was made contingent through observers' signals that later proved to be unnecessary, and the cues were eliminated. The cues were initially used to make the teachers aware of the contingencies.

Scientific Application (p. 332)

Example 30

Pinpoint: *Striking children with objects* (9-year-old boy)

Record: Boy hit other children five times during four free-play periods.

Consequate: Adult assigned in vicinity. Boys praised and given donut when playing properly, although when boy hit someone, supervisor instructed to hit him back with same object. During second supervised play period, boy hit another child in head with plastic baseball bat. Immediately, supervisor picked up bat and hit the boy. Explanation to child: "When people are hit, it hurts." This boy had been characterized as "having no conscience." It might be more accurate to say that he did not realize the consequences of his own actions regarding pain.

Evaluate: Boy never observed hitting another child.

Note: Although this consequate "worked," it easily could have created other problems. This example is included as a contingency that is not within the value structure of the authors. The authors believe that physical punishment should be used rarely, if at all. Again, the reader must discriminate. Just because something seems to work does not necessarily indicate that it should be used.

Professional Application

Example 31

Pinpoint: *Following instructions* (kindergarten, five students)

Record: Students followed teacher's instructions 60% of time during five days recording. Instructions included: pick up the toys, sit down, come and get a paper and pencil, write your name on the paper, fold your paper, bring your paper to my desk, put your chair on the table, get your mat out, lie down and be quiet.

Consequate : Teacher attended students who followed rules (within 15 seconds) by giving verbal approval. Teacher tried to catch children being good during act of following instructions (six days).

Evaluate : Instructions followed increased to average of 78%.

Consequate II: Teacher no longer caught students being good, acted as during Record phase (five days).

Evaluate II: Average instructions followed, 68.7%.

Consequate III: Attention given specific children for following rules again as in Consequate I.

Evaluate III: Average instructions followed, 83.7%.

Note: Instructions were followed when the teacher caught the children being good and gave verbal approval for following rules. Whether or not children continued to follow rules is specifically dependent upon the extent that consequences follow desired behavior.

Scientific Application (p. 332)

Example 32

Pinpoint: *Inappropriate behaviors* (third grade, adjustment class, 17-9-year-olds)

Record: Normal kinds of reinforcers (praise, grades) ineffective. Compliments from teacher resulted in children making faces at each other. Eight most disruptive children observed for one hour and forty minutes three days per week. Daily average of inappropriate behavior during three-week observation was 76% (range 61%-91%).

Consequate: Reward program instituted for afternoon hours; activities included stories, records, arithmetic instruction, and group reading. Reward procedures explained to children every day for one week prior to consequate. Small notebooks taped to child's desk. Every 20 minutes teacher gave each child a score from 1 to 10. Points exchanged for playthings at end of 1 hour and 40 minutes during first 3 days; days 4 through 9, points exchanged after 2 days. During next 15 days, delay stretched to 3-day period; and for last 24 days, a 4-day delay. In addition to individual rewards, *group* points earned and exchanged for Popsicle party end of each week.

Evaluate: Average inappropriate behavior decreased from 76% to 10% (range 3%-32%). Decline evident for every child.

Note: Teacher's reports and observer's records demonstrated profound difference in this classroom. The teacher also indicated that she had more time in which to teach. By pairing verbal praise with dispensing of points, the praise began to have a generalized effect even during the morning hours when the token system was not in operation. This program also "stretched" the reward system over ever increasing periods of time.

Scientific Application (p. 332)

Example 33

Pinpoint: *Failure to eat "nourishing" foods* (6-year-old girl)

Record: Mother reported continual nagging, longer periods taken to eat food (finishes last at supper)—four days; refused to eat vegetables—three days in one week.

Consequate: Mother told daughter one morning (during breakfast there were a few problems) that starting at noon the mother would no longer say anything about eating, but any food not finished would be saved and that same food would be her next meal. Girl didn't finish noon meal the first day; the mother presented plate directly from the refrigerator after having prepared the child's favorite evening meal. Girl just sat; still refused to eat. Mother re-presented the same meal the next morning; girl ate nothing. That noon, girl ate the old food.

Evaluate: Girl has never since refused meals. Mother later put a 2-minute time limit on eating with same contingency. Girl and family are now able to eat peacefully together.

Note: Many professionals believe that there should *never* be contingencies applied to eating food. This parent decided that the value of eating the food was important to her and that some negative consequences needed to be employed. Other parents may choose to ignore non-eating. Of course, once the value decision has been made as to *what* should be done and contingencies chosen, then consistency is critical. Rewarding eating rather than punishing non-eating could have developed a more positive approach. Again, caution is in order. Many adults have long-term problems because of well-intentioned parental intervention concerning their eating.

Professional Application

Example 34

Pinpoint: *Hyperactivity* (9-year-old boy, academic retardation)

Record: Home and classroom observations determined frequency and categories of hyperactive behavior-talking, pushing, hitting, pinching, moving, tapping, squirming, handling objects, that is, did not sit still.

Consequate: A box, 6" × 8" × 5", equipped with counter and light, installed in classroom. Following ten seconds of appropriate behavior, light flashed, counter advanced, and boy received M & M or penny. Accumulated awards divided among classmates. Thus, other children received rewards for ignoring. Training session varied from 5 to 30 minutes; average rewards dispensed 60 to 100.

Evaluate: Significant decrease in activity level (average decrease of 8.4 responses).

Note: The peer group in this study was used to reward the deviant boy. Thus, the group began to have a positive effect on him. Teachers can have an entire class help one or more children. Rewards can be given for both ignoring and paying attention. It is also suggested with *extremely* active children to: (1) use a stopwatch and start with as little as five seconds while counting to the child (verbal cues help the child perform in time) then reward immediately. Make sure the child does not get rewarded if he moves as much as an eyebrow. Gradually build the time sequence so child can remain still for thirty seconds or more; and (2) have the child practice the hyperactivity on purpose for five minutes a day to help the child discriminate between sitting still and moving.

Scientific Application (p. 332)

Example 35

Pinpoint: *Writing vulgar words* (8- and 9-year-old neighborhood boy and girl)

Record: Two letters found by parents within one week, eight vulgar words written by boy, six by girl.

Consequate: Parents talked to parents of boy. Boy's parents said, "You know kids nowadays, what can you do." Parents talked to daughter, explained proper time and place for verbal sexual discussion. Girl received special toys for bringing home notes.

Evaluate: Girl brought home four notes passed to her by same boy during next week. Wrote no more answers.

Note: Parents do not control all possible sources of reinforcement. Following the first week, parents discussed notes brought home and indicated girl should ignore any note-passing behavior. After initial incident they also spent time role playing with girl in how to ignore note-passing behavior. Although this contingency worked, it could have easily "backfired" in that the girl could have learned to increase bringing notes home in order to get rewarded. Adults should always think ahead. And then what might happen, and then what, and then what . . .

Professional Application

Example 36

Pinpoint: *Standing up, walking around* (first grade, 48 students, team-taught)

Record: Average of 2.9 children out of seats during each 10-second interval (291 children were counted [average] during 20-minute period-12 days.) Teachers told specific children to "sit down" an average of six times per 20 minutes. Whenever teacher told a child to sit down, the child did.

Consequate: Teachers instructed to tell children who stood up without good reason to sit down (average once every minute).

Evaluate: Amount of standing up *increased*. Each student sat down when told to sit down, but, overall, *more pupils stood up*. (Pupils standing per 10-second interval averaged 4.14.)

Consequate II: Procedure reversed, that is, children told to sit down only six times per 20 minutes.

Evaluate II: Standing decreased to approximately original level (3.14 pupils standing per 10-second interval).

Consequate III: To demonstrate that teachers' comments "caused" the children to stand up, teachers again told children who were up without good reason to "sit down" (average once every minute).

Evaluate III: Standing up again increased to about same level as the first time teachers "paid attention" (3.94 per 1 0-second interval).

Consequate IV: *Vicarious approval* introduced. Teachers praised good *sitting*. Whenever one child stood up or walked around, teacher "caught" a sitting student working diligently and praised the "good" child.

Evaluate IV: Standing *decreased* (1.89 average).

Note: Praise delivered to individuals who were *not* standing was very effective in controlling the entire class. (What teacher hasn't noticed that 30 backs straighten when one child is complimented for sitting up straight and paying attention?) In this study the "good" child was used as a model for the group. ("Watch how quietly Susie gets her math counter" "See how nicely Jim writes," etc.) Vicarious praise, however, was effective only for approximately 30 seconds. Even when first graders "know the rules," it is necessary to deliver praise comments very regularly. It should be remembered that attention is extremely important to most children. Sometimes by paying attention to *inappropriate* behavior, one might increase the very behavior one wishes to eliminate, especially when there is no approval for appropriate behavior.

Scientific Application (p. 332)

Example 37

Pinpoint: *Using subject matter to reinforce low-level subject matter* (third grade)

Record: Students working on individual prescriptions for math, pretest given covering music skills.

Consequate: Children divided into two groups: half of the students received no extra instruction, half of the students got to go to the "TV corner" upon meeting criterion for their individual work.

Evaluate: Students who "earned" music instruction via the television increased correct math problems. Additionally, those students who earned the TV corner gained significantly in music listening skills. Students who were not allowed to earn the TV corner actually decreased in correct math problems.

Note: Of constant concern to most educators is the development and maintenance of appropriate learning. Yet, after these learning contingencies have been established, one continues to encounter questions not only relating to "extrinsic contingencies" but also regarding the very nature of "behavioral rewards." Perhaps one of the best ways to solve some of these problems is to use "rewards" that not only provide some enjoyment, but teach something of importance as well.

Scientific Application (p. 333)

Example 38

Pinpoint: *Arson* (7-year-old boy)

Record: Boy setting fires for two years in home, always in presence of matches and absence of parents (average one to two times weekly).

Consequate: (1) Father informed son fire setting would result in loss of highly prized baseball mitt. (2) Matches or match cover brought to parents received small amount of money. Matches "planted" around house for boy to find, although told not to expect money *every* time. (3) Boy told he *could* strike full pack of matches under supervision, but for each match left unstruck he would receive money (4) Father gave verbal approval throughout program.

Evaluate: Boy brought all matches he could find to parents, stopped striking matches, ceased setting fires (entire instructional program only four weeks long); no fire-setting instances eight months later.

Note: Seeking and bringing matches to adults as well as thinking oneself "responsible" are incompatible with fire setting. The natural "approval" for setting fires (brightness, excitement, etc.) was made less desirable than the alternate approval from parents (praise and money) and, ultimately, self-approval. The end goal of self-approval is very important in that if this goal is not eventually achieved, the boy could conceivably have learned to increase his inappropriate behavior in order to get the monetary reward. It is also noted that parents taught boy when he could strike matches. The procedure was helped by the threat of disapproval (loss of glove).

Scientific Application (p. 333)

Example 39

Pinpoint: *Rest time disruptions* (first grade, 19 children)

Record: Average inappropriate behavior, 54% (trained observers, 10 days). Teacher gave praise or reprimands 12 times during 10 to 15-minute rest period.

Consequate: Teacher praised appropriate behavior, ignored disruptive behavior (12 praise comments per day—only two reprimands in eight-day observation).

Evaluate: Disruptive behavior averaged 32%.

Consequate II: Teacher reprimanded so no one except disruptive child could hear (11 per day—no praise seven days).

Evaluate II: Disruptive behavior averaged 39%.

Consequate III: Disapproval comments contingent on inappropriate behavior loud enough for entire class to hear (14 per day; no approval for five days).

Evaluate III: Disruptive behavior increased to an average of 53%.

Consequate IV: Teacher praised appropriate behavior, ignored inappropriate behavior (five days—12 approval comments).

Evaluate IV: Disruptive behavior averaged 35%.

Note: In this scientific study, the teacher controlled disruptive behavior by praising and reprimanding quietly. Loud reprimands (yelling) increased rather than decreased the inappropriate behavior. A combination of approval for appropriate behavior and firm statements to the individual offender usually serves to control young children very well. Quiet reprimands also eliminate the possibility of other children paying undue attention to the misbehaving child.

Scientific Application (p. 333)

Example 40

Pinpoint: *Teaching beginning reading* (10 research studies employing 400 children: retarded, slow readers, and unselected kindergarten and first grades.)

Record: Reading scores assessed prior to reading instruction.

Consequate: Programmed reading for periods of up to one semester.

Evaluate: No tutored children failed to read with exception of one "normal" first grader and some (but not all) children with IQ's below 50. One experiment showed relatively rapid acquisition of reading vocabulary by simple pairing of words with pictures. In another study, retarded children taught reading vocabulary to other retarded children with simple tutoring program. In other research, sight-reading vocabulary taught in sentence contexts to slow readers, retarded, and normal children. Two extension studies showed frequent alternation of programmed tutoring and classroom teachings more effective than less frequent alternation. One study indicated reinforcement proportion of approximately 20 percent more effective than higher levels.

Note: It appears that periodic withholding of approval develops a "hope" that is more effective than when the teacher reinforces all the time. The interested teacher can find literally hundreds of experiments in scientific journals concerning the effects of various reinforcement schedules. The central issues related to programmed instructions seem little different from any other teaching-learning sequence. One should begin where the student is. Learning steps should be small, and adequate reinforcement and feedback techniques should be employed. Every teacher can individualize instructions and follow these systematic procedures.

Scientific Application (p. 333)

Example 41

Pinpoint: *"Bad attitude"* (first-grade boy)

Record: Child continued maladaptive responses just a little past point of instruction. Thus, when teacher said, "Stop talking," he did but continued *almost* to point of being disobedient. When teacher said, "Do not pick the flowers," he picked leaves. When she said, "Come here," he walked very slowly. When she said, "Quiet down," he did—still slightly louder than the group, but not so loud as to receive punishment. This child (like so many others) delicately balanced upon the "edge of propriety." Punishment seemed not quite warranted, and reward seemed ridiculous.

Consequate: Teacher set up short lesson using *vicarious modeling*. Three names not duplicated in classroom were written on the board. The class was presented a new word, *attitude*. Teacher paired names with the new word: "George has a *bad attitude*; Sam has an *all right attitude*; Tommy has a *good attitude*. When their teacher tells these three boys, 'Let's all pick up the mess,' George tries to get out of work or hides his mess in the desk, Sam cleans up his own mess—only his own—, but Tommy cleans up his own mess and then helps other children." The teacher talked through two such specific examples, then let children say what they thought George, Sam, and Tommy would do. (Children are usually very correct in these assessments, especially as they describe their own problems.) Teacher made several praising comments, stating, "I liked Tommy the very, very best." She then asked problem boy whom he would want for a friend. (The teacher now had a word, *attitude*, that she could use to describe this boy's behaviors in specific and general contexts—"That's a good attitude, Cort.") She now began rewarding *good attitudes* instead of being frustrated at not being able to find responses to deal with this child.

Evaluate: Child in question changed "attitude" when rewarded for proper verbal and motor behavior.

Professional Application

Example 42

Pinpoint: *Thumb-sucking* (7-year-old girl)

Record: Thumb-sucking occurred 45% of time that the girl watched TV or read (mother's records). Dentist indicated "bite" was getting worse.

Consequate: Mother, after hearing PTA lecture on "A positive approach with record keeping," "caught" girl every time she had thumb in mouth. If thumb removed, girl received praise and special checks on prominently displayed chart in living room. (Checks were to be traded for bicycle—picture of bicycle at end of chart). Mother continued for 14 days.

Evaluate: Thumb-sucking *increased* to 75%. Mother sought professional help from behaviorally oriented counselor stating, "I tried, but bribery just doesn't work."

Note: A cause-and-effect approach rests on record keeping (data). In this case, the consequence did in fact work (changed behavior). Thumb-sucking *increased* 30%. The behavior change, however, was not in the direction desired by the mother (nor the dentist). Regarding the "bribery" issue, some people confuse the use of approval with a notion of "bribery." The girl in this case learned exactly what she was taught—(1) put thumb in mouth, (2) take thumb out of mouth, and (3) get rewarded. The girl was rewarded for what she was not supposed to do. Teachers must be careful not to reinforce the child by making a "deal" *after* the misbehavior has occurred or *after* the time for something to be done has passed. "If you stop dawdling and do your work, I'll give you free time," teaches dawdling. "Stop fighting, and you'll get a reward," teaches fighting. In each instance children are given approval to *stop* inappropriate behavior, but actually learn to *begin* the inappropriate behavior so they can make a "deal" to stop so they can get a reward. The reward is generally given on a partial schedule as we don't give in every time, and, thus, the child also learns persistence in misbehavior. Teachers should either use ignoring or disapproval to stop or extinguish the misbehavior. Teaching for incompatible responses using a positive approach involves setting up the reward beforehand.

Professional Application

Example 43

Pinpoint: *Unfinished assignments, bothering neighbors, playing* (second grade, two boys referred by teacher)

Record: Trained observers recorded average of 47% inappropriate behavior.

Consequate: Teacher and class formulated rules. Rules repeated six times per day for two weeks.

Evaluate: Little decrease in inappropriate behavior (average 40%).

Note: Apparently just knowing (being able to repeat rules) is not effective.

Consequate II: Teacher attempted to ignore inappropriate behaviors (teacher not entirely successful). Continued to repeat class rules every day.

Evaluate II: Behavior worsened. Average inappropriate behavior for four observations 69%.

Consequate III: Teacher praised pro-social behavior, repeated classroom rules, ignored inappropriate behavior.

Evaluate III: Inappropriate behavior *decreased* (average of 20%). Combination of procedures effective in reducing inappropriate behavior.

Consequate IV: Teacher instructed to act as she had in September. (Observers monitored entire year.)

Evaluate IV: Inappropriate behavior increased same day teacher changed (averaged 38%).

Consequate V: Rules, ignoring, and praise reinstated for remainder of school year.

Evaluate V: Inappropriate behavior again decreased (averaged only 15% for last eight-week period).

Note: Many teachers who believe they use more approval than disapproval actually do not (monitored by trained observers in classroom). It is necessary to practice delivering responses and to give yourself time cues or cues written on material you are teaching. A mark on every page can remind you to "catch someone being good." It is interesting to note that one boy reported in this study was seen during the entire year by a professional counselor. This boy responded in the same way to consequences, as did the other boy who was not seen. It would seem that the teacher is capable of handling many behavioral problems generally referred to counselors if responses are well developed and applied contingently.

Scientific Application (p. 333)

Example 44

Pinpoint: *"On-task" attention, academic accuracy* (14 third-grade children, age 10.1 average, IQ average 75, 2.58 arithmetic achievement level)

Record: Each day students worked 100 arithmetic problems drawn randomly from pool of 5,000 items containing equal numbers of addition, subtraction, multiplication, and division. Students worked 20 minutes per session. Average "on-task" behavior 80%, average disruptions 8%, median percent problems correct (number correct divided by number attempted) 55%, median number of correct problems 50% (six sessions).

Consequate : Teacher circulated through three rows of children once per minute, gave tokens for attending to work task. Each child earned 12-16 tokens per 20-minute session. Tokens exchanged for choice of candy, ice cream, inexpensive toys, high interest activities, field trips (14 sessions).

Evaluate : On-task attending behavior increased during seven days to over 90% last day, disruptions averaged less than one per day, median percent of problems correct remained approximately constant (54%) as did median number of correct problems (50%).

Consequate II: Teacher continued to circulate among three rows once each minute giving tokens not for attending, but for accuracy and rate of work. Students could now earn one token for seven correct problems, also bonus tokens (21-30% of problems worked correctly one token, 31-40% two tokens up to eight for 91-100% correct and two additional tokens for perfect paper). Students earned 10-18 per day (12 sessions).

Evaluate II: Attending behavior dropped to 50-70%, disruptions rose to high of 20%. However, median percent of problems correct rose to 76%, median number correct remained approximately constant (50%).

Consequate III: Teachers again gave tokens for attending, not for accuracy of work.

Evaluate III: Attending behavior rose slightly from previous phase (average approximately 73%, disruptions approximately 3%, median percent problems correct 72%, median number correct problems 50%.

Consequate IV: Teachers gave tokens both for attending and correct work.

Evaluate IV: Attending behavior increased to between 80-85%, disruptions decreased to 1%, median percent problems correct 80%. Median number of correct problems increased to approximately 65%.

Consequate V: Teachers again returned to giving tokens for correct work only, not for attending behavior.

Evaluate V: Attending behavior dropped to approximately 63%, disruptions rose to approximately 10%, median percent of problems correct rose to 83%, median number of correct problems approximately 56% (five sessions).

Consequate VI: Teachers again gave tokens both for attending and correct work.

Evaluate VI: Attending behavior increased steadily to a high of 86%, median percent problems correct 82%, median number of correct problems rose to high of 68% during last two sessions (seven sessions).

Note: This study and an additional study with the same age children demonstrated that reinforcement contingencies applied to on-task behavior consistently increased attending behavior and decreased disruptions, but had little effect on accuracy of math computations. Alternately, contingencies placed on correct work produced an increase in accuracy but the number of correct problems remained the same, attending behavior decreased while disruptions increased. Contingencies placed on both attending behavior and accuracy of work increased attending behavior, number of problems correctly completed as well as the percent of problems worked correctly. These two excellent studies indicate the importance of the teacher specifying the precise behaviors to be reinforced. The teacher should not expect automatic improvement in academic achievement if the teacher decreases or increases inappropriate social behavior. Conversely, the students will not magically behave in socially appropriate ways just because they are making accurate academic responses. The teacher must determine what is going to be reinforced in what combinations, and structure for *both* academic and social improvement.

Scientific Application (p. 333)

Example 45

Pinpoint: *Spelling accuracy* (10-year-old boy, 8.5-year-old girl, in psychiatric facility)

Record: Accurately spelled words: 3 of 15 for one child, 0 of 15 for the other.

Consequate: Alternating treatments design (two different consequates) used to compare "positive practice overcorrection" and positive practice *plus* positive reinforcement. During positive practice overcorrection, children had to (1) listen to word pronounced by teacher, (2) pronounce the word correctly, (3) say each letter of word aloud and (4) write word correctly 5 times for each misspelled word. During the positive reinforcement phase children received a star placed beside each correctly spelled word and praised for accomplishment.

Evaluate: The two consequates individually increased correct responses. For child 1, positive practice and positive reinforcement produced similar increases. For child 2, positive practice and positive reinforcement was slightly superior.

Consequate II: Positive practice combined with positive reinforcement was instituted for 3 sessions daily over 10 days for child 1 and 3 days with child 2 (child 2 was released early from the hospital setting).

Evaluate II: Child 1 spelled 8 to 9 of 10 words correctly, child 2 spelled 9 of 10 for 2 days and 10 of 10 the third day.

Note: *Combined* consequates produced an even higher rate for both children when used together. This method of alternating between two consequates provides the teacher with the opportunity of ascertaining the effectiveness of each single consequate as well as testing the effectiveness of both consequates when combined. See chapter 10 for another illustration of the alternative treatments design.

Scientific Application (p. 333)

Example 46

Pinpoint: *Stuttering* (8 6-to-10-year old children, 6 boys, 2 girls)

Record: Average duration of stuttering 3.9 years based on parental report. Audiotaped sessions from home were analyzed.

Consequate: Awareness training to assist parents and children in identifying stuttering by listening to audiotapes. Children were trained in relaxation, diaphragmatic breathing, and regulation of air flow over larynx when speaking. Social support was given by parent(s) who attended each session. Three sessions per week until children achieved criterion of stuttering less than 3%.

Evaluate: Rate of words spoken during treatment increased for all children with exception of a slight decrease for 2. Follow-up word rates increased from treatment sessions for all but 2 children, and were higher than the initial level for all but one child. Frequency of stuttering decreased to less than 3% for *all* children during the treatment phase and was maintained (except for 8 incidences) throughout the 10 to 13 month post-treatment phase. Stuttering also decreased for all 8 children outside the home treatment setting and generalized to other settings.

Note: Criterion of less than 3% stuttering was selected because normal adult speakers have 3% or less dysfluencies.

Scientific Application (p. 333)

UPPER PRIMARY EXAMPLES

Example 47

Pinpoint: *Bothering teacher at desk* (fourth grade)

Record: Students unnecessarily at teacher's desk (28% occurrences—one week)

Consequate: Teacher *ignored* all children who came to desk—made no eye contact, said nothing. Teacher recognized only those children who raised hands at seats.

Evaluate: Occurrences of students at teacher's desk steadily decreased. After two weeks, daily average between zero and one.

Note: Ignoring is one of the most effective techniques in eliminating the pay-off for inappropriate behavior and it may appear that it is easy for a teacher to do. While it may appear easy, it is the authors' experience that ignoring is the single most *difficult* behavioral technique to master. This is because it is the teacher who is providing the contingency for the inappropriate behavior. If the one who is providing a payoff for inappropriate behavior could easily ignore, the problem behavior would probably not exist. Consider the cliché "it takes two to argue." If this is the case, then either person could immediately end all arguing—just by stopping. Yet even when people try to ignore, they often extend the problem because they wait until "they just can't stand it any longer," before giving in. Of course, this teaches persistence and increases the problem.

Professional Application

Example 48

Pinpoint: *Teasing other children* (individual student, fourth grade)

Record: Disruptive behavior 83% (teacher's observation—two days)

Consequate: *Isolation.* A coatrack and bookcase rearranged in back of class-room making small isolation cubicle for child. Child sent to this "time-out place" for 10 minutes every time he disrupted class.

Evaluate: Disruptive behavior steadily *decreased.* After nine isolations (four during first day) disruptive behavior dropped to 10%.

Note: This child's teasing behavior was probably producing "payoff" from class (laughing, complaining, attending). Isolation is another form of removing reinforcement. It is highly effective if two conditions are met, 1) something in the regular classroom is, indeed, reinforcing and 2) the isolation is truly some form of "time out" and does not provide an alternative form of reinforcement.

Professional Application

Example 49

Pinpoint: *Child interfering with older child's play* (3- and 9-year-olds)

Record: Six instances in three days, older child complained to parent. Mother then recorded for five days-average of two to three "blowups" per day.

Consequate: Program developed to teach older child how and when to play with sibling. Older child instructed in techniques of attending younger child's play for short periods while giving approval to *facilitate the complete happiness of younger child*. Rewarded for *complete* attention to young child's happiness with special toys, separate play periods with own age peers after 20 minutes' play with brother. During separate times for older child, younger child kept entirely away; not allowed to interfere.

Evaluate: No instances of annoying interactions over one week.

Note: It is important for adults to realize that unless children are close in age it is difficult for each child to interact with equal benefit.

While it is possible for children to play *independently* side by side (many times this is desirable), great disparity in ages or other abilities usually necessitates that one child must entertain the other if children are to be in close proximity and "get along." Most parents believe that older children should establish these behaviors as well as derive joy from concerning oneself about younger siblings. Thus, parents try to promote children's "loving each other rather than fighting." Perhaps most "sibling rivalry" is caused by the hours, days, weeks, months, and years children actually compete with each other when left to their own resources. Regardless, it is imperative that the older child realize who is in control and take responsibility for the interaction.

Professional Application

Example 50

Pinpoint: *Overactivity* (six boys, 9 to 13 years, low-level intelligence)

Record: Boys observed in playroom for eight days

Consequate: Rewarded following 30 seconds of "quiet time" (tokens exchangeable for candy). Procedure continued 30 days; during last 4 days token given after 45 seconds.

Evaluate: Overactivity reduced 67%.

Note: Overactivity was still substantially decreased eight days later when *no rewards* were used.

Scientific Application (p. 333)

Example 51

Pinpoint: *Littering* (sixth grade)

Record: Materials not put away—25 daily (average one week)
Consequate: Large FRIDAY BOX instituted in classroom. Each student given responsibility for own materials—individually labeled. Materials not put away went in Friday Box. Friday Box opened one half-hour weekly— *only then could articles be recovered.*

Evaluate: After second week Friday Box, littering decreased to three incidents weekly.

Note: This procedure seems effective in all situations and at all age levels. An author had to wait four days to recover important research materials placed by his wife in the family Sunday Box. Also, the amount of material not taken from the box that is allowed to remain week after week provides a good indication of its worth to the litterer.

Professional Application

Example: 52

Pinpoint: *Homework completion and accuracy* (6th grade, 10 boys, 6 girls)

Record: Students divided into groups. Group 1 had an average of 31.8% homework assignments returned with 34% accuracy. Group 2 had 39.4% returned with 47.3% accuracy.

Consequate: Groups divided into two teams; teacher selected goals and student selected goals. All students told that they would be required to return at least 80% accurate homework to receive individual reinforcement, and team must average 80% accuracy to receive team reinforcement. After 3 days, teacher raised the criterion to 90% for Group 1. Group 2 teams selected own performance goal of daily points for each assignment returned by group members, and for 80%, 90%, and 100% accuracy levels depending on individual- and team-selected performance criteria, to earn reinforcers.

Evaluate: Teacher selected goal group increased completion to 64.6% and accuracy to 74.5%. Student group increased completion to 74.4% and 76.5% for accuracy.

Consequate II: No intervention.

Evaluate II: Teacher group completion decreased to 37.9% and accuracy to 69.8%. Student group decreased to 41.9% completion and 72.4% accuracy.

Consequate III: Intervention reinstituted for teacher-selected goals and student-selected goals.

Evaluate III: Teacher group completion was 56.6% with 77.8% accuracy. Student group was 73.9% completion with 82.9% accuracy.

Note: Team participation with self-management procedures was effective in increasing homework completion and accuracy in both teacher and student-selected goal groups. Parents of both groups reported less trouble relating to homework completion after consequates were initiated.

Scientific Application (p. 333)

Example 53

Pinpoint: *Disruptive classroom behavior* (9-year-old boy)

Record: Disruptions recorded by teacher.

Consequate: Disruptive behaviors ignored; appropriate behavior rewarded. Boy kept after school for extreme deviations and sent home on later bus. This put child with students he did not know and withdrew peer attention. Correct behaviors reinforced by teacher praise and peer approval (continuously in beginning, more infrequently later on). Also, job of blackboard monitor followed appropriate behavior.

Evaluate: Disruptive behaviors initially *increased* as payoff withdrawn. After initial rise, maladaptive behaviors progressively *decreased* and were eliminated by end of third week.

Scientific Application (p. 333)

Example 54

Pinpoint: *Positive piano practice* (9-year-old girl)

Record: New behavior.

Consequate: Piano purchased with contingency child would (1) instruct self through two beginner books to earn privilege of taking lessons and (2) pay small part of earned allowance to piano teacher every lesson for privilege of studying.

Evaluate: "Self-motivation" regarding practice—child practiced daily without admonition—three years.

Note: It was also decided in the above case to contract lessons through six-month periods with some weeks for rests, rather than just begin and act as though lessons might never stop. This obviates the need for children to view themselves as failures when they stop taking lessons. In music study it is curious that children must interpret their learning behavior as "defeat" when they have studied music successfully for from 6 months up to 10 years. It should also be mentioned that six piano teachers were contacted before one was found who immediately realized the importance of accepting the small part of the child's allowance every lesson from the child. Another interesting note concerns the day this child came home and reported to her parents in stark disbelief that "Julie wants to stop taking lessons. And gosh! She doesn't even have to help pay for hers."

Professional Application

Example 55

Pinpoint: *Failure to pass "key skills" entrance tests* (32 preschool children, 16 5th graders)

Record: All 32 children failed key skills test given to entering kindergarten children. Separate skills consisted of counting 1-10, recognition of colors, ordering all letters of the alphabet, etc.

Consequate: Kindergarten children divided into two groups, 16 received regular instruction from kindergarten teacher, 16 received regular instruction, plus individual tutoring from 16 5th graders. Older 5th graders had been assigned to a "special education" class because of severe academic and social problems. Fifth grade tutors planned intervention strategies implemented during a 10-week period, each working with one child. Contingency for older youngsters was to work with younger child in order to listen to preferred music via earphones after each tutoring session. Younger children had no contingency except being attended to by an older 5th grader.

Evaluate: All kindergarten children improved as expected. Children who were not tutored passed 10 key skills, yet those who were tutored passed 24 key skills.

Note: A videotaped analysis of the tutor/tutee dyads by a group of professionals indicated that they thought older students to be gifted, on-task, positive, socially appropriate, above grade level, and behaviorally normal. Additionally, what started out as a very strong contingency (listening to music) was superseded by an even stronger contingency relating to tutor/tutee bonding. Evidently the tutoring brought out the best in both older and younger children.

Scientific Application (p. 333)

Example 56

Pinpoint: *Disruptive noise* (large class)

Record: Absolute cacophony. No recording able to take place.

Consequate: Many children removed from class until class size became manageable. Teacher planned specific assignments and scheduled consequences.

After small number of children brought under control, one child at a time added to class. Procedure started with limited number of children during special period while others normally out of room—later extended to entire day.

Evaluate: Teachers indicated procedure very effective.

Note: Teachers also stated that initial control of the *entire* group was absolutely impossible. This procedure demands the cooperation of others who will care for the children who are removed.

Professional Application

Example 57

Pinpoint: *Reading "bad" literature* (10-year-old child)

Record: No instance of child reading "classic child stories" or factual book in two months.

Consequate: Parent paid child small amount of money per page to read any book in family library. Child could take earned money after 100 pages and spend it or buy any book of choice at a reduced cost.

Evaluate: Child read 62 pages of child's encyclopedia first week; thereafter, averaged approximately 50 pages per week from "good" books. Four-month follow-up indicated reading rate also increased. Child "hooked" on scientific book series.

Note: The child in this study kept the records personally. Completion of each 100 pages was countersigned by mother and presented to father for payment on a check-type book that became very important to the child. As with any such program, the payment(s) for reading should be gradually reduced and eventually ended in order that the child begin to read for the reinforcement of the reading material and not for the money.

Professional Application

Example 58

Pinpoint: *High noise level—lunchroom* (grade school)

Record: Generalized noise (talking) at high level observed by principal. Other maladaptive behaviors developing, that is, hitting, screaming, not staying at table until finished.

Consequate: Sound-activated switch (inexpensive circuit-breaker device) connected to lights in lunchroom. When noise reached preset level (first day, 90 decibels; second day, 85 decibels, etc.) lights went off. When noise dropped, lights came on.

Evaluate: Selected noise levels maintained without any instruction. Children learned quickly to stay just beneath sound-level setting.

Note: A similar device is available that can be set at any intensity level. This device sounds a shrill pitch until noise stops. Mechanical disciplinarians are absolute and effective. More important, they free a teacher's time for more productive interactions.

Professional Application

Example 59

Pinpoint: *Arithmetic achievement* (sixth grade, 13 boys)

Record: Assignments completed during arithmetic period preceding recess averaged 4.2 (approximately nine incomplete assignments). Recess activity closely observed. All boys played 100% of the time during two-week period.

Consequence: Boys told if assignments not completed, they could not go out to recess.

Evaluate: Only four incidents of recess participation were earned during the next week (three for one child). Arithmetic assignment completion did not increase following application of contingency.

If at first you don't succeed

Consequence II: All boys instructed to work through recess and *denied* recess privilege. However, each boy allowed five minutes' play in gym after finishing two arithmetic problems correctly.

Evaluate II: Completed arithmetic assignments increased to nine by end of first week. By Tuesday of second week, all 13 boys turned in assignments every day. After three weeks, accuracy reached an average of 80%.

Note: This application represents a discrimination many teachers fail to make. If the period of work is too long, the child cannot see the immediate rewards for his academic work; thus, behavior does not improve. It was apparent to the teacher that these thirteen boys (all below grade level in arithmetic) really enjoyed recess. The teacher used recess contingently, but it did not work. The time span of work without reward for these particular boys was too long. When the rewarding activity was given following a short period of work, they all produced even though regular recess was denied. To keep the boys coming back from the gym rapidly, the teacher occasionally rewarded them immediately with another period in the gym for prompt return. By the end of the second week, all boys were running back from the gym to work again. When using activities as rewards, it is important to pay very close attention to "structuring activities in time."

Professional Application

Example 60

Pinpoint: *Excessive dawdling* (fifth grade)

Record: Three to five minutes to get "on-task" in individual study. (Average over eight days.)

Consequate: Teacher instituted multiple divergent token systems. Some children received paper money that bought "surprise gifts" at end of day. Other children received candies on various time interval schedules. Some children accumulated points written in notebooks. Reinforcers changed constantly. Varying token reinforcers "stimulated interest and created mode of excitement in classroom."

Evaluate: Individual dawdling decreased to approximately thirty seconds (average three days).

Note: Expectation level increased general classroom excitement toward goal achievement (receiving tokens), which was later modified by stretching the time interval using only exchange tokens. If students have previously been on a single token system, sometimes it is wise to alter the routine.

Professional Application

Example 61

Pinpoint: *Teaching lying behavior* (11-year-old boy)

Record: Known misconduct; boy observed stealing money from sister's bedroom.

Consequate: Father took boy aside and with displeasure said, "Now, I want you to be honest with me, did you do it?"

Evaluate:	Lie 1	Child, "No."
		"Now, be honest!"
	Lie 2	"No, I didn't do it."
		"Don't lie to me."
	Lie 3	"I'm not, really I didn't do it."
		"I'm not going to tolerate any lying now."
	Lie 4	"I'm not lying."
		"Why were you in there?"
	Lie 5	"Where?"
		"The bedroom."

Lie 6   "Which bedroom?"
        "You know which bedroom."
Lie 7   "No, I don't."
        "Of course, you do."
Lie 8   "Dad, I really don't; I didn't do anything."
        "You took it."
Lie 9   "What?"
        "You know."
Lie 10   "I don't even have any money."
        "Ah! Who said anything about money?"
Lie 11   "You did."
        "No, I didn't."
Lie 12   "You said that I took Clara's money from her bedroom."
        "No, I didn't."
Lie 13   "Dad, I didn't take it."
        "How did you know it was money I was talking about?"
Lie 14   "I didn't."
        "You said, 'I didn't take Clara's money.' "
Lie 15   "No, I didn't say that."
        "What did you say?"
Lie 16   "I said, 'I didn't even know about Clara's money."
        "I'm not going to have you lie to me."
Lie 17   "I'm not lying, honest."
        "Now, once and for all, did you take it?"
Lie 18   "What?"
        "Clara's money."
Lie 19   "What money?"
        "I said I was not going to have any more lying!"
Lie 20   "I'm not lying."
        etc., etc., etc., until
Truth 1 "Okay, okay, I did it."

Consequate II: Next morning. "Son, your behavior makes me very ashamed of you. You took your sister's money without her permission. Very few things are as serious as stealing, especially from a loved one. I choose not to give you the privilege of interacting with the family or me until you make retribution to Clara and this family. I know that you will think about this for a long, long time; I also know that you will pay back Clara and apologize to her and to the rest of us. I hope you can also think of a positive project that will demonstrate to us all the kind of person I know you are; right now you make us very, very sad."

Evaluate II: Boy exhibited "guilt" and engaged in project to earn back respect, that is, positive familial interaction.

Note: Obviously consequate II should have been consequate I. Nothing is gained by playing detective or cross-examiner, except to increase lying. Even though most people can be caught in lies because they do not have good memories and/or are afraid and/or are young, this questioning process does not usually represent a worthwhile pursuit. If one knows for certain that a child has committed an inappropriate act, then the adult should act on that basis. It does little good to get the child to "admit it." If the adult is not sure, the adult should think through the possible consequences of the questioning process, that is, to unwittingly teach lying. Additionally, the "guilt" exhibited by the boy was effective in changing his behavior. Many people have a problem with "guilt" and believe that it should never be used, yet it is often the guilt that one feels that mitigates inappropriate behavior.

Professional Application

Example 62

Pinpoint: *Inappropriate oral hygiene* (12-year-old boy and 10-year-old girl)

Record: Brushing done only at parental insistence. (Recording over two-week period.)

Consequate: Two-track program devised: (1) Children directed (by father—one week) to brush after breakfast and dinner and "feel your teeth with your tongue and smell your own breath." (2) During second day of second week father "caught" children after observing tooth brushing. Father said, "If you've brushed, you may open my hand and have the prize inside" (a small amount of money) once daily. During same week father "caught" children when brushing was omitted and said same thing, but when children said, "I haven't," the father said, "Open my hand anyway and see what you might have had."

Evaluate: "Brushing" behavior amplified to operational point of acceptability (i.e., four forgets each week).

Note: Children can be taught to appreciate the "good" smell of their breath as well as the "feel" of clean teeth.

Professional Application

Example 63

Pinpoint: *Classroom "out of control"* (sixth grade, 30 students, beginning teacher)

Record: Average classroom study rate during first hour 25% (four days).

Consequate: Teacher had two conferences with principal, wrote assignments on board, changed class seating arrangement, watched a helping teacher demonstration (study rate 90% during demonstration).

Evaluate: Average classroom study rate increased to 48% (13 days). Teacher averaged only 1.4 contingent approval comments per day to entire class during the period.

Consequate II: Teacher instructed in principles of contingent approval; contingent approval comments increased to average of 13 per session.

Evaluate II: Average study rate rose to 67% (14 days).

Consequate III: Teacher discontinued contingent approval comments.

Evaluate III: Study behavior decreased steadily to 45% by sixth day.

Consequate IV: Teacher reinstated contingent approval averaging 17 per session; decreased disapproval comments following non-study behavior.

Evaluate IV: Study behavior increased average 77% (14 days).

Note: Three post-experimental observations indicated the study rates were being maintained at approximately the same level.

Scientific Application (p. 334)

Example 64

Pinpoint: *Negative comments and high-intensity "screaming" among family members prior to evening meal* (father, mother, children ages 5, 9, 13, and 16)

Record: Thirty-minute observations prior to evening meal (five days). Average 64.3 disapproving comments (38.6 high intensity "screaming" and 8.7 accompanied by parental motor disapproval—"hitting"; 43.1 comments per day by children and 21.2 by parents).

Consequate: Parents decided every time anyone yelled, the father would deliver severe reprimand accompanied "when appropriate" by motor disapproval (spanking).

Evaluate: Disapproving comments by children *increased* (58.6) and disapproving comments by parents increased (44.3, mostly by the father).

Consequate II: Timer set on kitchen stove thirty minutes before meal, anyone who engaged in quiet talk during that time received a special treat *prior* to supper. Family role-played how to ignore, disapprove, and praise quiet talk using examples from daily records. Father "caught the youngest child in quiet talk" and gave a special treat during the 30-minute period; others waited.

Evaluate II: Disapproval comments by children *decreased* (13.2 average first week and 5.6 second week). Disapproval comments by parents decreased (3.3 average first week and 1.8 second week).

Note: Loud reprimands defined as disapproval by the parents may not be disapproving. Here they served to increase the very behavior the parents were trying to control. "Modeling" also occurs; children observe parents yell and scream and in turn yell and scream. Discrimination was taught using role playing, and speaking quietly received approval. Parents presented dessert prior to dinner in small segments. In this case a quiet tranquil house was valued more than a traditional eating sequence.

Professional Application

Example 65

Pinpoint: *Volunteering answers* (sixth grade, social studies class, four girls)

Record: Number of times girls volunteered during two-week period: zero. Only six questions answered when specifically directed toward them. Sociograms indicated girls were isolated.

Consequate: Activities developed with approval from teacher and classmates. Girls recited alone from assigned book, read passages for parents, who praised accomplishment, then read for teacher alone. Girls' voices recorded and positive verbal approval given by teacher for effective talking. Recording later played for entire class, who praised performance. Teacher also praised interaction with other children. Additionally, small groups of girls worked on projects. Each group started with one fearful girl and one girl who modeled appropriate behaviors—number of students gradually increased.

Evaluate: Volunteering in class increased from nothing to an average slightly below rest of class.

Note: These procedures are closely related to many learning situations in which initial fear is gradually reduced by participating in the fear-producing activity (or approaching the feared objects) in small steps, receiving approval for behavior that is incompatible with avoidance.

Professional Application

Example 66

Pinpoint: *Bed-wetting (enuresis)* (47 children, ages 8 through 11)

Record: Average of five nights per week including all age groups.

Consequate: Twofold program: (1) To teach child to take responsibility for own bed-wetting behavior and (2) train child to wake up when the bladder pressure is high just prior to urination. Parents purchased a simple battery operated device that consists of a battery case with speaker and two leads that attach to two flexible metal sheets placed on the bed separated by thin porous paper sheets (available commercially). When the urine passed through the sheet it closed the circuit (no chance occurred for electrical shock as the circuit was both low amperage and low voltage) and rang the buzzer, which awakened the child whereupon he went to the bathroom. When accidents occurred the child changed his own bedding, clothing, and helped reset the alarm. (Depending on child's age, the procedures are done alone or with help of parents.) Most parents also placed charts in bedroom with prizes to be given after 2, 6, 9, 15, 18, 21, and 30 dry nights.

Evaluate: Forty-four children eliminated or decreased bed-wetting to one accident within 30 days of starting the procedure.

Note: When using such procedures, many parents make the mistake of limiting the child's liquid intake. This is detrimental in two ways: the acid percentage of the urine will increase and may induce urination, but more importantly the child cannot learn to "get up" with bladder pressure unless bladder pressure is increased. The buzzer procedure is built upon the principle that the child will learn to respond to internal physiological cues (increased bladder pressure) and awakening will occur earlier and earlier in the sequence until the awakening will precede the buzzer whereupon the problem will be solved. Therefore, it is important for the parent to give as much liquid as possible just before bedtime and for most efficient use also to give as much liquid as possible every time the buzzer awakens the child. It is also important for the child to wake up to the buzzer *before* the learning procedure is employed. Put the child to bed and wait until sleep is deep, start the buzzer, leave it sounding and make certain the child is awake (sometimes with "sound" sleepers ice on the stomach is effective), have the child go to the bathroom (do not take hands or lead him), simulate or actually engage in urination, and then let him go back to bed himself, after which the buzzer is turned off and reset. Continue this wake-up routine until you are certain that the buzzer *always* wakes up the child (generally this takes between 3 and 24 experiences). Next, give increased liquid, send the child to bed, and wait for the buzzer. (It was found that with seven children increased liquid intake and wake-up procedure alone resulted in termination of bed-wetting.)

Should parents not have the monetary resources to purchase the buzzer, another routine built upon the same principles may be employed. The child is given increased liquid and the parents awaken the child after approximately 120 minutes. Should urination occur prior to this time wake the child up on an earlier schedule. The child should go to the bathroom by himself/herself, drink as much liquid as possible, go back to bed, and be awakened in another 120 minutes. This should be repeated every two hours all night for seven days. (The idea is the same as above, that is, ensure the bladder is full and awaken the child.) Next, parents should increase the time before waking up the child by 15 minutes (2 hours and 15 minutes) for the next seven days and add 15 more minutes each week until the child gets up on own initiative. A good physical exam should precede any application of the above routines, but parents should not worry about any special significance concerning bed-wetting. Getting up to go to the bathroom behavior is learned just like any other behavior. If it has not been learned or the learning has been slow, then we should assume the child deserves to be taught. However, we recommend waiting until children are at least three years old or old enough to get themselves to and from the bathroom before this routine is begun.

Professional Application

Example 67

Pinpoint: *Academic underachievement* (25 underachievers, 8 to 12-year-olds, average age, 10.1)

Record: Thirty children originally selected for summer program, five moved. Average educational level of mothers 7.0, fathers 7.2. Low average income and 40% of children from broken homes (separation, divorce, or death). California Achievement Test 1.5 years average below norms. Overall grade point average for preceding year 1.47 (D grades). Total work time (percent of assigned classroom time engaged in academic activities) averaged 39% (dropped last day to 18%). Rate of work output (number of exercises and problems done divided by number of minutes) averaged 1.40 problems attempted per minute. Accuracy of output (number of problems and exercises done correctly divided by total attempted) averaged 50% (15 days recording of all 25 students). Teachers and aides averaged 13 approvals per hour, 27 disapprovals per hour. Instructional responses (requests, commands, and rules) averaged 55 per hour.

Consequate I: Students given personalized booklets with 50 squares per page (three colors of pages). Points awarded by teacher checking appropriate number of squares in booklet. Academic work reinforced by assigning points for *accuracy* (two-thirds of total) and *speed* of working (one-third of points). Social behavior reinforced by getting to work quickly (20 points), working for 10-20 minutes continuously (20 points), working while fight or noise going on nearby (10 points), raising hand (5 points), obtaining permission to leave desk (5 points). Inappropriate behaviors were given warning first and then 10-50 points fine taken, two fines resulting in "time-out" with contingency to finish one assignment without points to work way back into system. Points redeemable as follows: First 25 points (green) paid for lunch (no child missed lunch entire summer); yellow points earned school store (candy, gum, toys, supplies, goldfish, clothes, jewelry, makeup kits, baseballs, games of many kinds, etc.); red points earned field trips occurring on Friday afternoon (fishing, boating, swimming parties, farm trip, bank, hospital, and pet shop). Teachers passed out store items while giving approval and urging continued success. Teachers and aides paired approvals for academic and social behaviors while giving points in books. Program lasted for 29 days of summer term.

Evaluate I: Total work time increased from average of 39 to 57%. Rate of work increased from 1.4 assigned problems attempted per minute to an average of 3.35. (SRA reading workbook .97 to 2.9, SRA spelling .90 to 2.34, SRA Reading Lab .28 to 1.43, Merril Workbook 1.37 to 2.7, spelling workbook .80 to 1.72, math workbook 2.01 to 6.19, math worksheets 2.65 to 4.84). Accuracy increased from 50% correct to 70% correct (SRA Reading workbook 32.4% to 62.2%, SRA reading lab 30.9% to 64.9%, Merril workbook 53.3% to 68.2%, spelling workbook 52% to 68%, math workbook 51.6% to 72.9%, math worksheets 58.7% to 75.1%, spelling tests 46.7% to 71.9%). Teachers and aides during Consequate I averaged 47 approvals per hour, 7 disapprovals per hour and 17 requests, commands, and rules per hour.

Consequate II: Teachers eliminated point system but continued approval for appropriate academic and social behavior (children received candy, toys, lunch without contingencies during nine days of program as during Record phase).

Evaluate II: Time at work average dropped to 42%. Problems attempted per minute *increased* to 5.5. Accuracy increased to 73%. Teachers and aides decreased approvals to 27 per hour, disapprovals increased to 9 per hour, and requests, commands, and rules to 16 per hour. CAT scores averaged .42 year higher at end of summer than at beginning.

Note: The normal classroom routines during the record phase were producing less and less work prior to the introduction of the point system. There followed a substantial increase in achievement with the dual introduction of the points and change in teacher verbal approval from an approval ratio of approximately 33% to 87%. Six weeks of contingent points and high verbal approval did not maintain a high work rate after the points were withdrawn. These teachers unfortunately did not maintain the same high approval rate during Consequate II. Perhaps if the teachers had maintained the same rate and ratio of approvals the work time might have remained as high after the points were withdrawn. The rate of work output increased steadily during the six weeks of contingent points and stayed even after the points were withdrawn. It appears that six weeks of contingent reinforcement was able to maintain a high rate of work output even after withdrawing the reinforcers (things and activities), provided that teachers remain predominately positive and use verbal approval. The same is indicated for accurate work. Students reached a high level of accuracy during the point system and maintained the same level with social and academic verbal contingencies. The authors also report that during the record phase teachers were spending much more time in trying to eliminate disruptive inappropriate behaviors, but during the consequate phase shifted to teaching behaviors. The students were also able to learn to interact in positive ways with teachers and academic materials. Even though the work time dropped after the point system was withdrawn, students maintained a high work rate and high accuracy rate perhaps indicating that the interaction with academic materials became more reinforcing to the students. It is interesting to note that the students were able to maintain accuracy and rate of problems completed using less time in "on-task" work. Perhaps, as with the teachers, the students were able to spend less time and achieve better results following a precise and well-implemented program of contingent reinforcement.

Scientific Application (p. 334)

Example 68

Pinpoint: *Talking out, standing* (fifth grade, 28 students)

Record: Students averaged 43.3% talk-outs, 5.5% out-of-seat behaviors during English period and 39.2% talk-outs, 10.0% out-of-seat during math period (14 days observation).

Consequate I: Individual contingencies applied only during English period. Reinforcement included free time with choice to participate in desired activities (tutoring, reading, assisting teachers, record listening, viewing filmstrips, etc.).

Evaluate I: Average talk-outs decreased to 2.8%, out-of-seat decreased to .3% during English period. Observations during math indicated talk-outs 24.8%, out-of-seat 4.1%. Individual contingencies during English only, slightly modified the same behaviors during math.

Consequate II: Contingencies removed (five days).

Evaluate II: During English talk-outs increased to 24.8%, average out-of-seat to 6.6%. During math period talk-outs averaged 30.2%, out-of-seat 8.8%.

Consequate III: Group contingency applied to English period only. Five or more rule violations for entire class resulted in entire class losing free-time privileges (five days).

Evaluate III: During English period average talk-outs decreased to 1.8%, out-of-seat to .1%. During math period talk-outs averaged 15.0%, out-of-seat 1.7%.

Consequate IV: Contingencies removed from English class.

Evaluate IV: Talk-outs 3.4%, out-of-seat .4% during English. During math period talk-outs averaged 20.1%, out-of-seat .3%.

Consequate V: Group contingency reapplied to both English period and math period. Five violations for entire class resulted in entire class losing free-time privilege (five days).

Evaluate V: Inappropriate behavior decreased to lowest level during both English and math periods. During English talk-outs averaged .4%, out-of-seat, 0%. During math period talk-outs averaged 1.0%, out-of-seat 0%.

Note: Both the individual and group contingencies had an impressive effect in reducing two bothersome behaviors. When the actual number of talk-outs is counted (rather than percentage of observed intervals) the results are even more impressive. During an average 40-minute English or math period there was a difference of at least 180 fewer talk-outs during the least effective contingency. Results also indicate some carryover to math period when contingencies were applied to English. Group contingencies are easier to apply than individual contingencies (record keeping) and both were equally effective.

Scientific Application (p. 334)

Example 69

Pinpoint: *Tardiness following recess* (fifth grade, 25 students)

Record: Teacher and one student recorded number of students late for noon, morning, and afternoon recesses. Average number of students late for noon recess 7.2 (13 days). Average number late for morning recess 3.7 (21 days). Average number late for afternoon recess 3.9 (27 days).

Consequate I: Students studying patriots and excited about being Today's Patriot. Teacher introduced Today's Patriot Chart. Chart (posted on the board at the end of each day) listed those who got back to classroom on time after noon recess. Chart only for noon recess, did not include morning and afternoon recesses.

Evaluate I: Students late decreased dramatically. Only three students late after noon recess during 19 days chart in effect. However, average number late after morning recess 3.3, after afternoon recess, 3.7.

Consequate II: Patriots Chart expanded to include morning recess. Names appeared on chart only if students on time for both morning and noon recesses.

Evaluate II: No student late during 10 days chart in effect for either morning or noon recesses. Average 3.2 students continued to be late for afternoon recess.

Consequate III: Teacher again raised criterion for inclusion on Patriots Chart to on time for all three recess periods.

Evaluate III: No one late after any recess period during five days criterion.

Consequate IV: Teacher informed class that students had done so well chart no longer needed. Teacher could "count on them" to remain patriots.

Evaluate IV: Noon tardiness averaged 5.0 for five days, tardiness after morning recess, 2.6, and after afternoon recess, 2.6.

Consequate V: Teacher reinstated chart for all three recess periods.

Evaluate V: Not one person late after any recess during five days chart in effect.

Consequate VI: Class voted to post a Un-Patriots Chart (those students who were *late*) instead of Patriots Chart. Teacher posted chart every second day for six days, every third day for six days, and every fifth day for last week of project.

Evaluate VI: One student late after one recess during final 18 days of project.

Note: This study indicated that many teachers could carry out very specific projects without the help of outside observers. Also, if a consequence is used that has some meaning to the student and is consistently applied, the results are predictable. Many teachers have used "good" charts but they are seldom as precise and consistently applied. The specific name given to the charts is meaningful to the students. They might help decide the name of the chart as well as criteria for being included on the chart.

Scientific Application (p. 334)

Example 70

Pinpoint: *Remediation of mutually aversive interactions between a problem student and four teachers* (13-year-old girl)

Record: High level of student disapproval, high level of teacher disapproval.

Consequate: *Student* was taught to give approval statements to teachers (cued by a tape recorder and earplug) that earned tokens exchangeable for records, extra gym periods, lunches with the English teacher, and extra credit toward English grade.

Evaluate: Student approval increased for all teachers, disapproval decreased. Teachers approval increased, disapproval decreased.

Consequate II: *Student* reversed procedures. Gave three of four teachers more disapproval than approval.

Evaluate II: Two of the teachers then changed back, giving more disapproval than approval.

Consequate III: *Student* again gave more approval to all four teachers, gave low disapproval.

Evaluate III: All four teachers gave high approval to student, low disapproval.

Note: A post-check without cues or tokens for the student indicated that for two teachers where the student was still giving high approval and low disapproval, the teachers were reciprocating in kind. The two teachers where the student was equally mixed were giving the same mixed approval/disapproval back to the student. However, all these interactions were still better than baseline. During the post-check teachers commented on the student's "remarkable socialization" and new-found "maturity."

Scientific Application (p. 334)

MIDDLE SCHOOL/JUNIOR HIGH SCHOOL EXAMPLES

Example 71

Pinpoint: *Homework study time* (11- and 13-year-olds)

Record: Average 4.5 minutes homework per child per school day after four weeks' recording according to child's records. Parent's spot checks averaged 3.8 minutes.

Consequate: Television viewing time made contingent on homework time *whether or not assigned*. Each minute of homework or review time redeemable for six minutes of viewing time. Children kept own time logs. Given extra monetary reward when parents record within two minutes of child's report.

Evaluate: Homework study time increased to 32 minutes per child per day at which time parents changed the study/viewing ratio to 3-1 with no decrease in study time.

Note: In this study homework time was mandated whether or not assigned. Often, parents/children get into arguments concerning the actual assignment of any homework. This procedure alleviates this potential problem.

Professional Application

Example 72

Pinpoint: *Low-level skill achievement* (ninth grade, industrial arts class)

Record: No evidence of completed individual project or increased skills after fourth week of term.

Consequate: Teacher continually threatened students with failing final grades for lack of industry and productivity.

Evaluate: Only *one* student of eight finished final project.

Note: Anxiety increases were observed during the last few days of class, as students frantically tried to finish projects. One boy was cut with a band saw two days before term ended. Students complained that they tried, but "didn't really know what the teacher wanted." This represents a situation where the teacher "did not start where the student is." Thus, threats of disapproval did not produce constructive behavior; rather, threats produced anxiety and subsequent physical harm.

Professional Application

Example 73

Pinpoint: *Noisy transition changing classes* (eighth grade)

Record: Length of time after bell rang that students took to be in seats steadily increased to eight minutes.

Consequate: "Record party" contingent on all students being in seats before final bell. One "pop" record (brought by students) played during Friday's class for each day all students in seats before final bell.

Evaluate: Extended record parties by end of third week.

Note: A decrease in other maladaptive responses was observed when one record was *deducted* from "Friday's list" for antisocial behavior from any student.

Professional Application

Example 74

Pinpoint: *Chewing-gum vandalism* (eighth grade, Special Education class)

Record: Five (average) gum wads under each desk. Gum wrappers observed on floor (6 to 10 daily).

Consequate: Gum privilege extended with admonition to "be responsible."

Evaluate: Six (average) gum wads under each desk. Gum wrappers on floor (8 to 11 daily).

If at first you don't succeed

Consequate 11: Group gum chewing Monday, Wednesday, Friday contingent upon rules: Rule 1—"If an individual is caught chewing Tuesday or Thursday, individual will lose privileges of chewing gum for one week and must also clean five wads from under desk." Rule 2—"If more than two wrappers are found on floor Monday, Wednesday, or Friday, *entire class* loses gum chewing privileges for one day."

Evaluate 11: After three weeks all gum wads removed from under all desks. Two wrappers Monday, Wednesday, and Friday observed on floor.

Note: If contingency would have stipulated no gum wrappers, probably all wrappers would have been put away.

Professional Application

Example 75

Pinpoint: *High level off-task* (3 emotionally disturbed males 14-15 years old)

Record: Average off-task 92%, 95%, and 76% for students 1, 2, and 3, respectively. High level of socially inappropriate behavior in class, when teacher out of room and when changing classes.

Consequate I: Training in appropriate social skills over a 5-week period. Program consisted of social skills and self-management training and was reinforced by point system. Treatment procedures included instruction, modeling, and role-playing of social skills, as well as self-assessment, self-recording, and self-reinforcement for correct approximations of these skills. Point system exchangeable for rewards and activities. Points earned through teacher assessment (1–4 scale) and matching self-assessment with teacher assessment.

Evaluate I: In-class inappropriate behavior decreased to 3.3%, 6.3%, and 1.8% for students 1, 2, and 3, respectively. Yet, inappropriate behavior between classes was still high, decreasing from 100% to 89.2% for student 1, *increasing* from 77.5% to 90.8% for student 2, and decreasing from 35% to 31.6% for student 3.

Consequate II: Students instructed to self-assess their between-class behavior and add points for appropriate behavior to their daily classroom points earned.

Evaluate II: Socially inappropriate behavior between classes decreased to near 0 for all students.

Note: Minimal transfer was made by these students to improve their between class behavior until they were directly instructed to do so. Often teachers assume that students will make transfers automatically. Most often this is not the case. This study was very successful in facilitating improved conduct to a setting where no societal agent was present.

Scientific Application (p. 334)

Example 76

Pinpoint: *Off-task individual study* (seventh grade, Special Education class)

Record: Completion of work taking longer each day and extending into next period. (Average time increase—20 minutes by end of third week.)

Consequate: All water-drinking privileges made contingent on finishing work on time. Water-drinking frequency increased considerably, but functioned as a positive reward.

Evaluate: Increase in finished work in allotted time by end of fourth day.

Note: The contingent delivery of other materials previously not associated with proper study (crayons, pencils, and watercolors) was later introduced to reward other academic behaviors. The use of water as a contingency may *not* be a desirable contingency regardless of whether or not it works. Perhaps this teacher should have started with crayons, pencils, and watercolors.

Professional Application

Example 77

Pinpoint: *Constant talking out and disturbing others* (15-year-old boy, math class)

Record: On-task study behavior ranged from 3 to 45% with an average of approximately 25%.

Consequate: Boy took daily report card for teacher to check. Teacher marked yes or no to such items as acceptable use of class time; assignments completed on time; homework assignments; overall behavior good. When student earned all yesses, he received snacks, TV, and permission to go outdoors. Even one "no" resulted in loss of privileges. (Child lived in a foster home for pre-delinquent boys.)

Evaluate: Study behavior rose to 95%; it remained high for six days of observation.

Consequence II: Student no longer received teacher's checks; he was told he would be granted privileges anyway.

Evaluate II: Study time dropped to 25% the first day, 10% the second day, and boy also got into one fight.

Consequence III: Privileges again made contingent on card signatures.

Evaluate III: Study time increased to 80% first day, dropped for three days until teacher assigned one "no" whereupon on-task study time increased to 100% and remained high for remainder of term.

Note: It is often extremely difficult to "control" behavior that takes place somewhere else. This study indicates that home-based rewards can maintain on-task school behavior. Rewards were on a daily basis as it was necessary for the teacher as well as foster parents to "prove" that they would, or could, be consistent.

Scientific Application (p. 334)

Example 78

Pinpoint: *Fighting during recess* (12-year-old boy)

Record: Teacher watched through window and recorded number of days boy hit other children (four out of six days observed).

Consequence: Every time boy hit another child, he was taken into principal's office and given one hard swat with paddle.

Evaluate: Playground fighting *increased* after consequences.

Consequence II: Procedures changed. Boy allowed talking privileges (five minutes) with principal every day he behaved well on playground.

Evaluate: Fighting behavior decreased to zero over four weeks.

Note: Sometimes severe punishment can be actually rewarding to a child. There are children who associate any attention given by authorities or adults as indications of approval. (This is not as absurd as it seems—remember, we discipline those we care about.) Some children receive only negative attention. The application of approval following good behavior changes this wrong association.

Professional Application

Example 79

Pinpoint: *Vandalism* (seventh grade)

Record: Seven students wrote on or destroyed: (1) desks, (2) walls, and (3) school equipment.

Consequate: (1) Desks—students sanded and re-varnished damaged desks, plus two others. (2) Walls—students washed *entire* wall. (3) School equipment—students contributed double financial value. All work strictly supervised and completed to satisfaction of teacher. Thereafter, students responsible for property upkeep, regardless of who caused damage. Parents *not allowed* to contribute to restitution in any manner.

Evaluate: Vandalism eliminated. Students' supervision of school property established.

Note: This is perhaps one of the oldest and most effective discipline procedures.

Professional Application

Example 80

Pinpoint: *Disruptive behaviors*—talking, fighting, out of seat throwing objects, noisy (seventh grade, 30 students, beginning teacher)

Record: Class met daily for 40 minutes; had 5-minute break followed by a 45-minute session. Observation during first 30 minutes of session showed study behavior to average 47% (25 days). Teacher gave contingent approval average of 6 times, disapproval for disruptive behaviors over 20 times per session.

Consequate: Teacher increased attention to study behavior, decreased attention to off-task behavior. Contingent approval increased to nine times per session, disapproval to nine per session.

Evaluate: Study behavior increased to average of 65% (six days). Noise level, disruptive behavior remained high.

Consequate II: Teacher placed chalk mark on board when students disturbed class. Each mark reduced class break 10 seconds (24 marks canceled break).

Evaluate II: Study behavior increased to 76% (24 days). Noise dropped.

Consequate III: Teacher eliminated disapproval contingencies (chalk marks). Attention to disruptive behavior was increased.

Evaluate III: Study average dropped immediately; noise level increased.

Consequate IV: All procedures reinstated.

Evaluate IV: Study rate increased to 81% (maintained for remainder of study).

Note: The overall noise level remained high even when there was a large gain in on-task study behavior. It was necessary in this well-controlled scientific study to add a disapproval contingency (deprivation of break time for inappropriate behavior) before the classroom was brought under control. It should be emphasized that approval for good behavior can provide a positive atmosphere for learning even when disapproval procedures are employed.

Scientific Application (p. 334)

Example 81

Pinpoint: *"Joy-riding"* (15-year-old boy)

Record: Picked up by police on first offense.

Consequate: Juvenile judge placed boy on probation in care of parents with charge to supply appropriate disapproval. Parents restricted boy to house except for school, but purchased highly desired article to "prove they still loved him in spite of the problem."

Evaluate: Boy continued to get in trouble—three serious instances during the next three months.

Note: Parents inadvertently rewarded boy for getting into trouble with "love present" and boy learned that "when you do bad things, good things happen to you."

Professional Application

Example 82

Pinpoint: *Disruptive social talking* (junior high school, six girls)

Record: Talking recorded on sheet of paper taped to teacher's desk (77% of time, three days).

Consequate: Teacher explained to class that talking during study time interfered with completion of work assignments (this had been done before).

Class discussed importance of rules for study, agreed something must be done, and suggested very extreme alternatives. Teacher then stated, "Anyone caught talking in class during study time must leave the room." Five girls sent out during next two days.

Evaluate: Eight-fold *decrease* in talking followed four weeks of contingency.

Note: One caution in using this type of procedure should be mentioned. The technique of removing students from a classroom (isolation) is effective *only* when the classroom provides many positive consequences (i.e., the student would rather spend time in the classroom than be isolated). The girls in this classroom were *very concerned* with receiving approval from one another as well as from the teacher; thus, isolation was effective.

Professional Application

Example 83

Pinpoint: *Juvenile offender* (14-year-old boy)

Record: Many disruptions at home—came before court on two separate occasions: one theft, one ungovernable charge.

Consequate: Summer vacation: spending money contingent upon no more offenses and finishing summer school.

Evaluate: No arrests, although summer school not finished.

Consequate II: Boy placed in County Detention Center during family's vacation.

Evaluate II: Boy left home, went to live with friend's parents.

Consequate III: Kicked out after four weeks—moved to another friend's parents.

Evaluate III: Kicked out after 13 days—went traveling.

Consequate IV: Called father long distance (collect) for money to come home; received money, but did not come home.

Evaluate IV: Unknown.

Note: In this case the juvenile was placed by his counselor in the County Detention Center during the family's two-week vacation. It was only then he began to believe that he could not get his own way and thus wanted to live elsewhere. It should be noted that although this boy had just failed all prescribed contingencies regarding summer school work, his parents still planned to take him on vacation in order to "develop a fresh rapport." The above juvenile court counselor reported many failures because of well-intentioned parents who allow children's friends to live with them after these children have run away or been purposely ostracized by their own parents.

Professional Application

Example 84

Pinpoint: *Disruptive school bus behavior* (6th grade, approx. 44 students)

Record: Bus selected because of complaints by bus driver. Average of 624.1 noise outbursts (62.3 seconds per trip) that exceeded the threshold of 86-87 dB on each of 13 trips as measured by sound level meter ("Noise Guard").

Consequate I: Students were instructed concerning safety issues and told that they would receive free music on the first day, but thereafter, they would receive music only if noise levels on the preceding day had not exceeded cutoff criterion. Panel of lights provided feedback as to noise level that could terminate the next day's listening if threshold was exceeded. Additionally, a raffle for hamburger coupons was available if the preceding day's level was attained. After five consecutive successful days, there would also be a raffle for movie tickets. Students could exceed sound threshold for a limited time before the music and raffle privileges for the following day were forfeited; the cut-off criterion was adjusted downward until after 3 days it remained at 5.0 seconds. Students told that if a particular student deliberately activated the lights, that student would be sent to the principal.

Evaluate I: Noise outbursts exceeding threshold level decreased to an average of 27.7 per trip, lasting an average of 1.6 seconds per trip. Excessive noise remained below criterion 100% of the trips and thus reinforcement was provided.

Consequate II: Original (baseline) conditions reinstated for 10 days.

Evaluate II: Noise outbursts increased to average of 437.9 occurrences, 49.4 seconds per trip.

Consequate III: Music and raffles reintroduced (54 days).

Evaluate III: Noise outbursts decreased to an average of 89.2 instances lasting 7.2 seconds per trip. Excessive noise remained below criterion on 75% of trips.

Consequate IV: Phaseout and elimination of hamburger raffle and adjustment of movie raffle schedule (12 days).

Evaluate IV: Noise exceeded threshold 68.5 times lasting 4.6 seconds. Duration of excessive noise remained below the cutoff criterion of 5 seconds (and reinforcement was provided) on a majority of bus trip conditions.

Note: In addition to a reduction in excessive noise during all of the conse-quates, out-of-seat behavior and "horseplay" were also reduced. Another positive side effect resulting from the interventions was a reduction in fre-quency of the bus driver's coercions. Because the driver's voice could acti-vate the lights, the students readily followed her instructions. An extension study determined that the music contingency alone maintained appropriate behavior, even without the raffles.

Scientific Application (p. 334)

Example 85

Pinpoint: *Teaching contractual agreements* (ninth grade, civics)

Record: Nothing

Consequate: Beginning of term each student wrote contract including amount of work to be completed for special class project as well as evaluation crite-ria for determining student's grade. Individual contracts exchanged among students. Entire class then chose a project and wrote one contractual agree-ment determining individual and collective responsibilities, including penal-ties for "illegal" behaviors. Teacher assumed role of interested bystander as students pursued class project. Disputes during course of project adjudicated in "class court" (some students did not do their share of work).

Evaluate: Effective learning judged by teacher on basis of *ex post facto* essays written by students.

Note: It is interesting that the predominant theme of most essays concerned "fairness." Written contractual agreements are very effective for this age group and can concern any cause-and-effect relationship between the parties (teacher/student, parent/student). Contracts specify contingencies ("If I do my work you promise to pay me," etc.) and may be used for individuals and/or groups. Exactly the same benefits accrue from such written contracts as from similar, more sophisticated adult agreements.

Professional Application

Example 86

Pinpoint: *Academic failure* (general—12 students, different classrooms, age range 11-14)

Record: Each student failed at least two academic subjects.

Consequate: Individual work-play routines developed with consent of par-ents. Students given special after-school assignments (approximately 30 minutes). Work immediately checked by parents, and points assigned.

Points were totaled each day to "buy" privileges and things (TV watching, outside peer playtime; two children received money; one child–supper; one student–Saturday hiking plus one television program nightly; one student–time using "ham radio"). Time ratio for work-play approximately 1:4 in most cases. Thus, 30 minutes on-task work carried points worth two hours' activity or other reward.

Evaluate: Eleven of 12 students improved (average increase 1.5 letter grades in four months) One 14-year-old ran away from home—this student entirely on money contingency—parents later admitted they began to pay him before, rather than after, study sessions, that is, he was manipulating them, rather than vice versa.

Note: This program is effective, but demands absolute cooperation from parents. Many parents will respond to such a program when they: (1) admit their child has a problem, (2) have some confidence in the programmer (teacher/counselor), and (3) will be *honest* in dispensing rewards.

Professional Application

Example 87

Pinpoint: *Rebelliousness, disagreements, and refusal to talk to parents* (11.5-year-old boy, large for age)

Record: Summer camp and school behavior in sharp contrast to misbehavior at home. (Young man reported camp and school misbehavior punished immediately; related interesting activities contingent on good behavior; therefore, no problem.) Boy indicated obedience only when father angry as father oblivious to misbehavior except when in a "sour mood."

Consequate: Counselor enlisted boy's aid in "experiments." Boy to be on lookout for situations when he could disagree or disobey, then to stop and imagine to himself that father was so angry he was ready to attack verbally and physically. It was explained that if he could control his behavior by imagining an angry father, probably he would not have to face an actual one. Role-playing practice in imagery produced reactions similar to when he actually faced an angry father. Further treatment focused on the boy accepting authority of his father, even when unreasonable.

Evaluate: Home situation improved. First nine days boy reported using the "little trick" anywhere from 10 to 25 times. The first week father had even taken him to an auto show and spent an enjoyable day. (It was pointed out that present obedience and restriction in freedom would result in more freedom later—delay of gratification.) Following some weeks boy took father more into account (turned down volume on record player so it wouldn't disturb father, etc.). During the fourth week an argument developed that was so violent the boy didn't want to return home. Father stayed away from boy for several days with improvement in relations continuing. Boy received more freedom; it became unnecessary to use "imagining father angry" technique as father became more reasonable and son less inclined to disagree on every little thing.

Note: A professional behavioral therapist helped this boy over a five-month period. The most significant factor appears to be that the boy, by pretending the father was angry, was able to tell himself that disobedience would lead to disapproval. This method of having children "talk to themselves and imagine potentially good or bad results" is a method of assisting in the development of self-control especially if the thoughts are immediately followed by approval. This technique can be enhanced as parents teach children to "label" many aspects of their behavior and follow the reproduction with approval. The results may not be as dramatic as the present case where the use of a thought "trick" improved a terrible home situation, but with continued communication parents are able to assist children in self-control procedures.

Scientific Application (p. 334)

Example 88

Pinpoint: *Increasing math responses* (middle school, 88 students)

Record: One hour spent on individualized math kit. 33.21 average correct responses.

Consequate: Correct responses during 20 minute work session earned 10 minutes of (1) nothing, (2) math games, (3) earphone music listening, (4) group dance.

Evaluate: Gain scores for correct responses after one week: (1) no reward, -2.86; (2) math games, -.41; (3) earphone music listening, 26.05; (4) group dance, 16.00.

Note: The contingent application of reward (music) served to cut the math period in half and still increase correct responses. It is interesting that individual earphone listening, which can be easily dispensed, was actually superior to the group dance in increasing correct math responses. Also, the teacher had been using math games "to help motivate," but, upon analysis, math games did not function to increase responses.

Scientific Application (p. 334)

Example 89

Pinpoint: *Low arithmetic achievement* (7th grade boy, 13 years old).

Record: Number of completed correct problems per minute .47, attention to assigned work averaged 51% (five days recording). Each day's assignment corrected and returned the following day.

Consequate I: Student given immediate praise, correct answers marked for each two problems completed (two days), four problems completed (next two days), eight problems (next two days). Final two days of treatment student completed 16 problems before receiving approval.

Evaluate I: Correct answers per minute increased to 1.36. Average percentage attending behavior increased to 97%.

Consequate II: Teacher returned to original procedure: gave student daily worksheet, corrected assignment, and handed back the following day without immediate approval (five days).

Evaluate II: Rate of correct answers decreased to .98. Percentage of attending behavior *decreased* to 82%.

Consequate III: Teacher again instituted immediate feedback. Five problems prior to approval (first day), 10 (second day), 15 (third day). Student completed all 20 problems before receiving approval (last two days).

Evaluate III: Correct arithmetic answers per minute increased to 1.44. Percentage of average attending behavior increased to 97%.

Note: This study demonstrates that when the teacher starts where the student is and gradually trains the student to delay feedback, the student's on-task behaviors may increase at the same time. The teacher in this case used a "fixed-ratio" schedule that was adjusted either every day or every other day.

Scientific Application (p. 335)

Example 90

Pinpoint: *Obesity* (64 individuals, 5 to 57 pounds overweight, where medical examination revealed no medical problem and physician supervised medical aspects of diets)

Record: Many *environmental stimuli*, as well as some bodily responses *(emotions)*, have become connected with eating in previous history of overweight person. (Many eat when angry, or perhaps when sad, or just plain tired, "I always feel better if I have something to eat.") In addition, certain activities are generally associated with eating or drinking—TV viewing, fixing meals, "I have to see what it tastes like," during coffee breaks, hard work, "A cold beer sure tastes good after work," cocktail parties, "I really shouldn't, but just to be sociable," card parties, and so on. Generally normal everyday activities are associated with food or liquid intake.

Consequate:

1. *Eating place*

The first step is to designate a place (specific chair at a specific table) where eating will occur. This place should be maintained with rare exceptions until weight is down. Engage only in eating at that particular place (i.e., no reading, studying, working, or playing). Henceforth, this is your *eating place*. All meals, snacks, and drinks (other than water or low-calorie liquids) should be consumed in this specific location.

2. *Eat on purpose*

Most of us have become used to engaging in many other behaviors other than eating during meal or snack time. People talk, work, play, watch, listen, and exercise at the same time they eat. Weight control under these conditions is difficult. Therefore, discriminations need to be made. To build discriminations one must *eat on purpose*. Do not be distracted from eating in the "eating place." Try to contemplate every spoonful, forked morsel, or swallow. One way is to talk to yourself about eating as it occurs. This behavior is incompatible with many other behaviors during mealtime. As you look at a morsel of food say, "Now I'm going to cut my meat. I must pick up my knife and fork and cut my meat so I can eat it. Now I'm picking up my knife and fork, and now I am cutting my meat so it can be eaten. I lay down my knife, pick up my meat, and take it to my mouth." Stop just before the food gets to the mouth and say, "This meat is now going to be chewed and swallowed." Place the food in the mouth and think about chewing the food and say sub-vocally, "Now I am chewing my food" (chew 20 times counting and thinking how good the food is), next as you swallow say, "Now I have swallowed the food, and I am going to get the benefit from that bit of food." This procedure should be followed every meal for a period of two weeks before any diet is started. This procedure ensures that food taken into the mouth will get into the mouth *on purpose*. This also serves to bring eating behavior under the control of your intentions and to break learned connections between eating and other behaviors. Repeated chewing also slows the rate of eating.

3. *Weight chart*

During the two weeks that you eat on purpose in your designated place, take your morning nude weight every day at the same time (preferably just after getting up in the morning). It is important to record your weight every day.

For reliability you might have someone watch you weigh. The two-week chart will give you a baseline from which to measure progress and the reliability person (mother, spouse, partner, etc.) will give supportive incentive to reduce. Make certain the chart is attached to the wall in a prominent place where you can see it as you get ready for the day's activities. Some people also find it helpful to include a measurement chart (waist, etc.).

4. *Breakfast*

Breakfast should be considered a reward for looking neat and clean. Often, a sloppy appearance is conducive to gaining weight (even though you stay at home). Wear clean clothes and engage in appropriate sprucing.

5. *Eating Cue*

Use something at the table that is always present when you eat. For example, use a small hourglass or brightly colored napkin or conspicuous charm (any brightly colored object will do). When you sit down to eat, take the object, place it in view, and say, "This gives me permission to eat," look at the object, and go through the *eating on purpose* routine. The object of the card provides a "transfer" to other situations, and you may come to feel guilty if it is not being used.

6. *Eat off schedule*

Schedule meals at variable times during the day and stick to your *variable schedule*. If other members of the family are unable to meet your schedule, then it is better to eat by yourself. *This does not mean to snack between your variable schedule.* Eating off schedule helps break the bodily cycle of getting hungry at certain time periods. It also helps establish the *eating on purpose* routine.

7. *Calorie chart*

All food, especially tiny portions, should be logged with number of calories when eaten on an intake chart that shows your quota for each day.

8. *Additional helps*

    a.   If you shop, shop by list only, and never allow yourself to buy anything that is not on your list.

    b.   Prepare the shopping list immediately after dinner.

    c.   Food should be out of sight when beginning the program except when actually eating or preparing meals.

    d.   One-half hour before each mealtime take a small 6-ounce glass of juice or appropriate liquid. Thus, you will probably not be as hungry when mealtime arrives.

e.   Remember to get your diet from a doctor and stay under supervision during your behavioral program.

Evaluate: All individuals lost weight (average 15 pounds) from following the above procedures. In combination these procedures are extremely effective; some people report weight loss by using just one of the above.

Professional Application

Example 91

Pinpoint: *Negative verbalizations* (three youngsters—9, 12, and 14 years old)

Record: One hundred nineteen occurrences in one week counted during afternoon and evening.

Consequate: *(Negative modeling.)* Bad examples illustrated using TV commercials (e.g., "My wash is whiter than your wash." "Isn't Gladys fat, oh! here she comes . . . tried that old (product) time and time" "Okay, have it your way—you'll see." (Later) "See I told you so, you never listen." "Husbands can't do anything—let me do it—see," etc.)

Evaluate: Youngsters began to become sensitized to their verbalizations and actually started keeping records to help each other decrease "nasty" comments. Only five comments counted during the fifth week.

Note: Television provides an excellent source for both positive and negative behaviors. TV can be used to sensitize as well as shape both appropriate and inappropriate behaviors. Adults must be present, however, if they want to take part in the definition.

Professional Application

Example 92

Pinpoint: *Physical abuse of mother* (15-year-old boy)

Record: Boy placed in county juvenile detention center for physical abuse of widowed mother, throwing her out of house, threatening others with a gun. Boy stated that he only wanted to play his guitar and be left entirely alone.

Consequate: (1) Guitar lessons contingent on assigned work tasks. Guitar removed if tasks not completed. (2) Communication sessions developed between mother and son, using boy's music as subject matter. Also, music paired with talk sessions to decrease high emotional responses. (3) Role-playing sessions between counselor and mother to establish correct verbalizations.

Evaluate: Case terminated after four weeks (guitar was removed once); no beatings, arrests, or verbal abuses.

Note: The mother in this case was being unwittingly controlled by her son. In her words, "Every time I try to talk with Fred and explain how I feel, he somehow turns my words against me and then goes into his room to listen to music; I am deeply concerned that he just doesn't understand me." Many adults, as the widow in this case, try to reason and explain their feelings, yet become "used" by young people. Reinforcing this insensitive behavior is certainly unproductive for adults and does little but produce a kind of "sadism." It seems extremely unproductive when adults allow young people to use divorce, adoption, lack of love, peer or sibling comparisons, and so on, to get their way. In this case, the mother had fallen into the trap of "trying even harder to make her son understand her." It should be noted that after the boy's verbal and physical abuse stopped and he was rewarded for *appropriate* behavior (i.e., household duties, clearing the yard, not arguing, etc.), he did start to "understand" his mother.

Scientific Application (p. 335)

Example 93

Pinpoint: *Off-task, low-achieving students* (seventh grade, 12 students)

Record: Students off-task 56.4%, teacher academic approval 44.9, teacher social approval ratio 3.0 (10 days observation).

Consequate I: Eight students taken from room and received daily group counseling (four were given behavioral counseling through role playing, modeling appropriate classroom behaviors, and reinforcement for verbalizing appropriate classroom behavior; four students were given "client-centered" counseling and helped to verbalize and interpret classroom behavior). Four students remained in room as a control group to check effects of group counseling.

Evaluate I: Four students in behavioral counseling increased on-task behavior 6.8%. Four students in client-centered counseling increased on-task behavior 2.2%. Control group decreased on-task behavior 11.3% (average on-task for all 12 was 57%). Teachers' academic approval ratio was 11.7 and social approval ratio was 1.5.

Consequate II: Counseling continued for both groups (four weeks of treatment); teacher instructed in contingent use of approval techniques (one week).

Evaluate II: Behavioral counseling group increased on-task behavior an additional 38.1%, client-centered counseling group increased on-task behavior an additional 27.7%, no-contact control group increased on-task behavior 40.7% (average on-task for all 12 was 21.3%). Teacher academic approval ratio was 62.2%, social approval ratio was 62.4%.

Consequate III: Counseling continued, teacher continued attention for both academic and social behavior, also instituted a token reinforcement system (tokens were given for appropriate social behavior, redeemable on Friday afternoons for donuts and soda pop, 2 weeks).

Evaluate III: Behavioral counseling group increased on-task behavior another 7.8% (2.1% total off-task), client-centered increased on-task behavior another 10.8% (total off-task 18.5%), control group increased on-task another 5.7% (total off-task 19.6%). Average off-task for all twelve was 13.4%. Teacher academic approval ratio was 76.3%, social approval ratio was 86.7%.

Consequate IV: Counseling discontinued, teacher instructed to behave as before the study began (one week).

Evaluate IV: All 12 students increased inappropriate behavior (41.2% off-task). No significant difference between three counseling groups.

Consequate V: Teacher re-instituted approving academic and social behavior, also reinstated token system.

Evaluate V: Average on-task behavior for all 12 students averaged 93.2%. Teacher's academic approval ratio averaged 42.8%, social approval ratio averaged 91.1%.

Note: This study indicates that the teacher is the major instigator of both appropriate and inappropriate behavior even on the seventh-grade level. It also indicates that counseling outside the classroom for classroom behavioral problems is probably not effective unless the teacher reinforces appropriate classroom behavior. Even though behavioral counseling was more effective than client-centered counseling, behavioral counseling had little effect until the teacher used contingent approval. The study also indicated that the teacher is better able to change behavior where the problem occurs (in the classroom).

Scientific Application (p. 335)

HIGH SCHOOL/ADULT EXAMPLES

Example 94

Pinpoint: *School failure* (16-year-old boy)

Record: Failed all academic subjects first half of year. Parents and teachers unable to "motivate studying."

Consequate: School counselor developed system with parents' cooperation. Every teacher signed individual *daily progress report* (one small sheet) after each class. Decision of signing for appropriate social and academic behaviors based on teacher's criteria. Allowance, social engagements, car privileges contingent on number of signatures earned each day.

Evaluate: Better grades. C+ average attained for last six-week period of same year.

Note: Many parents offer rewards for good grades, but cannot find a way to cut down the time interval so that rewards are meaningful in motivating the student. A complete academic term is very long for a student who cannot exhibit correct study patterns throughout one day.

Professional Application

Example 95

Pinpoint: *"Love note" passing—boy-girl talking* (eleventh grade, biology class)

Record: Five intercepted notes in one week (three innocuous, two vulgar). Twenty incidents of talking during one class period.

Consequate: Friday field trip privilege contingent upon "no more talking or letter writing."

Evaluate: Friday field trip *denied* two consecutive weeks, given third week after talking and letter writing stopped.

Note: Field trips were continued throughout year. However, trips were subsequently denied four times for talking—sometimes students forget. Even though the above contingencies were effective, it is usually unwise to attempt to "control" note and letter writing for students at advanced grade levels. Most often contingencies are either ineffective or may even backfire, producing other inappropriate behavior.

Professional Application

Example 96

Pinpoint: *Homework study* (high school, 17-year-old girl)

Record: Grades monitored for one semester. Average grades D- with frequent failures.

Consequate: Flash cards developed by student to assist study in history, civics, Latin. Meals contingent (except breakfast) on success in responses to cards.

Evaluate: Within eight weeks grades rose from a D to a B-average.

Note: Researchers noted the flash cards might have been reinforcing instead of the food. However, a follow-up at a later semester indicated grades had returned to a D average. Obviously, cards or grades alone were not sufficient rewards for this girl. Motivation must come from without before it gets "in." The question of how long it takes for motivation to "get in" for each individual is not known. However, it would appear that even constant rewarding is better than constant failure.

Scientific Application (p. 335)

Example 97

Pinpoint: *Boredom* (tenth grade, Spanish)

Record: Lack of enthusiasm for subject-matter acquisition—only 2 of 23 assignments completed in two-week period

Consequate: Friday football game instituted: teams chosen, rules established, points, yards, substitutions, and so on, developed for correct *academic* responses. Game played on chalkboard with losing team providing "treat" for winners.

Evaluate: "Enthusiasm replaced boredom"—all assignments completed by second Friday.

Note: Any game can be used for any subject matter. It is best to choose a game specifically appropriate to the general outside interests of the student age group and having enough status that they will not think that it is "silly."

Professional Application

Example 98

Pinpoint: *Loud disruptive laughing* (tenth grade, six boys)

Record: Girl's recitations elicited loud laughing from boys.

Consequate: Boys collectively taken out of room—brought back individually in front of class as girls applauded. Seating arrangements also changed to place each boy among group of girls.

Evaluate: Loud inappropriate laughing ended.

Note: The same procedure of boy-girl seating was employed for the student body during general assemblies, resulting in considerable decrease in catcalls and noise. It also helped boy-girl socialization. Arranging the total environment, including seating arrangements decreases many inappropriate school behaviors.

Professional Application

Example 99

Pinpoint: *Positive verbalizations about oneself and positive social interactions* (16-year-old boy)

Record: Boy avoided peer interaction; stated he did not like himself because his parents couldn't stand him; stated he was no good and no one could possibly like him (self-records indicated over 20 times per day debased self and no positive peer or adult contact—two weeks' records).

Consequate: To teach good "self-concept" (appropriate self-labeling), boy was instructed to: (1) record positive verbalizations, (2) list hierarchy of interests and good points (himself and parents), (3) carry list in pocket and read list whenever he caught himself in self-abasement (incompatible response), (4) initiate peer contact (one per day) based on similar peer interests, and (5) interact verbally with parents 10 minutes per day in a positive manner.

Evaluate: One close friendship within six weeks (average three to four positive contacts daily); joined boy's science club. After three weeks, he talked positively regarding parents.

Note: "Self-concept" usually relates to cognitive behavior and to a phenomenon called *labeling,* that is, "I am a good person" as opposed to "I am no good" or "My student is a good person" versus "He is just a bad boy." Some research regarding "labeling" suggests a cause-and-effect relationship between labels and behavior. If a student gets the idea that he (she) is a "bad person," this might influence his (her) behavior. That is, the student will behave in accordance with this "self-concept."

Professional Application

Example 100

Pinpoint: *Non-cooperation* (eleventh grade, English, five boys)

Record: No English assignments completed during two-week period. Students also refused to recite orally. Boys caught "shooting craps" in back of room.

Consequate: All boys sent to principal's office and given a "good talking to" concerning classroom responsibilities and advantages of learning English.

Evaluate: No change occurred in behavior. Boys became more noncooperative and began to mimic female teacher. Caught shooting craps twice during following week.

If at first you don't succeed . . .

Consequate II: Teacher began to praise every class member who cooperated in giving oral recitations from selected literature.

Evaluate II: No change noted. Not one boy volunteered to participate in oral recitations. Teacher saw dice once, but didn't catch boys in any games.

Consequate III: Everyone who participated in oral recitations allowed to bring any book or magazine to class for 30 minutes of private reading.

Evaluate III: One noncooperative boy brought a *Playboy* magazine to teacher after class and asked sarcastically: "If I read aloud from your book, can I read mine?" Teacher agreed. Next session he did. Within four weeks all boys recited.

Note: The teacher was also able to shift these boys' interests from *Playboy* to *Hot Rod*, and, after four months, to sophisticated sports magazines found in the school library. This case demonstrates effective use of peer contingencies and approximations toward better literature through lack of censorship. However, this procedure might be extremely problematic for a teacher if not supported by supervisor.

Professional Application

Example 101

Pinpoint: *Use of illegal drugs* (17-year-old boy)

Record: "Pot," three to four times weekly; LSD, two occurrences.

Consequate: Boy began research on effects of drugs and was paid for each two-page paper written.

Evaluate: LSD discontinued.

Note: This boy stated he found what he considered good evidence for discontinuing LSD, but found conflicting evidence on the dangers of marijuana, so he decided not to stop. Others with similar contingencies have decided to give up all drugs because of legal, occupational, religious, and/or societal consequences. Yet, the use of illegal drugs is widespread and the age of users is becoming progressively younger. New "designer drugs" are being manufactured and used indiscriminately and many times there is not scientific data available as in the above case. PCP "angel dust," cocaine, crack, as well as other drugs, are becoming more prevalent. While media reports attest to the dangers of drugs, almost all users know (or think they know) what drugs will or will not hurt them. Most often this information comes from other participants. As has been repeatedly stated, the effects of "modeling" are tremendously powerful and this is especially true from peers. Regardless, solid information concerning drugs when available (e.g., differentiating among drugs), and *early preventative* measures seem most effective.

Professional Application

Example 102

Pinpoint: *Cocaine and marijuana dependence* (two adult men, 28 and 35)

Record: Subject 1 reported 3 years cocaine use (8g previous week), latest use was 3 of prior 30 day period. Seventeen years of marijuana use (14g per week), latest use was 27 of 30 previous days. Subject 2 reported 10 years cocaine use, consuming 7g per week, latest use was 29 of past 30 days. Fifteen years of marijuana use (4g per week), latest use was 10 of prior 30 days.

Consequate I: Cocaine-abstinence phase (12 weeks). Subjects received a *community based reinforcement* (CRA) intervention consisting of two behavior therapy sessions each week. For both men, sessions involved functional analysis of cocaine use, stimulus-control training, employment and career counseling, assertiveness training, AIDS education, relaxation training, and counseling targeting increased participation in non-drug-related recreational and social activities. One man had six sessions involving reciprocal relationship counseling with his girlfriend. During this phase, girlfriend was telephoned immediately following each urinalysis test and informed of results. If negative, she performed an agreed-upon positive activity. Urine specimens collected and analyzed for cocaine use 4 times per week, other drug use once per week. Negative samples earned increasingly more points with each point redeemable for small amount of money. Points also traded for prosocial activities. Four consecutive negative tests earned bonus points.

Evaluate I: Both men tested positive for marijuana use, *negative* for all other drugs (except S1 had a positive cocaine test during week 1). Both men reported working—S1 for 28, and S2 for 22, of last 30 days.

Consequate II: Cocaine-maintenance phase (S1=3.5 weeks, S2=7.5 weeks). Urine tested twice per week. One lottery ticket was given for negative specimens. CRA behavior therapy sessions reduced to 30 minutes each week, focused on maintaining behavior changes from first phase, and strategies for marijuana abstinence.

Evaluate II: Complete cocaine abstinence although regular marijuana use; tested negative for all other drugs.

Consequate III: Cocaine-marijuana-abstinence phase (12 weeks). Urine tested twice per week. Vouchers only given for both negative marijuana and negative cocaine tests. 30-minute therapy sessions weekly or bi-weekly, maintaining previous behavior changes.

Evaluate III: S1 provided 96% and 92% negative specimens for cocaine and marijuana, respectively; S2 specimens 100% negative for cocaine and marijuana. Both reported working 24 of final 30 days. One- and 5-month follow-ups indicated that cocaine abstinence continued, but marijuana smoking resumed.

Note: This behavioral program was nested in the natural environment of these men. Feedback was very specific and the interventions appeared to be effective. However, follow-up indicated that marijuana use continued after the interventions. It should be noted that neither man sought treatment for marijuana use at the beginning of the program but agreed to its institution prior to initiation of the cocaine-marijuana-abstinence phase.

Scientific Application (p. 335)

Example 103

Pinpoint: *Fear of failure, worrying* (17-year-old girl)

Record: Girl reported "worrying constantly." Mother recorded average of 12 times per day daughter talked about upcoming "problems."

Consequate: (1) Time set for 15 minutes of daily worry. Must worry "hard" during this time, imagining all the bad things that might happen. (2) Rank ordered all possible outcomes of failure in upcoming events. (3) Instructed to say "stop," sub-vocally, every time worrying started during other times of day and change to organized study routine immediately after recording one instance of worrying on worry card carried by girl.

Evaluate: Worrying increased to "constantly" (daughter's own statement, no actual record). Worrying during prescribed time seemed "silly."

Consequate II: Girl told worrying had probably actually decreased from "constantly," had actual record been made, to point that she could discriminate between when she was or was not worrying; therefore, worry could be counted.

Evaluate II: Worrying decreased to twice daily; 15-minute worrying period decreased to 5 minutes (worry time became negative).

Note: Eventually the worrying time became extremely silly as girl learned to plan constructive activities, and worry time was discontinued.

Professional Application

Example: 104

Pinpoint: *Increasing salad purchase at two fast-food restaurants.*

Record: Salad and side salad summed sales (corrected percentages) combined for both restaurants were calculated (100% was statistically determined as the baseline figure).

Consequate I: Two posters stating "Be Fit & Healthy; Eat a low-fat SALAD as your meal or add a side salad" with a picture of a salad, located near cash register. Table tent cards with same message placed on each table; banner and streamers at restaurant entrance stating "Eat Salads" (3 weeks).

Evaluate I: Corrected percentage of salad sales rose to 115%.

Consequate II: Visual prompts removed (1 week).

Evaluate II: Corrected percentage was 90% of baseline percentage.

Consequate III: Visual prompts reinstated (1 week).

Evaluate III: Corrected percentage increased to 109%.

Consequate IV: No signs (follow-up after one month).

Evaluate IV: Corrected percentage was 99%.

Note: Hamburger sales throughout the study remained relatively constant as control data. Data for this study were taken from the computer and while this method of data collection is accurate and easy, additional information might include aspects relating to individual people. For example, are some choosing salads but using a large amount of high calorie dressing, or are those who most need a low-fat alternative the ones who choose it? Regardless, this study demonstrates the effectiveness of rather simple procedures.

Scientific Application (p. 335)

Example 105

Pinpoint: *Rehearsal effectiveness* (high school band)

Record: *All* stops by conductor constituted disapproval responses (traditional rehearsing procedure).

Consequate: Band director marked two notated musical scores (equal difficulty and unfamiliar to band) with periodic pencil checks that divided musical phrases. During first score, director stopped at each checkpoint, delivered *disapproval* responses regardless of performance quality. During second score, director stopped at checks and delivered specific compliments to performers or gave approval gestures (expressions) *during* the performance.

Evaluate: Compliments produced "a better performance and rehearsal attitude." Rehearsal time judged for equal performance level: disapproval 33 minutes, approval 19 minutes.

Note: When anyone is engaging in a self-selected "pleasurable activity" there is usually a tremendous amount of reinforcement coming from the activity itself. In the above activity students could be receiving reinforcement from a variety of separate and collect sources. For example, a person could be reinforced by manipulating fingers to make sounds come out of a horn, the physical pleasure of "blowing" an instrument, making/listening to beautiful sounds, pleasing the conductor, looking forward to a performance or to a trip, getting to wear a uniform, sitting next to a special person, etc. Indeed there are many potential "natural" reinforcers within most activities and not all of the approval/disapproval is coming from the conductor/teacher.

Professional Application

Example 106

Pinpoint: *Using adoption to control adults* (16-year-old girl)

Record: Girl used statements concerning her adoption to "get her way." Engaged parents in "proving their love" and providing "payoff" (seven instances in one month).

Consequate: Parents instructed to ignore all talk concerning adoption, to leave girl's presence when subject brought up unless girl verbalized approval statements, and to prepare for extreme test.

Evaluate: Girl ran away; she returned the following weekend.

Consequate II: Girl instructed by parents that parental approval would continue to be contingent on good behavior, not on genetic involvement.

Evaluate II: The use of "adoption" to control parents ceased.

Note: Many children (at all ages) use adult concern, worry, or guilt to change the adult's behavior. The child learns one of several perverted associations. "When I get punished and act hurt long enough, someone will give in," that is, good things happen after I suffer. "They love me, so if I act nasty long enough they'll give up," that is, to stop the negative behavior adults provide payoff. This reinforces the adults as obnoxious behavior stops, but children are reinforced for persisting in negative behavior for longer and longer periods. "When I get their goat anything is likely to happen." Thus, the child's payoff *is* the anger of the adults (parents or teachers).

Professional Application

Example: 107

Pinpoint: *Pedestrian crosswalk safety* (reducing conflicts on a six-lane crosswalk)

Record: Average of 8.1 motorist-pedestrian conflicts per day for first 30 pedestrians monitored. Conflicts recorded when motorist braked, changed lanes abruptly, or pedestrian jumped to avoid being hit, or when vehicle passed within less than 1 lane distance from pedestrian, or when vehicle passed in lane immediately to left of another vehicle that yielded to pedestrian.

Consequate I: Advance *stop lines* and *sign prompts* instituted. Two signs stating "STOP HERE FOR PEDESTRIANS" posted 50 meters before crosswalk on 2 separate streets combined with advance stop line painted across 3 lanes at same distance as signs.

Evaluate I: Daily motorist-pedestrian conflicts decreased to 2.5 per 30 people in crosswalk (69% reduction during 8 days).

Consequate II: Signs and lines removed.

Evaluate II: Daily conflicts increased to 4 per 30 people in crosswalk (9 days).

Consequate III: Signs and lines reinstated.

Evaluate III: Daily conflicts returned to 2.5 per 30 people in crosswalk (5 days).

Consequate IV: Signs and lines removed.

Evaluate IV: Daily conflict increased to 5.8 per 30 people in crosswalk (7 days).

Consequate V: Sign and lines reinstated.

Evaluate V: Daily conflict decreased to 1.7 per 30 people in crosswalk (44 days).

Note: The higher number of pedestrians hit by vehicles resulting in death and serious injury shows importance of simple inexpensive and effective interventions such as this one that included advance stop lines and sign prompts.

Professional Application

Example 108

Pinpoint: *Garbage removal from kitchen* (15-year-old boy)

Record: Mother recorded reminding boy to take out garbage an average of five times prior to any action.

Consequate: If garbage not removed prior to supper, garbage can was placed on boy's chair at evening meal.

Evaluate: Entire family laughed the first time son discovered the can. Boy promptly took the can outside and returned to the kitchen. Three days later the same procedure was employed. Following six instances (during three-week period), boy decided to give himself reminder cues and constructed a sign in bedroom: "empty the trash." Job completed with no relapses.

Note: In this case, parents were able to remove themselves from an unpleasant disapproval and interact in joking fashion while still making it very clear the job should be completed. Similar techniques have been used for other household chores. One father put his 16-year-old's dinner on a tray and placed it under her bed behind some dirty clothes. The clothes had to be removed before the dinner was obtained. With older children these consequences primarily serve as reminders. However, when inappropriate behaviors have reached a frequency and magnitude that is severe, this type of "reminder" might not function. In the above case the boy could have emptied the trash on the table.

Professional Application

Example 109

Pinpoint: *Embarrassment* (tenth grade music, three girls)

Record: Self-evaluation indicated students possessed "no musical talent." Students refrained from individual singing stating "My voice sounds funny," or "I cannot carry a tune."

Consequate: Twofold program to: (1) teach all students discrimination between (a) possessing ability and (b) performing before class, and (2) teach entire class role playing to deliver approval feedback to "insecure students."

Evaluate: Students learned to participate in activities, even though they did not possess even moderate "talents." Class also taught to smile, nod heads, keep eye contact, and approvingly reinforce a terrible performance. Teacher played role of extremely poor singer while class learned to "put a performer at ease" by *not* responding to performer's fear and avoidance with fear and avoidance, but with approving reinforcement. Shy performers began participating regularly. One girl stated: "I have always known I've had a lousy voice, but now I love to sing."

Note: Older students who have a problem with embarrassment in relation to any activity have *learned* this embarrassment from someone. It is usually learned traumatically. For example, the young child sings and enjoys it until one shocking day someone says that her/his voice sounds terrible, whereupon singing stops—often for a long, long time. Unfortunately, some teachers do not understand the importance of teaching discriminations, and, therefore, continuously prepare many youngsters for disillusionment—some for catastrophe. Dedicated to well-intended censorship, many teachers pretend that no one is different from anyone else. "Celia has only one arm, but in my classroom she has two, just like everyone else." "Fred has a lisp, but in my classroom we ignored his impediment—it does not exist." "Spencer is the only black child in my room, yet in my classroom there is no skin color, everyone's skin is exactly the same." It is unfortunate that these children must get out on the playground where other children do not censor: "Hey, Celia, what happened to your arm?" "Gosh, Fred, you talk funny." "Why are your hands white, Spencer?" Some children even make fun of these differences. Yet, where can children learn to accept differences proudly and not make fun? Certainly not in a classroom in which differences *do not exist*. Children can easily be taught discrimination of differences. Much more importantly, they can be taught *acceptance* and *respect* for differences. This learning, however, will not come from censorship.

Professional Application

Example 110

Pinpoint: *Inappropriate sexual advances* (15-year-old girl)

Record: Four cases of boys responding with sexually aggressive behavior opposite to that desired by girl (following recent move to new school).

Consequate: Girl practiced role playing in delivering verbal response and changing bodily responses in order to elicit more "appropriate," fewer "inappropriate" responses from male peers. Also instructed to report any sexual misbehavior to authorities.

Evaluate: "Inappropriate" sexual behavior decreased to zero after four weeks. Girl also became more isolated.

Note: Obviously, the boys in the above case needed intervention in not behaving inappropriately. Inappropriate sexual behavior should *never* be condoned in society, and especially in schools. Yet many youngsters report being regularly sexually accosted, sometimes beginning in grade school. The girl in this case was extremely reluctant to report any misbehavior. Effective social behavior is made up of correctly interpreting and giving cues, yet learning *appropriate* behavior is difficult for some students. Even in the absence of cues, people are subjected to sexual aggression. Every youngster needs to develop techniques to deal with these inappropriate behaviors—techniques for self-protection as well as techniques in reporting them to authorities. Teachers should provide strong support and appropriate modeling for all such behavior, especially in reporting transgressions and following through. Additionally, all students should be instructed at an early age that no should always mean no—and stop always means stop!

Professional Application

Example 111

Pinpoint: *Illegal parking in handicapped spaces* (432 vehicle drivers in, 4 spaces)

Record: Violation rate of 51.3% while vertical sign (international symbol for handicapped parking) displayed (8 days).

Consequence I: Message posted below the vertical symbol, "Warning: this space watched by concerned citizens."

Evaluate I: Parking violation rate decreased to 37.3%.

Consequence II: Vertical sign only.

Evaluate II: Parking violations increased to 50.4%.

Consequence III: Vertical sign plus addition of a message box below the sign, "Warning: This space watched and ticketed by concerned citizens."

Evaluate III: Parking violations decreased to 24.5%.

Consequence IV: Vertical sign only.

Evaluate IV: Parking violations increased to 57%.

Consequence V: Vertical sign and message box dispenser.

Evaluate V: Parking violations decreased to 23.7%.

Consequate VI: Vertical sign only.

Evaluate VI: Parking violations increased to 37.3%.

Note: During the final period illegal parking did not return to initial rates with the vertical sign only.

Scientific Application (p. 335)

Example 112

Pinpoint: *Lawbreaking* (40 delinquent boys, average age 17.8, lower socioeconomic level)

Record: Average age at first arrest 13.5; average number arrests 8.2; total time incarceration 15.1 months. All boys arrested approximately same age, same nationality, equal number of months in jail, similar residence and religious preferences.

Consequate: One group participated in consequences, one "control" group did not. Boys were not in school (most of them should have been) and met on street corners or other places of frequent occupancy. Each boy was offered job and told that the researcher wanted to know "how teenagers felt about things." Boys who participated were rewarded with food, cokes, money, or tokens, depending on each individual case. No punishment was employed. Occasionally, bonus rewards given for prompt arrival, proper verbalizations, and spontaneous interest.

Evaluate: Groups were compared three years later. Consequate group averaged 2.4 arrests, other group 4.7; average number of months in jail 3.5 for consequate group, 6.9 for other group. Illegal acts committed by consequate group less frequent and much less severe.

Note: In this particular study, consequences were not directed toward criminal behavior itself but represented an attempt to teach prosocial behavioral patterns. When a boy did not appear, the researcher would meet him out on the street and bring him to the lab. It is sometimes important for the teacher to go after a child and bring him where he should be. Any peer group such as the above juvenile group can exercise tremendous pressure toward group conformity. Often peer rewards must be broken down or changed if the teacher is to succeed.

Scientific Application (p. 335)

Example 113

Pinpoint: *Excessive local directory-assistance telephone calls* (over one million persons in a large city area)

Record: Telephone directory-assistance calls monitored over 25 years.

Consequate: Telephone subscribers allowed three local directory assistance calls per month. Subscribers were then charged for each additional local directory-assistance call. No change was placed on long-distance directory-assistance calls.

Evaluate: Frequency of local calls dropped markedly (60,000 per day). Frequency of long-distance directory-assistance calls remained the same.

Note: The above charge fits the description of a *response cost* procedure. That is, the charge is contingent on the response of making a directory-assistance call. Many similar response cost procedures have been used in educational token systems. Often the *response cost* represents the most viable alternative to punishment (e.g., taking away tokens for cheating or breaking rules).

Scientific Application (p. 335)

Example 114

Pinpoint: *Low-level English achievement* (high school dropouts, 17 students)

Record: No academic performance, all students out of school during summer.

Consequate: Students contacted on city streets during summer induced to "try coming to school a few days for rewards." Local merchants donated (1) food—hamburgers, cokes, malts, sandwiches, etc., and (2) music—records and theatre passes. These were compared with (3) free time; (4) teacher attention and (5) grades. Students assigned a different consequence each day.

Evaluate: Fourteen boys completed English requirements during regular year, decided to return to high school in fall.

Note: Of special interest in this study was the disparity between stated preferences and actual behavior. At first of summer all boys were presented paired items from reinforcement menu and asked which they would work for (e.g., would you work harder for a McDonald's hamburger or 10 minutes of free time). All classes of items were paired with all other classes. The order of preference at the beginning of the summer was (1) food, (2) music records and passes, (3) free time, (4) grades, (5) teacher attention. At the end of the summer the same questionnaire was given all boys. The order of preference as stated by the boys was exactly the same at the beginning of the summer as at the end. However, accurate records kept on the actual work output of each boy indicated that during the first week of summer school they did indeed work harder for material rewards and food, but during the last week of summer school, while the stated preference had not changed, the most work was actually produced when followed by *teacher attention.*

Professional Application

Example 115

Pinpoint: *Increasing athletic performance* (21-year old male pole-vaulter)

Record: Successful pole vault dependent upon arm extension and maximum pole height at take-off. Vaulter's ground-to-pole angle at take-off lacked consistency with maximum angle never displayed. Mean hand height at take-off was 2.25 meters (14 sessions).

Consequate: Goal was to develop and maintain (at maximum height) the position of the pole during take-off (2.54 m.). Intervention based on a changing criterion design including 200 sessions over 18 months. Photoelectric beam set across runway at 2.3 m. Verbal prompt "reach" shouted to vaulter when running down runway at 9 m distance from plant box. Additionally, vaulter given feedback in form of a beep when photoelectric beam broken, indicating vaulter had achieved desired height. Beam raised to 2.35, 2.4, 2.45, 2.5, and 2.52 m. when vaulter stabilized each preceding performance level at 90% criterion.

Evaluate: Vaulter obtained 90% level at all heights except 2.52 m, reported responding to the photoelectric beam like a competitor.

Note: Beep seemed to operate as a conditioned positive reinforcer for arm extension. Vaulter increased his height from 5.15 meters during baseline to 5.37 following intervention.

Scientific Application (p. 335)

Example 116

Pinpoint: *Decreasing vascular headaches* (5 women, aged 33 to 56 years)

Record: Reported headache history ranging from 9 to 40 years. All diagnosed by physician as having vascular headache and a minimum of 1 headache per month. Exercise averaged 0.8 Cooper Points (standardized measure of aerobic benefit; score of 8 equivalent to 1.5 miles in 10-12 minutes) per week.

Consequate: Behavioral adherence package including instructions, modeling, behavioral contracting, goal setting, stimulus control, performance feedback and praise, shaping, and verbal strategies. Exercise selected by subjects included jogging, walking, exercise biking, and aerobic dancing.

Subjects paid a large monetary fee, refunded in small increments for each exercise session completed to increasingly demanding criterion. Engaged in one on-site exercise session per week, given contingent feedback and praise while exercising, exercise recorded and publicly displayed. Also encouraged to focus on pleasantness of environment, not aversive stimuli or self-defeating thoughts. Expected to exercise twice per week on own, encouraged to lay out exercise clothes night before. Also, significant others (who were trained to record exercise for reliability purposes) prompted and gave reinforcement, telephone prompts also provided encouragement.

Evaluate: Weekly average of 23.6 Cooper Points during last 2 weeks of training, 14.9 at 3-month follow-up, and 9.0 at 6-month post-training follow-up. Four subjects reported continued exercise at 3 months, 3 at 6 months. Three subjects reported full weeks without headaches after beginning exercise, four reported headache reductions during training and reduced medication. One person reported being headache free at end of training but headaches returned to pre-training level during exercise lapse.

Note: Not only did four of five subjects experience reductions in headaches that had previously interfered with daily life, but they also improved overall levels of fitness through aerobic exercise.

Scientific Application (p.335)

Example 117

Pinpoint: *Academic "apathy"* (eleventh grade, history, poverty-level backgrounds)

Record: *No* evidence of *any* study behavior. Five days constant harassment.

Consequate: Teacher left *all* books and teaching materials home, sat at the desk, looked at students, and said nothing. Teacher continued procedure day after day throughout *one entire week.* Did not attempt to teach, control class, or respond in any way.

Evaluate: During the second week, two students timidly brought books to class and asked what to do. Teacher brought the two students to front of room and began teaching. As days passed, other students joined the small learning group. By end of six weeks, every student was involved. Last seven students came into learning group on same day.

Note: Much is said in education about students establishing their own goals. This study is an excellent example of this concept at its most basic level, for there is an infinite distance between zero and one. Most students do not know what their goals are. If they can engage a teacher in battle, this often becomes their goal. In the above case, students were left with nothing. In time, they began to want something, anything, even school-work. Ignoring takes a temporal patience many teachers could well develop. Concerning these students, it should be noted that children who live in extreme deprivation meet boredom and apathy as an "old friend." Perhaps more sophisticated students would have developed goals during this long period that excluded the teacher entirely.

When a teacher decides to accept the contingencies (goals) of the student peer group, the teacher should do so in full knowledge of possible results. When speaking of "children establishing their own goals," it would seem wise for teachers to think through this concept carefully. Most often this cliché indicates that the teacher *decides* to let children *decide* certain innocuous things. "You may choose any color you wish—you may not color on the wall." If, from the beginning, goals were left *entirely* to children, formal education would cease to exist. Knowledge and/or decisions cannot exist in a vacuum—"Tell me something you *do not know*."

Professional Application

Example 118

Pinpoint: *On-task versus cluttered communication* (13-, 15-, and 17-year-old teenagers, adults)

Record: "Lack of communication" reported by teenagers and parents after initial misunderstandings regarding use of car, hour of return from dates, work responsibilities at home, and schoolwork. Discussions characterized by noise, interruptions, TV, telephone, loud talking, etc. (80 occurrences in three two-hour periods).

Consequate: Family communication sessions instituted with rules: (1) we speak softly, (2) we speak one at a time, (3) we listen carefully, (4) we do not contradict, (5) we might have to *agree to disagree* on some issues, and (6) we will verbalize opposite viewpoint to satisfaction of other person to prove we understand. Sessions free from any extrinsic interruptions set up daily after dinner beginning with 5 minutes (oven timer set) and gradually increasing to 25 minutes.

Evaluate: "On-task" communication. No interruptions during communication times—other problems decreased.

Note: As adults, it is important to help children (perhaps even ourselves) to make some basic discriminations. On-task communication, for example, does not automatically occur just because two people are in proximity to one another. Time must be scheduled that ideally has no interruptions. On-task communication does not occur in movie houses, while watching television, or necessarily even when families take some time off and spend a weekend or longer vacation together.

Although worthwhile activities should be given the time and attention deserved, on-task communication should not be confused with other activities. The classic example is the father who wondered why he couldn't communicate with his son after eight years of weekend fishing together. Many parents, as well as older children, actually believe that going to the movies together, camping together, attending school functions, going to church together, and so on, are prerequisites for, or somehow take the place of, communication and other important interactions. The boy in the above example could fish very well.

Certainly activities may give an impetus to start communication, but human beings are not able to be on-task to two things at precisely the same time and do justice to both. When people enjoy activities, they should not confuse the emotional involvement of "feeling good" while engaged in the activity with other important behaviors (communication). There are individuals who appear never to engage in any family activities, yet are on-task in time spent communicating, teaching kindness, and maintaining extremely satisfying lives with significant others.

Professional Application

Example 119

Pinpoint: *Developing a study routine* (36 teenage students, girls and boys)

Record: Average grade level considered by both teachers and parents to be at least one letter grade below potential (average grades C-).

Consequate: Students were asked to indicate amount of time each felt appropriate to achieve goal (raising grades). Total time indicated was cut by 40%, after which a contract signed by pupil, teacher, and parent. Specific routines developed to aid in concentration:

1. *Concentration*

The important aspects of study are *on-task* concentration and repetition of materials not fully learned (asking oneself questions and answering as the material is studied; talking to oneself). On-task study time determined by each student before beginning to study material. Students also noted the number of their distracting thoughts (no student was able to complete six minutes of study time with fewer than eight distraction marks). On-task study time was increased in following manner: Each student purchased a timer (kitchen timer) and set aside only weekday study times that fit individual schedule (weekends free from nagging parents appealed to all students).

2. *Study place*

Students chose a "study place" where only study would take place. If necessary, other members of family used the same spot, but the student with the problem could study only there and nowhere else in the house. A straight-backed chair was chosen, with attempts made to place chair facing a corner or blank wall. Prominent signs were constructed warning family members (including parents) to stay away during study time. Distractions such as music were eliminated (these do *not* increase studying effectiveness). Only one book or one set of materials was taken to study place for each study session.

3. *Distraction cards*

Students used 5 × 8 inch cards labeled with date, time started, time finished, session number, as well as open space for distractions (distracting thoughts or interruptions). Students chose a pleasant activity to engage in during break times (reading, eating, listening to music, talking with friends, telephone calls, etc.), got materials ready, removed watches and other indicators of time, filled in the card, set kitchen timer for six minutes, and began to study. Whenever the student was distracted in any way (defined by student to help teach discrimination between on-task and off-task behavior), the student marked in space provided for distractions and also wrote in longhand at the bottom of card, "Get back to work." After having first noticed a distraction (competing sound, daydreaming, etc.), the initial inclination is to go back to work; writing little note "Get back to work" prevents this for a moment and serves to make concentration more desirable, discriminations more complete.

4. *Timer* (positioned so students couldn't see face)

When the timer rang, the students stood up immediately, took the timer, and moved away from study area. Reset timer for two minutes, then engaged in "fun" activity until timer again sounded, whereupon students went through same routine filling in new card. This procedure was repeated until the total time period allotted for study passed. Students changed from six-minute study session to nine-minute study session when number of distraction marks (and corresponding self-written work instructions) numbered two or fewer.

5. *Study schedules*

Students were permitted 3-minute break for 9-minute study period. Each time distracters had been reduced to 2 or below, students moved up scale (study 6, break 2; study 9, break 3; study 12, break 4; study 15, break 5; study 18, break 6; study 21, break 7; study 24, break 8; study 27, break 9; study 30, break 10; study 33, break 11; study 36, break 12; study 39, break

13; study 42, break 14; study 45, break 15) until reaching maximum. Students were strongly encouraged to never study longer than 45 minutes while using a 15-minute break for pleasant activities. This routine builds strong study skills as well as gives approval rewards following each small study session.

6. *External rewards*

Some parents/students used extra incentives (movies, car privileges, staying out time, money, and family outings) for moving up study scale *while maintaining absolute honesty.* Of course, many students were delighted with a routine that didn't start with amount of homework to be finished, but with amount of time to be studied (when no homework was available or required, student reviewed materials for test).

Evaluate: Average grades (31 students) increased to B within the school terms. Follow-up indicated 24 students maintained this level or above during entire following school year. Five students who did *not* improve admitted to never getting with the program. Seven students who did not *maintain* grade level did not consistently adhere to program primarily as results of parents who did not change their normally punitive, nagging reaction—who expressed doubts as to mental capabilities of their children or effectiveness of program and who did not encourage positively through words and extra incentives. Five students with parents falling into above category succeeded in spite of parental negativism and lack of support. (All later confided to school personnel they were going to prove to their parents that they were not "stupid" and continued the program in spite of lack of support. Three of these finally set up study places in friend's or relative's homes away from "distracting" influence of negative parents.)

Note: This routine has been used successfully with junior high students, upper-level grade school students, college students, and professionals who need to learn discrimination between on-task study as opposed to clutter. Most students do not enjoy their rest or fun times because they begin to feel "guilty" about not doing work. Alternately, when they attempt to study, they begin to feel sorry for themselves because they are not out having a good time!

Professional Application

Example 120

Pinpoint: *Dishonesty* (any classroom, anywhere)

Record: Three students caught cheating on first exam of term.

Consequate: F grades assigned without explanation.

Evaluate: Same three students caught stealing "ditto master" of second exam from typist's wastebasket.

Consequence II: Each student asked to write short theme stating reasons for cheating.

Evaluate II: Same three students caught cheating in falsifying laboratory manual.

Consequence III: Students asked to prepare confessional speech to be delivered before entire class. Parents of two students strongly objected, stating such treatment "would not only be a terrible experience, but damage children's reputations." Principal received call from school board member, after which students, parents, and teachers instructed to meet in principal's office. At meeting, all students denied any cheating whatsoever. Teacher presented first themes of confession. Parents of one student immediately placed her in private school. Parents of second student persuaded principal to allow daughter to withdraw from course. Parents of third student did not come to meeting. Teacher required this girl to make confessional statement before class. She did, but broke down crying before finishing. She later told teacher it was the worst thing she ever did in her life. Much later, she told the teacher that it was the second worst thing she ever did in her life.

Evaluate III, IV, V, VI, etc.: The science of behavior is predictable. You know all three of these students, regardless of age, sex, or position.

Fictional Application

STUDY GUIDE FOR CHAPTER 6

Questions:

Answer all questions and then check your answers by locating the appropriate pinpoint in Part II. Correct every false answer and rewrite so that the statement becomes true, or write 30 additional true-false statements using pinpoints (Examples) not previously used in this activity.

True-False

1. Overt behaviors, such as teasing, probably elicit payoffs from classmates.

2. Behaviors that have been diminished (such as reducing activity to a more appropriate level) may be internalized to the point that they are self-reinforcing.

3. Students learn more effectively if initially taught abstract concepts rather than specifics.

4. Long-term observational feedback increases teacher effectiveness more than daily observational feedback.

5. Student repair of damaged equipment and/or financial restitution rarely stops vandalism.

6. Special activities, such as field trips, may be made contingent on appropriate classroom behavior.

7. Research indicates that teacher approval is always the best reinforcer for controlling classroom behavior.

8. Inconsistent rules are more likely to be manipulated by students.

9. Specific situational rules are made to be broken.

10. Loud reprimands often tend to increase, rather than decrease, disruptive classroom behavior.

11. The technique of removing students from a classroom as punishment is effective only when the classroom provides positive consequences for the student.

12. Some content areas do not lend themselves to making a game out of learning.

13. Academically related materials (pencils, crayons, paper, books, and experiments) may be used as reinforcers for appropriate academic behaviors.

14. Rewards following student behavior are more meaningful when given at appropriate time intervals.

15. Children do not learn specific behavioral discrimination through negative practice.

16. Most teachers mistakenly feel that they use more approval than disapproval in the classroom.

17. Practice and/or role playing in delivery of approval or disapproval responses is not necessary for the experienced teacher who can apply these responses intuitively.

18. If students are to learn appropriate discriminations, they must be taught to discern differences.

19. Young students, if given no instruction, are capable of establishing all of their own goals.

20. Once the behavior to be changed is pinpointed and records taken treatment must be consistent and persistent to be effective.

21. Behavior that has been reinforced in the past may persist even when the specific reinforcers used to establish the behavior are no longer given.

22. Many rewards offered by teachers and parents for appropriate behavior are ineffective because the time interval between the behavior and the reward is too long.

23. Some scientific studies apply contingencies to classroom behavior and then take them out again in an attempt to hide research results from the classroom teacher.

24. Hitting and other aggressive behaviors are to be expected from young children, as these behaviors are innate.

25. Attitudes are probably learned through behavioral principles much as other behaviors.

26. The ability to choose specific reinforcers is very important when interacting with older students.

27. Attention to inappropriate behavior may increase rather than decrease behavior the teacher desires to reduce.

28. Withdrawal of approval may be ineffective if the teacher uses predominantly disapproval to control inappropriate behavior.

29. Children may be taught to ignore inappropriate behavior from each other.

30. Many times, it is necessary for the teacher to remediate social behavior before the subject material can be learned.

LEARNING ACTIVITY I I—PINPOINT RANKING EXERCISE

A behavior is anything a person does that can be observed and measured. Ideas (values) are generally made more and more behavioral as behaviors are specified in observable and measurable terms; consider for example the following Values (Ideas)-Behaviors-Values (Goals) Chart.

Definitions lead from inferential non-behavioral ideas (C) toward very specific observable and measurable behaviors (A).

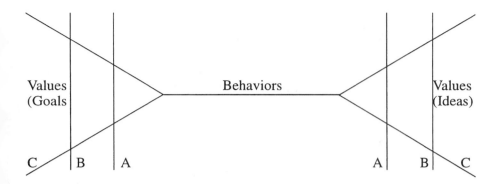

A-Pinpoint defined in terms of specific behaviors. Behavior is both observable and measurable and therefore overtly demonstrable. It can be observed without further definition (nonambiguous).

B-Pinpoint somewhat inferential, some ambiguity involved. Additional definition or more specific delineation necessary before precise observation and recording can take place.

C-Pinpoint definitely an inference, is non-observable, and non-measurable as stated.

Task 1: Assign a definitional category to the pinpoints for the 120 examples in Part II, pages **91-188**, using the A, B, and C code given above, adding pluses and minuses as needed (A-, B+, B-, C+, C-). Use only the information given in each Pinpoint section of the Examples.

Task 2: After all pinpoints have been ranked using the A, B, and C code, check each pinpoint ranked lower than an A-. Go back to the appropriate page in Part II and reread any information given in the Record section. When the new information serves to further specify the behavior involved, then re-rank the pinpoint. For Example 47, Bothering Teacher at Desk, the first ranking might be B; re-ranking after reading the Record could give it a B+.

First Ranking Totals	Re-Ranking Totals
120 = % A pinpoints	120 = % A pinpoints
120 = % B pinpoints	120 = % B pinpoints
120 = % C pinpoints	120 = % C pinpoints

Additional practice in specifying overt behaviors in observable and measurable pinpoints may be acquired by referring to the behaviors you have written in completing Learning Activity 5 and rewriting each pinpointed behavior that does not qualify as an A so that it can be readily observed and counted.

LEARNING ACTIVITY 12— SELF-MODIFICATION

Principles are generally more useful after one has used them on oneself. Therefore, include all four aspects of the teaching principles (pinpoint, record, consequate, and evaluate) and develop some specific procedures to change one of your own behaviors:

1. An inappropriate behavior you choose to decrease in yourself
2. An appropriate behavior you choose to increase in yourself
3. A behavior either appropriate or inappropriate you desire to change in another person: child, supervisor, spouse, roommate, or fiance. It is assumed that any attempt to change behaviors of others will be discussed with the person involved and consent obtained prior to beginning any program.

Remember to pinpoint the precise behavior(s) that will be recorded and set up an observational recording system with specific time intervals and specific times of the day when recording will take place. Record the occurrence of the behavioral pinpoint for at least five observational periods (in some instances more than one can occur on the same day), so adequate recording (baseline data) can take place prior to institution of the consequences. Consequences should be honestly applied and recorded for at least five days or longer before evaluation takes place. If the behavior does not change in the desired direction with the contingencies as applied then "Try, try again" by implementing additional consequences.

General Objectives: The student will conduct a behavioral change project on a child, another student or friend, or him/herself. Any project on another person must be preceded by a permission form signed by that person or, in the case of a child, by the child's legal guardian. This permission form must include the behavior to be changed and a brief description of the method.

Project Description: The project is to include at least 15 days of data taken at least once per day. Five days of "baseline" data is to be recorded before any program of contingencies is instituted, and at least 10 days of data are to be obtained after the contingencies are begun. If possible, there is to be at least one "reliability check," that is, another person independently taking data at the same time in the same place, and so on.

Contents of Final Report: The report will consist of four sections: (1) pinpoint, (2) record, (3) consequate, and (4) evaluate. Each part will contain the following information:

Pinpoint: A. A brief description of the subject including age, sex, major (if appropriate), and so on. B. A brief description of the history of the problem. C. A behavioral description of the problem to be changed. D. The desired direction of change.

Record: A. The unit of behavior being recorded. B. The unit of time of observation. C. The precise observation procedure, that is, exactly what was done to record the behavior. D. How the reliability check was made.

Consequate: A. A precise description of what the subject must do to earn the rewards or punishers, and so on.

Evaluate: A graph of the 15 days of data, the baseline data separated by a vertical line. The occurrences of behavior should be on the ordinate, that is, up and down on the vertical axis and the units of time on the abscissa, that is, across on the horizontal axis. See the example below.

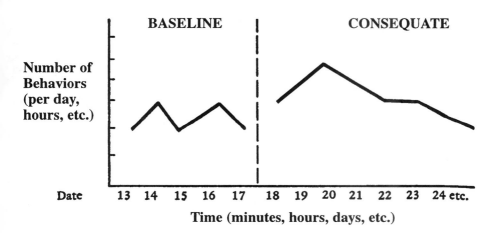

PART III

A POSITIVE
APPROACH

Developing Responses

One has many potential reinforcers that can be used contingently across time to teach desired behaviors. However, merely reading, talking, and thinking about consequential responses does not produce optimum results. The development of effective responses takes practice. Consider for a moment the tremendous practice it takes for a poet to choose the precise word, for a musician to turn a beautiful phrase, for an actor to deliver a line effectively. Practice in developing responses cannot be overemphasized. Just talking to yourself while looking into a mirror is very effective. A tape recorder can also be valuable in developing response skills. At first you will notice some tension—you will feel awkward and perhaps a little childish. Nevertheless, practice. A good place to start is with the words "thank you." Practice saying "thank you" with as many inflections as possible— from extreme sarcasm to sincere appreciation.

If one desires to express a sincere feeling, one must make sure the real intent will be expressed. Those people whom we consider warm and sensitive are people who have developed great skill in expression. Most often, expressions are not overtly practiced, yet all teachers (having been often misunderstood) should be sure to communicate their thoughts and feelings most effectively. Considering all the time we spend in front of the mirror on physical appearances, is it not incongruous that we do not use some of this time to develop effective personal responses? After patient practice in role playing, the teacher will begin to notice exciting new skill in the development of responses. Sometimes one may choose to practice developing responses with another person who will be helpful in giving appropriate feedback.

Other than subject matter itself, available responses can be classified in five categories: (1) words (spoken-written), (2) physical expressions (facial-bodily), (3) closeness (nearness-touching), (4) activities (social-individual), and (5) things (materials, food, playthings, awards). The following lists have been developed as possible approval models. One should select and develop those reinforcers deemed usable as specific behavioral contingencies for the age and grade level of persons involved. Start with one or two responses, develop thoroughly, and evaluate before developing others.

WARNING—As you go through the following approval lists you will find that some of the responses will seem very inappropriate to you. Some of the sayings are regional, some will seem very "mushy" and some should be used only with very small children. It is important that you develop only those responses that "fit" you. You should develop only those potential reinforcers that you believe will enhance your effectiveness. Indeed, a reinforcer is defined by its effectiveness. Again, discrimination is important.

APPROVAL RESPONSES

Words Spoken: Approval

Words

Yes	Correct
Good	Excellent
Neat	That's right
Nice	Perfect
O.K.	Satisfactory
Great	How true
Fascinating	Absolutely
Charming	Keep going
Commendable	Good responses
Delightful	How beautiful!
Brilliant	Wonderful job!
Fine answer	Fantastic!
Uh-huh	Terrific!
Positively!	Swell
Go ahead	Beautiful work
Yeah!	Tasty
All right	Marvelous!
Nifty	Exciting!
Exactly	Pleasant
Of course	Delicious
Cool	Fabulous
Likeable	Splendid
Wonderful	Well-mannered
Outstanding work	Thinking
Of course!	

Sentences

That's clever.
I'm pleased.
Thank you.
I'm glad you're here.
That's a prize of a job.
You make us happy.
That shows thought.
We think a lot of you.
You're tops on our list.
That's good work.
That's remarkably well done.
You're very pleasant.
That shows a great deal of work.
Yes, I think you should continue.
That's a good way of putting it.
I like the way (name) explained it.
That is a feather in your cap.
You are very friendly.
That's an excellent goal.
Nice speaking voice.
That's a nice expression.
It is a pleasure having you as a student.
That's interesting.
You make being a teacher very worthwhile.
That's sweet of you.
That's well thought out.
Show us how.
You're doing better.
You are improving.
You're doing fine.
You perform very well, (name).
That's very good, (name).
I'm so proud of you.
I like that.
This is the best yet.
That's the correct way.
That's very choice.
You do so well.
You're polite.
Thinking!

Relationships
Nice things happen to nice children.
That is very imaginative.
You are worthy of my love.
That will be of great benefit to the class.
I admire it when you work like that.
That is original work.
I appreciate your attention.
You've been a fine credit to your class.
I commend your outstanding work.
We are proud to honor your achievement.
That was very kind of you.
You catch on very quickly.
Obedience makes me happy.
That deserves my respect.
You demonstrate fine ability.
That is clear thinking.
You should be very proud of this.
That was nice of you to loan her your _____.
I wish you would show me and the class how you got such an
interesting effect.
I like that—I didn't know it could be done that way.
Permission granted.
That's a good job—other children can look up to you.
Let's watch him do it.
He accepts responsibility.
That was a good choice.
Show this to your parents.
I know how you feel—should we continue?
I'm happy your desk is in order.
Why don't you show the class how you got the answer?
That's a good point to bring up, (name), I agree.
Let's put this somewhere special.
I'd like this in my own house.
My, you have a nice attitude.
Now you're really trying.
Keep working hard, (name).
You've improved.
Your work appears so neat.
You're a good person.
If at first you don't succeed, try, try again.
Thinking!

Words and Symbols Written: Approval

Bravo!	Good work!
Improvement	★
Fine	Correct
Good	+
Neat	Satisfactory
Very good	Nicely done
O.K.	Very concise
Passing	Complete
*	A, B, C, D
X	Enjoyable
✓	Excellent
Thoughtful	Outstanding
100%	
Good paper	[Colored Pencil markings]
Very colorful	Superior
☺	Congratulations
Well done	Yeah
Great!	Show this to your parents.
Wow!	[Honor rolls]
A-1	For display
Perceptive	[Rubber stamps]

Rules

In formulating rules, remember to:

1. Involve the group in making up the rules.
2. Keep the rules short and to the point.
3. Phrase rules, where possible, in a positive way. ("Sit quietly while working" instead of "Don't talk to your neighbors.")
4. Remind the group of the rules at times other than when someone has misbehaved.
5. Make different sets of rules for varied activities.
6. Let people know when different rules apply (work-play).
7. Post rules in a conspicuous place and review regularly.
8. Keep a sheet on your desk and record the number of times you review rules.

Expressions: Approval

Facial

Looking	Widening eyes
Smiling	Wrinkling nose
Winking	Blinking rapidly

Nodding
Grinning
Raising eyebrows
Forming kiss
Opening eyes
Slowly closing eyes
Laughing (happy)
Chuckling

Giggling
Whistling
Cheering
Licking lips
Smacking lips
Pressing lips affirmatively
Rolling eyes enthusiastically

Bodily

Clapping hands
Raising arms
Shaking fist
Signaling O.K.
Cocking head
Skipping
Rubbing stomach
Thumbs up
Shaking head
Jumping up and down
Shrugging shoulders
Circling hand through air
(encouragement to continue)

Hand/finger to face, eyebrows,
eyes, nose, ears, mouth, cheek,
lips, hair, forehead
Grabbing
Bouncing
Dancing
Stroking motions
Opening hands
Flipping head
Taking a fast breath
Expansive movements of hands
Hugging self

Closeness: Approval

Nearness

Nearness concerns physical proximity and ranges from geographical
   separation—through noticeable contact—to embracing.
Interacting with class at recess
Eating with children
Sitting on desk near students
Sitting within the student group
Standing alongside
Walking among students
Gently guiding
Pausing while transferring objects

Touching

Hand on hand
Ruffling hair
Touching head
Patting head
Pinching chin
Touching nose

Walking alongside
Combing hair
Tying shoes
Quick squeeze
Dancing
Rubbing back of neck

Patting back	Gently raising chin
Patting shoulder	Leaning over
Touching arm	Touching a hurt
Straightening clothes	Kissing hurt
Hugging	Putting face next to child
Touching hand	Tweaking nose
Shaking hands	Tickling
Squeezing hand	Cupping face in hands
Patting cheek	Gentle pull at hair
Nudging	Running finger down person's nose
Helping put on coats	Guiding with hand
Retying sashes	

Activities and Privileges: Approval
Individual

Leading student groups
Representing group in school activities
Displaying student's work (any subject matter)
Straightening up for teacher
Putting away materials
Running errands
Caring for class pets, flowers, etc.
Collecting materials (papers, workbooks, assignments, etc.)
Choosing activities
Show and tell (any level)
Constructing school materials
Dusting, erasing, cleaning, arranging chairs, etc.
Helping other children (drinking, lavatory, cleaning, etc.)
Reading a story
Exempting a test
Working problems on the board
Answering questions
Outside supervising (patrols, directing parking, ushering, etc.)
Classroom supervision
Omitting specific assignments
First in line
Assisting teacher teach
Leading discussions
Making gifts
Recognizing birthdays
Grading papers
Special seating arrangements
Responsibility for ongoing activities during school holidays
    (pets, plants, assignments)

Decorating room
Presenting hobby to class
"Citizen of the Week" or "Best Kid of the Day"

Social

Movies
Decorating classroom
Presenting skits
Playing records
Puppet shows
Preparing for holidays (Christmas, Thanksgiving, Valentine's Day)
Making a game of subject matter
Outdoor lessons
Visiting another class
Field trips (subject matter)
Planning daily schedules
Musical chairs
Competing with other classes
Performing for PTA, PTO
Dancing
Going to museums, fire stations, courthouses, picnics, etc.
"Senior Skip Day"
Participating in group organizations (music, speech, athletics,
     social clubs)
Talking periods
Recess or play periods
Early dismissal
Parties
Talent shows (jokes, readings, music, etc.)

Things: Approval

Materials

Books (appropriate level)	Talking books
Beads	Bookcovers
Gum ball machine	Balls
Book markers	Sand toys (bucket, shovel, etc.)
Coloring books	Play money
Crayons	Banks
Paints	Peg board and peg towns
Personalized pencils	Telephones
Chalk	Play Putty
Buttons	Play Dough
Pins	Pick-up sticks

Pictures
Colored paper
Flowers
Counting beads
Games
Stuffed animals
Cards
Stars
Chips
Kites
Balloons
Jacks
Striped straws
Windmills
Miniature animals
Farm set and farm animals
Plastic toys (animals,
  soldiers, etc.)
Jump ropes
Musical toys
Wind-up toys
Hand puppets
Marbles
Building blocks
Lego
Electronic games
Building logs
Flashlight
Strollers
Kitchen equipment (play stove,
  sink, refrigerator)
Comic books
Food mixes
Utensil sets
Household items (pots, coffee
  can, paper rolls, cardboard
  boxes, etc.)
Dishes
Money (exchangeable, token)
Stamps
Cleaning sets (carpet sweepers,
  brooms, etc.)
Play furniture (table, chairs, etc.)

Blocks
Jack 'n box
Bath toys (boats, rubber ducks)
C/D player
Pounding blocks
Doctor kits
Nurse kits
Tops
Tool bench and tools
Tinker toys
Fire engine
Yo-Yo
Boats
Trains and equipment
Bean bags
Cars and gas stations
Racing cars
Trucks
Tractors
Steam shovels
Dolls and equipment (bottles,
  clothes, etc.)
Doll houses
Doll furniture
Talking toys
Electronic music instruments
Kaleidoscopes
Music tape
Playing cards
Record player
Walkie-talkie
Records
Stationery
Calendars
Acoustic musical instruments
Bulletin boards
Desk organizers (notes, books,
  pencils, etc.)
Cameras and equipment
Photo album
Label maker
Pencil sharpener
Stapler

Purses
Umbrellas
Costumes
Jumping beans
Ice cream maker
Popcorn maker
Cotton candy maker
Cash register
Switch board
Electronic games football, -
  baseball, basketball, hockey
Cowboy toys and equipment
Knights, castles, and equipment
Model kits (cars, planes, ships,
  etc.)
Pinball machine
Bicycle
Tricycle
Music boxes
Rocking horse
Bird houses
Ant houses
Bug houses
Suitcases
Wall decorations
Knickknacks
Sewing machine
Sewing boxes
World globe
View master
Telescope
Microscope
Erector set
Trains
Science kits
Experiential language kit(s)
Chemistry set
Slide preparing kit
Geologist's kit
Biological kit
Radio kit
Computer kit
Electric builder kit

Autograph book
Date book
Address books
Pencils
Pens
Radios
Tape recorders
Watches
Vanity sets
Jewelry
Masks and wax disguises
Perfume
Bath powder
Bath oil
Hats and clothes
Make up
Hair ribbons
Hair bands
Hair barrels
Hairdryers
Belts
Jewelry boxes
Puzzles jigsaw, trauma tower,
  dice cube, wooden cube,
  solitaire, pyramid, mad maze,
  dimensional, etc.)
Collections (coins, rocks, glass,
  leaves, stamps, etc.)
Art sets
Oils
Watercolors
Pastels
Chalk
Colored pencils
Bowling equipment (ball, shoes,
  etc.)
Swimming equipment (fins, face
  mask, etc.)
Kickball
Golf equipment (clubs, balls,
  etc.)
Ping pong equipment
  Pool table

Rock identification kit
Magnetic kit
Body kits (man, woman, heart, head, skeleton, eye, ear, etc.)
Creative craft kits
Origami (paper-folding)
Wood burning
Hand bag decorating
Embroidery
Decoupage
Wall decorations
Mosaics
Pillow
Clay
Yarn
Ceramics
Beads
Leather
Colored pipe cleaners
Cloth
Rock polishing
Papier mache
Wood
Felt
Tile
Glass
Paper

Football equipment
Baseball equipment
Tennis equipment
Skiing equipment
Ice skates
Roller skates
Scuba diving equipment
Sleigh
Toboggan
Class pictures
Swing
Slide
Boxing gloves
Computer programs
Body building equipment
Horse shoe set
Croquet set
Badminton set
Swing sets
Darts
Tether ball
Camping equipment (sleeping bag, lantern, stove, etc.)
Fishing equipment (rod, reel, etc.)
Aquariums
Money
Juke box

Food

Jaw breakers
Chocolate creams
Cake
Lemonade
Popcorn
Peanuts
Ice cream
Cookies
Sugar-coated cereals
Apples
Crackers
Raisins
Candy kisses
Fruit
Life savers

Lemon drops
Cereal
Candied apples
Candy canes
Candy corn
Animal crackers
Soft drinks
Milk
Marshmallows
Gum
Juices
Lollipops
Popsicles
Candy bars
Potato chips

Awards

Citations	Medals
Athletic letters	Cups
Plaques	Report cards
Pins	"Good-Deed" charts
Subject-matter prizes (books, science hardware, subscriptions, etc.)	

DISAPPROVAL RESPONSES

The following lists gleaned from actual classroom observations contain disapproval responses. The teacher should study these lists carefully in order to achieve two important discriminations: (1) to recognize responses that one may be unwittingly using and wish to eliminate or replace with incompatible approval responses (this is the reason that the lists are purposely long) and (2) to plan carefully, responsibly, and cautiously the application of disapproval. WARNING: The authors believe most of the following should never be used. The teacher must discriminate. Even a pleasant "hello" can be a scathing indictment if the tone and intensity of the voice cause that effect.

Words Spoken: Disapproval

This list includes naggings, sarcasms, bitternesses, dishonesties, and other ineffectual teacher responses whose angry delivery generally demonstrates that the teacher, not the student, has the problem.

Impractical
Be prompt
Work faster
Try to understand
Do your homework
Do your best
Unclear explanation
Don't you want to do things right?
It can't be that difficult
You're too slow
Stop talking
Behave
Pay attention
Don't
Wrong
Stupid

Be still
Follow directions
Think for a change
Use some thought
No, that's not what I said
Would you like to get paddled?
You don't understand because you don't listen!
If I find you chewing gum once more, you'll wear it on your nose
Be quiet and sit down
You're gutless
That's ridiculous
Meaningless
Absurd
Bad
Nonsense
Too vague
Try harder
Unacceptable
That's not right
Incorrect
Needs improving
Unsatisfactory
Poor
Undesirable
You should be ashamed
Useless
That's not clear
I dislike that
Don't be silly
That's terrible
What is this?
Is this something?
Quit making messes
Let's throw this away
That's not mature
I can't read anything you write
Haven't you learned how to spell?
Grow up
You're not doing as well as you used to
Horrible
Absolutely not!
Shh!
Stop

Listen to me
Maddening
Be quiet
Raise your hand
Stop that laughing
I'll have no more talking
Apologize now
Sloppy
Shut up!
I'll show you who's boss
One more time and you'll get it
  from me
Finish it now
No talking
I'll slap you silly
Look for the answer
Leave her alone
You march straight to the office
Keep your eyes on your own paper
You lack interest
I'll give you something to cry about
You couldn't have done worse
I do not like this
It's not up to requirements
I will not repeat it
I'm not telling you again
You're dull
That's ugly
You idiot
You're a laughingstock
It's hopeless for you
Why are you a fraidycat?
You're cheap
Snob
You're worthless
You're rude
Don't be crabby
You're disgusting
You little monster
Don't laugh at me
Cut it out
You're dumb
You're filthy

You naughty boy
Mock me and you won't hear the
end of it
You're narrow-minded
That's childish
Simple Simon
No! No!! No!!!
You haven't applied yourself
Your work isn't acceptable
Get your parent to sign this bad
  paper
What do you mean you're not fin-
ished?
Stand up straight
Just try that once more
Anyone else!
Learn that!
You'd better get on the stick
So you're tardy again!
Speak when you're spoken to
Smart alec
You must be confused
I don't see your point
You know what happened the last
  time you did that
You do this over
You know better than that
Play fair
Don't cause problems
You're never dependable
That wasn't the right thing to do
Well, we'll never do this again
If you had a brain in your head, you
  wouldn't say that
Do it!
You think you're the only one here?
You're bad
Poor stupid oaf
Wrong again
You're doomed to failure
You're wrong all the time
You don't know anything
You make me sick

You're just an inadequate person
Impertinent
You're not thinking
You haven't been paying attention
Wipe that silly grin off your face
I guess I shouldn't expect any more from you
You're just plain boring
You have a dirty mind
Terrible! Terrible!
This isn't what I had in mind
You know that's wrong
Stupid nonsense
You'd better try harder
People never change

Expressions: Disapproval

Frowning	Puckering lips
Curling lip	Wrinkling nose
Lifting eyebrows	Pounding fists on table
Looking at ceiling	Laughing
Furrowing brows	Shaking head
Smirking	Turning away
Lowering eyebrows	Gritting teeth
Shaking finger or fist	Biting lips
Wrinkling mouth	Squinting eyebrows
Squinting eyes	Looking sideways
Staring	Closing eyes
Wrinkling forehead	Clicking tongue
Nose in air	Pushing mouth to one side
Pointing finger	Turning head away
Putting hand behind ear	Letting out breath
Grimacing	Raising lips
Sniffing	Hissing
Tightening jaw	Fingers in fronts of lips
Sticking out tongue	Nodding head (no)
Twisting side of mouth	Showing teeth
Cackling	Pulling in bottom lip
Snickering	

Closeness: Disapproval

Closeness disapproval concerns corporal punishment and ranges from threatening approaches—through spankings—to severe physical beatings.

Activities and Privileges: Disapproval

Disapproval concerning activities and privileges constitutes various degrees of deprivation. Deprivation ranges from withholding of privileges—through isolation—to social incarceration.

Isolation
Ostracism
Silence periods
Sitting in corner
Staying after class
Waiting misbehaviors
Standing in front of class
Leaving room
Extra work
Staying in from play
Being last to leave
Sitting in hall
Being sent to principal
Eating alone in lunchroom
Away from friends
Pointing out bad examples
Apologizing to class
Writing letters of apology
Bringing parents to school

Things: Disapproval

Concerning things, disapproval refers to inanimate materials that are damaging to the body: (1) intense noises (ear damage), (2) heat (fires and stoves), (3) chemicals (poisons), and (4) objects in motion (knives, cars, bullets, radiation). Obviously none of these should ever be used (even washing a child's mouth out with soap can sometimes cause tissue damage).

CONCLUSION

Teaching and learning should be exciting and satisfying for both teacher and student. The innovative person has too many positive and effective resources available to resort to shoddy and punitive measures. Many experienced teachers state that almost all of their earlier punitive consequences could have been handled in a more positive manner. A person who truly cares will practice developing positive responses.

STUDY GUIDE FOR CHAPTER 7

Questions:

1. What do you think would be the long-term effect(s) of strong approval?

2. What do you think would be the effect(s) of strong disapproval?

3. Do you believe in corporal punishment? Why? Why not?

4. Is corporal punishment legal in your state? Should it be? Why?

5. List several positive reinforcers that would be appropriate for a high school senior of your same sex. List five for the opposite sex.

6. Why will one type of approval "work" for one student and not for another?

7. If a child has been physically abused, what ought to be the teacher's responses to get this student to do the difficult tasks?

8. Why is it that some of the preceding lists of approval applications seem so "mushy?"

9. What type of disapproval are you used to giving when you are frustrated? When you are trying to get someone to correct an injustice or rectify a mistake, what do you use?

10. Do you believe that people who are "naturally" negative should go into teaching? What should one do if one is "naturally" negative?

LEARNING ACTIVITY 13— CHOICE OF REINFORCERS

1. For all of the following pinpoints (actual observed incidents), determine three different procedures (logical consequences) that could be used to increase or decrease the pinpointed behavior. Be as specific as possible and specify at least one approval and one disapproval technique for each pinpoint. (Instructors and/or students may choose to make up their own pinpoints.)

2. State one good reason for the selection of each consequence. Indicate whether the consequence is (a) approval, (b) withdrawal of approval, (c) disapproval, (d) threat of disapproval or (e) ignoring.

3. When all pinpoints have been consequated and designations as to approval/disapproval completed, then categorize the specific reinforcers used for each separate consequate using the following categories:

   a) Words
   b) Closeness
   c) Bodily expressions
   d) Activities
   e) Things

1. Pinpoint: Refusal to go outdoors for recess (seven-year-old girl)

   Record: Child refuses to go outside during morning or afternoon recess.

   Consequate: 1.

                      2.

                      3.

2. Pinpoint: School phobia (seven-year-old boy)

   Record: Child refuses to go to school; protests with disruptive behavior (crying, screaming).

   Consequate: 1.

                      2.

                      3.

3. Pinpoint: Blanket bringing behavior (six-year-old)

   Record: Child insists on bringing "security" blanket to school at the beginning of the second school year. The behavior was not observed during the first year of school.

   Consequate: 1.

                      2.

                      3.

4. Pinpoint: Headaches (second-grade girl)

   Record: Girl complains of headaches during language arts period a total of twelve times in five sessions.

Consequate: 1.

                     2.

                     3.

5. Pinpoint: Teasing handicapped child (third and fourth graders)

    Record: Several boys and girls make fun of handicapped younger child every recess period.

    Consequate: 1.

                         2.

                         3.

6. Pinpoint: Pants wetting (kindergarten)

    Record: Teacher noticed wet dress of child seven times during one week.

    Consequate: 1.

                         2.

                         3.

7. Pinpoint: Tattling (elementary grades)

    Record: Child observed to "tell" on others in class 23 times in one week.

    Consequate: 1.

                         2.

                         3.

8. Pinpoint: Book stealing from library.

    Record: Ten books missing during the first week of school.

    Consequate: 1.

                         2.

                         3.

9. Pinpoint: Damaged musical instruments.

    Record: Fourteen instruments damaged in one week.

    Consequate: 1.

                         2.

                         3.

10. Pinpoint: Damage to teachers' automobiles.

    Record: Eight tires slashed, 4 radio antennas bent, and 18 windows broken during one week of school.

    Consequate: 1.

                         2.

                         3.

11. Pinpoint: Book slamming (ninth-grade boys, English class)

    Record: Six boys slam books down on desk upon entering English class, a total of 32 times in one week.

    Consequate: 1.

                         2.

                         3.

12. Pinpoint: Lunch stealing (seventh-grade boys)

    Record: Three seventh-grade boys are observed stealing fifth graders' lunches every day for one week.

    Consequate: 1.

                         2.

                         3.

13. Pinpoint: Kissing in halls

    Record: Seven couples observed kissing in the hall during lunch period two consecutive days.

    Consequate: 1.

                         2.

                         3.

14. Pinpoint: Turning in assignments late

    Record: Teacher notes student delinquent in turning in math homework nine times in one month.

    Consequate: 1.

                         2.

                         3.

15. Pinpoint: Graffiti

    Record: Writing noted on the boys' restroom walls after each cleaning.

    Consequate: 1.

                           2.

                           3.

16. Pinpoint: Teacher mimicry (16-year-old boy, math class)

    Record: Student mimics 15 sentences of female math teacher during three math classes.

    Consequate: 1.

                           2.

                           3.

17. Pinpoint: Teacher threats (18-year-old male student, English class)

    Record: Student threatens to "get even" with teacher if she fails him.

    Consequate: 1.

                           2.

                           3.

18. Pinpoint: Book tearing

    Record: Four male students have 10 page tearing "accidents" in literature class during one week.

    Consequate: 1.

                           2.

                           3.

19. Pinpoint: Glue sniffing

    Record: Four high school seniors caught sniffing glue in the boys' restroom.

    Consequate: 1.

                           2.

                           3.

20. Pinpoint: Profane language

    Record: Female social studies teacher records 45 outbursts of profanity during her lectures in a two-week period.

    Consequate: 1.

                     2.

                     3.

21. Pinpoint: Abuse of privileges

    Record: Two girls use Honor Society work as an excuse to leave chemistry class six times in one month.

    Consequate: 1.

                     2.

                     3.

LEARNING ACTIVITY 14—TEST ON TEACHING/DISCIPLINE (CHAPTERS 1-7)

Please circle the answer that best completes the statement.

1. The foremost question regarding discipline in the classroom is one pertaining to

    a)   strict relationships.
    b)   strict and permissive relationships.
    c)   cause-and-effect relationships.
    d)   interpersonal relationships.
    e)   strict versus permissive control.

2. The teacher's personal approval is a most effective reward for most children and should be given

    a)   discriminately.
    b)   noncontingently.
    c)   approvingly.
    d)   partially.
    e)   all of the above.

3.   To solve a student's inappropriate behavior, the teacher should

   a)   know the reinforcement history of the student.
   b)   do something to change the student's behavior.
   c)   try to understand the behavior on the basis of previous test results.
   d)   seek evaluation of the student's personality.
   e)   none of the above.

4.   A very simple behavioral principle used to teach children to respond appropriately is

   a)   "when you do bad things, bad things happen to you."
   b)   "no matter what you do, nice things happen to you."
   c)   "when you do nice things, nice things happen to you."
   d)   "no matter what you do, bad things happen to you."
   e)   both a and c.

5.   Why is the principle of specificity important in behavior modification?

   a)   The teacher can only deal with specified traits.
   b)   Only specified overt behaviors can be dealt with.
   c)   The word discipline is a specific category.
   d)   Generalized behavior is amenable to modification.
   e)   After the behavior is specified, the student will improve.

6.   Human behavior can be measured

   a)   in time intervals.
   b)   within discrete pinpointed categories.
   c)   for specific academic responses.
   d)   following appropriate student behavior.
   e)   all of the above.

7.   Partial reinforcement

   a)   may refer to inconsistency in responding.
   b)   often prolongs inappropriate behavior.
   c)   often prolongs appropriate behavior.
   d)   may refer to consistency in responding.
   e)   all of the above.

8. If a teacher inadvertently gives approval to a student following an inappropriate response

   a) new contingencies may be structured immediately.
   b) it will not function as an error because it was unwitting.
   c) the student will likely repeat the response.
   d) the teacher should disapprove the next time.
   e) both a and c.

9. Disapproval may be used effectively in modifying inappropriate behavior except when

   a) its magnitude is too great.
   b) it functions as a payoff for the inappropriate response.
   c) it is given on a partial schedule.
   d) it is used as a follow-through after a threat.
   e) none of the above.

10. An issue that teachers should consider carefully is that it seems easier for one to_____ one's way into a new way of _____than to _____ one's way into a new way of _____.

   a) think/acting/act/thinking
   b) talk/feeling/feel/talking
   c) work/studying/study/working
   d) act/thinking/think/acting
   e) both c and d.

11. If contingent rewards/punishments are to be effective, they should generally take place

   a) immediately.
   b) with a reward hierarchy in mind.
   c) consistently.
   d) without verbal explanation.
   e) all of the above.

12. _____ is anything a person does, says, or thinks that can be observed directly and/or indirectly.

   a) Data
   b) Reality
   c) Behavior
   d) Behavior modification
   e) Association

13. _____ is defined as a change or modification of behavior.

    a) Contingency management
    b) Reinforcement
    c) Learning
    d) Teaching
    e) None of the above.

14. Some students may become upset if a teacher makes a class privilege contingent upon the behavior of a few students. Students who become upset are probably concerned with

    a) strictness of control.
    b) peer approval.
    c) group discipline.
    d) fairness.
    e) threat of disapproval.

15. "Making a game out of learning" may involve

    a) structuring learning material.
    b) establishing rewards.
    c) manipulating the environment.
    d) maintaining contingencies
    e) all of the above.

16. When a teacher says, "I don't like all that structure and those behavioral techniques. I don't want my students to have to sit quietly all day," he/she is confusing

    a) facts with values.
    b) techniques with values.
    c) social with academic behavior.
    d) rules with how to enforce them.
    e) both b and d.

17. If creativity can be taught and learned then the educator needs to be concerned with

    a) at what point further teaching might inhibit creativity.
    b) whether students can create from nothing.
    c) what information and materials students need to get started.
    d) the situation in which learning occurs.
    e) all of the above.

18. If a teacher noncontingently reinforces all of the student's creative products because the teacher feels the child needs it, the child will probably learn

    a) to love himself contingently.
    b) to discriminate the quality of his classmates' products.
    c) lack of social discrimination.
    d) lack of discrimination concerning his work.
    e) none of the above.

19. Many teachers quit the teaching profession because of

    a) anxiety relating to teaching pressures.
    b) lack of education in coping with special problems.
    c) inability to discipline.
    d) loss of motivation after initial teaching experience.
    e) personality problems.

20. Motivation is

    a) shaped by strict discipline.
    b) taught by manipulating the external environment.
    c) based on personality factors.
    d) based upon student interest and background variables.
    e) innate within every student.

21. Within the classroom, "being approved of" is probably controlled by

    a) the teacher.
    b) partial reinforcement.
    c) both teacher and students.
    d) self-concept.
    e) the student.

22. Desire to learn is

    a) innate, except for special problems.
    b) universal if students are left alone.
    c) taught, but not learned.
    d) necessary in all situations.
    e) none of the above.

23. While handwriting is an appropriate learned behavior, yelling out the answer is often a(n) _____ behavior.

    a) cued
    b) more desirable
    c) innate
    d) more spontaneous
    e) inappropriate

24. Three things are necessary for learning to take place—

    a) motivation, assimilation, and reinforcement.
    b) experience, discrimination, and association.
    c) proper set, attention, and deduction.
    d) accommodation, reward, and adaptation.
    e) attention, reinforcement, and discipline.

25. A behavior that results in pleasant consequences will likely be

    a) forgotten.
    b) appropriate
    c) repeated.
    d) reinforced.
    e) assimilated.

Below are listed five examples of classroom contingencies. In the blank space after each statement, indicate by letter, the particular contingency situation.

    a) approval following appropriate behavior
    b) withholding approval
    c) disapproval following inappropriate behavior
    d) threat of disapproval
    e) ignoring

26. Making the student sit in a corner facing the wall because he threw spitballs at another student. _disapproval following inappropriate behavior_

27. Inattention following a student's verbalizations.
    ignoring

28. Having the student continue working on arithmetic problems until he finishes them, and telling him that only then may he go out to recess.
    withholding approval

29. Providing special activities for every correct arithmetic problem completed. _approval following appropriate behavior_

30. Telling the student that he will be sent to the principal's office if he doesn't stop talking. _threat of disapproval_

31. "You have not followed the rules today, Fred. Therefore, I am sending you to the time-out room." _disapproval following innappropriate Behavior_

32. "You have not completed any science problems. You may go to band when you have correctly completed all the problems."
Withholding approval

33. "Good work, Jane. You have completed your homework assignment and handed it in on time." _approval following appropriate behavior_

34. "If you do not finish these problems correctly in five minutes, I am going to make you sit in the corner by yourself."
threat of disapproval

35."I am sorry Mary did not sit still. We will have the party later, if everyone is still." _disapproval following innappropriate behavior_
withholding

What is the consequence to pinpoints found in the text (not necessarily the one that worked)?

PINPOINT	CONSEQUENCE
_a._ 36. dishonesty	a) Grade assigned without explanation.
_c._ 37. nail biting	b) Teacher instituted multiple divergent token systems. Some children received paper money that bought surprise gifts at end of day. Other children received candies on various time interval schedules. Some children accumulated points written on notebook. Reinforcers changed constantly.

_e._ 38. fear in young children

_b._ 39. excessive dawdling

_d._ 40. bothering teacher at desk

_d_ 41. children manipulating

_b_ 42. standing up walking around

_e_ 43. striking other children
        with objects

_a_ 44. aggressive hitting

c) Negative practice-students practice inappropriate behavior at specific times (e.g., 8 A.M. for five minutes) in front of mirror. Parent or teacher delivered disapproval responses during sessions.

d) Teacher ignored all children, made no eye contact, said nothing, only recognized children who raised hands at seats.

e) Incompatible response-object or situation gradually introduced into child's presence while child engaged in fun activity. Gradual approach—child led by degrees, over number of days, to come closer and closer to activity or object made readily accessible to child while other children participated enjoyably.

*****

a) Large punching bag dummy with red nose installed on playground.

b) None apply.

c) Twofold program to teach all students discrimination between possessing ability and performing before class, and teach entire class role playing to deliver approval feedback to insecure students.

d) Mothers (1) instructed in delivery of approval techniques, (2) taught to ignore inappropriate behavior, and (3) responded with praise and affection for appropriate behavior.

_C_ 45. embarrassment

e) Adult assigned in vicinity; child praised and given a donut when playing properly, although when boy hit someone supervisor hit him back with same object.

*****

_e_ 46. boredom

a) School counselor developed system with parents' cooperation. Every teacher signed individual daily progress report (one small sheet) after each class. Decision of signing for appropriate social and academic behaviors based on teacher's criteria. Allowance, social engagements, car privileges contingent upon number of signatures earned each day.

_a_ 47. school failure

b) Teacher explained to class that talking during study time interfered with completion of work assignments (this had been done before). Class discussed importance of rules for study, agreed something must be done, and suggested very extreme alternatives.

_d_ 48. disruptive classroom behavior

c) If assignments not competed, no recess.

_C_ 49. arithmetic achievement

d) Disruptive behavior ignored, appropriate behavior rewarded. Boy kept after school for extreme deviations and sent home on later bus. This put child with students he did not know and withdrew peer attention. Correct behaviors reinforced by teacher praise and peer approval (continuously in beginning, more infrequently later on). Also, job of chalkboard monitor followed appropriate behavior.

_b_ 50. disruptive social talking

e) Friday football game instituted, teams chosen, rules established for points, yards, substitutions, etc., developed for correct academic responses. Game played on chalkboard with losing team providing treat for winners.

OBSERVATION MANUAL

Learning Through Observation

It has been stressed repeatedly by those interested in behavioral analyses that data must be collected regarding overt demonstrable behaviors. Often teachers in the field are able to devise their own recording instruments in regard to specific problems to be corrected within their own classroom. In most cases this is preferable, but to sensitize the teacher or potential teacher to individual effects of reinforcement, more elaborate procedures should be used. In addition, researchers must maintain even greater rigor as well as some uniformity in observation data in order that their findings may be transmitted in a systematic manner to others in the area. Regardless of intent or dissemination, observational data must be both accurate and reliable.

CATEGORY DEVELOPMENT

Prerequisites to accurate behavioral observations include mutually exclusive category definitions that are precise enough to allow observers to note and record the behavior reliably. The general rules that are followed in developing observational categories for inappropriate student behaviors are categories that should:

1. Reflect behaviors that interfere with classroom learning by limiting the time (individual or group) students are on-task in the classroom.

2. Involve behaviors that violate rules, written or implied, established by the teacher.

3. Reflect particular behaviors a teacher desires to change (increase or decrease).

4.   Refer to overt behaviors that can actually be observed in order to limit the potential for inferences made by the person doing the observing.

5.   Be similar in some important way—either topographically (appearing similar) or logically (conceptual class).

6.   Be mutually exclusive so that observational recording of one category of behavior will not be confused with another category.

7.   Be limited so that the observer can rapidly decide and record the classes of behaviors observed.

Observation that is accurate and reliable requires observers who are extremely proficient in recording procedures. Indeed, recording of behavior should become almost automatic. Therefore careful study of behavioral categories as well as continued practice either in the classroom or with videotape is required.

OBSERVER MATERIALS AND RULES

Each observer should be equipped with (1) a pencil (always better than a pen as corrections are sometimes required), (2) something to write upon (a clipboard is generally best), (3) a means for accurately assessing the passage of small increments of time,* (4) observation sheets with space for the date, time, activity, person or persons being observed, and a section for inferences or other comments, and (5) a pair of sunglasses. Observers should always record all information never leave any item blank.

Observers need a special signal that identifies them readily to school personnel and also serves as a signal for teachers and students to refrain from interacting with them. Sunglasses are excellent for this purpose. Sunglasses also partially hide the observer's eyes from the teacher and class so that the person being observed is generally unaware of the scrutiny. Teachers should be instructed to refrain from introducing or otherwise referring to the observers when they come into the classroom. Teachers should also be instructed to say nothing and ask no questions of any observer when the sunglasses are over the eyes. When the observer is part of the school staff, for

---

*Equipment might include electronic recording devices or prerecorded cassette tape signals for observation. Also, two or more observers listening to the same cassette eliminate unreliability due to time differences as the signals can state, "Line one, observe . . . Record. . . . Line two, observe. . . . Record. . . , and so on. Small timed lights have also been used successfully.

example, a counselor, psychologist, or administrator, the observer will remove the sunglasses before speaking to any of the students or teachers. Thus the sunglasses serve a dual purpose in identifying the observer and signaling to inhibit verbal interaction. Research within many classrooms indicates that observers are effectively ignored by the students in primary classes after about three or four hours of observation, while intermediate and high school classes take about four to eight hours of observation and teachers somewhat longer.

It is axiomatic that observations are not as accurate (valid) prior to the time the class and teacher became accustomed to observers taking data. But, even though interaction patterns are somewhat less frequent during the first phases of observation, the general ratio of approval/disapproval reinforcement is generally similar even during initial observations.

The goal for observers is to become as unobtrusive as a piece of furniture. Teachers should try to be as natural as possible with the class and, except for brief answers to observer's questions prior or subsequent to observation, refrain from interacting with or even mentioning the observers, especially when the class is watching. It is preferred that teachers who are to be observed not have a specific time schedule for the observations. This would only increase initial anxiety and limit observational accuracy. It is recommended that teachers understand the purpose of the observation and be given feedback as soon as possible concerning the results of the observations, preferably immediately following observations.

Observer instruction summary

Observers should be provided with the following instructions:

1. During the time of the observation there should be *no* talking or interaction with the teacher, and questions or recording problems should be settled before entering the classroom whenever possible. If teacher interactions become necessary, make certain that observations cease for a short time. Should a teacher initiate interaction during an observation, generally ignore it until the observation is concluded.

2. Sit silently and as immobile as possible when observing. Change location quietly and only when absolutely necessary. If you are observing a particular student or students who change locations then you may have to change if you are unable to hear the verbal interactions.

3. Your goal as an observer is to become a piece of furniture. Take great care that you do not become a reinforcement variable with reference to the behavior of students or teachers in the classroom.

4. Make no differential responses to students, that is, laughing at wise-cracks, answering questions directed toward you, smiling at student's responses, or changing position of head or eyes when addressed. Make the minimal movement necessary to see the student, teacher, or other person you are recording. Social behaviors by students either on entering or leaving the classroom or the school should be ignored as well as behaviors directed toward you while you are in the halls.

5. Discussion of any student, by name or otherwise, except with proper school personnel or your immediate supervisor, is a breach of professional conduct.

6. Please conform to the general faculty dress standards of the school in order that your dress does not become a variable and/or interfere with the task of observation.

7. Look only at observation forms during recording intervals and ignore any noises from the person or persons observed.

8. Remain as unsubjective and unbiased as possible at all times. The main objective is for two people watching the same behavior to agree that the same behaviors occurred (reliability). Record what the person does without trying to think what he should have done. Your time will come.

Teacher observation forms

Teacher forms are self-contained and provide for a complete analysis that can later be graphed, summarized, or presented verbally to the teacher who has been observed. Observations of teacher reinforcements following student behavior are more easily understood when the appropriate symbols are related to the two-by-two teacher contingency table (page 235). The teacher observation symbols are placed in the appropriate boxes to facilitate learning. The order of the symbols is identical to the placement on all teacher observation forms; therefore, symbols are directly transferred from the following contingency table to the observation forms whenever an observer is recording teacher reinforcement.

RECORDING PROCEDURES

Before observation begins, all identifying data should be completed. This generally includes recording the name of the teacher(s) and/or student(s) being observed, the date, the time, and name of the observer.

The general activity is recorded at the top of the sheet and the nature of the ongoing classroom (for individual) activity is recorded under the column marked activity. Each time there is a change in activity, such as from reading to math or from group discussion to seatwork, this change should be recorded in the activity column. Activities can be recorded using a number and letter code.

The *first* number recorded in the activity column indicates the number of students with whom the teacher is interacting for that time period. In most classrooms this may change constantly—the teacher may be working with an individual child, then a small group, and perhaps later conduct a class discussion. Record the exact number of students for each line of intervals.

The *second* entry should indicate the content area the teacher is pursuing with the students being instructed. The code indicates only the academic activity of the group or individual with whom the teacher is interacting; other students may be engaged in other activities. An illustrative code that has been used in elementary schools follows:

LA-Language arts M-Mathematics Sc-Science SS-Social Studies
PE-Physical Education Mu-Music A-Art R-Recreation Sp-Spelling
W-Writing F-Free time, play, student-selected activity, Re-Rest
L-Lunch

Behavioral Contingency Interactions: Table 8-1

| | | SOCIETAL AGENTS BEHAVIOR | |
		Approval	Disapproval
STUDENT BEHAVIOR	APPROPRIATE (On-Task — Social and Academic	**YES** (No When No Disapproval) (1)	**NO** (Mistake) (2)
	INAPPROPRIATE (Off-Task— Social and Academic)	**NO** (Mistake) (3)	**YES** (No if Payoff Or When No Approval (4)

Form A: Teacher Observation

Observer_____   Teacher _____
Reliability Observer_____   Grade or Subject _____
No. in Class or Group_____   Date _____
General Activity_____   Time: Start____End _____
Length of Observational Intervals in Seconds _____
Record Intervals in Seconds _____   Page _____of _____

TIME	ACTIVITY CODE	(1)	2-RECORD	(3)	4-RECORD	(5)	6-RECORD	COMMENTS
					INTERVALS			
1			As Aa Ds Da / As Aa Ds Da		As Aa Ds Da / As Aa Ds Da		As Aa Ds Da / As Aa Ds Da	
2		OBSERVE NOW	As Aa Ds Da / As Aa Ds Da	OBSERVE NOW	As Aa Ds Da / As Aa Ds Da	OBSERVE NOW	As Aa Ds Da / As Aa Ds Da	
3			As Aa Ds Da / As Aa Ds Da		As Aa Ds Da / As Aa Ds Da		As Aa Ds Da / As Aa Ds Da	
4			As Aa Ds Da / As Aa Ds Da		As Aa Ds Da / As Aa Ds Da		As Aa Ds Da / As Aa Ds Da	
5			As Aa Ds Da / As Aa Ds Da		As Aa Ds Da / As Aa Ds Da		As Aa Ds Da / As Aa Ds Da	
6			As Aa Ds Da / As Aa Ds Da		As Aa Ds Da / As Aa Ds Da		As Aa Ds Da / As Aa Ds Da	
7			As Aa Ds Da / As Aa Ds Da		As Aa Ds Da / As Aa Ds Da		As Aa Ds Da / As Aa Ds Da	
8		OBSERVE NOW	As Aa Ds Da / As Aa Ds Da	OBSERVE NOW	As Aa Ds Da / As Aa Ds Da	OBSERVE NOW	As Aa Ds Da / As Aa Ds Da	
9			As Aa Ds Da / As Aa Ds Da		As Aa Ds Da / As Aa Ds Da		As Aa Ds Da / As Aa Ds Da	
10			As Aa Ds Da / As Aa Ds Da		As Aa Ds Da / As Aa Ds Da		As Aa Ds Da / As Aa Ds Da	
11			As Aa Ds Da / As Aa Ds Da		As Aa Ds Da / As Aa Ds Da		As Aa Ds Da / As Aa Ds Da	
12			As Aa Ds Da / As Aa Ds Da		As Aa Ds Da / As Aa Ds Da		As Aa Ds Da / As Aa Ds Da	
13			As Aa Ds Da / As Aa Ds Da		As Aa Ds Da / As Aa Ds Da		As Aa Ds Da / As Aa Ds Da	
14		OBSERVE NOW	As Aa Ds Da / As Aa Ds Da	OBSERVE NOW	As Aa Ds Da / As Aa Ds Da	OBSERVE NOW	As Aa Ds Da / As Aa Ds Da	
15			As Aa Ds Da / As Aa Ds Da		As Aa Ds Da / As Aa Ds Da		As Aa Ds Da / As Aa Ds Da	
16			As Aa Ds Da / As Aa Ds Da		As Aa Ds Da / As Aa Ds Da		As Aa Ds Da / As Aa Ds Da	
17			As Aa Ds Da / As Aa Ds Da		As Aa Ds Da / As Aa Ds Da	TOTALS:		

TOTALS:
As_____ Aa_____ Ds_____ Da_____
As_____ Aa_____ Ds_____ Da_____

Form B:Teacher Observation

Observer_____   Teacher_____
Reliability Observer_____   Grade or Subject _____
Number in Class or Group_____   Date_____
General Activity_____   Time Start_____Time End _____
Length of Observation Intervals in Seconds _____
Record Intervals in Seconds _____   Page_____ of_____

TIME	ACTIVITY CODE	1 - Record	2 - Record	3 - Record	4 - Record	5 - Record	Comment
1		As Aa Ds Da / As Aa Ds Da	As Aa Ds Da / As Aa Ds Da	As Aa Ds Da / As Aa Ds Da	As Aa Ds Da / As Aa Ds Da	As Aa Ds Da / As Aa Ds Da	
2		As Aa Ds Da / As Aa Ds Da	As Aa Ds Da / As Aa Ds Da	As Aa Ds Da / As Aa Ds Da	As Aa Ds Da / As Aa Ds Da	As Aa Ds Da / As Aa Ds Da	
3		As Aa Ds Da / As Aa Ds Da	As Aa Ds Da / As Aa Ds Da	As Aa Ds Da / As Aa Ds Da	As Aa Ds Da / As Aa Ds Da	As Aa Ds Da / As Aa Ds Da	
4		As Aa Ds Da / As Aa Ds Da	As Aa Ds Da / As Aa Ds Da	As Aa Ds Da / As Aa Ds Da	As Aa Ds Da / As Aa Ds Da	As Aa Ds Da / As Aa Ds Da	
5		As Aa Ds Da / As Aa Ds Da	As Aa Ds Da / As Aa Ds Da	As Aa Ds Da / As Aa Ds Da	As Aa Ds Da / As Aa Ds Da	As Aa Ds Da / As Aa Ds Da	
6		As Aa Ds Da / As Aa Ds Da	As Aa Ds Da / As Aa Ds Da	As Aa Ds Da / As Aa Ds Da	As Aa Ds Da / As Aa Ds Da	As Aa Ds Da / As Aa Ds Da	
7		As Aa Ds Da / As Aa Ds Da	As Aa Ds Da / As Aa Ds Da	As Aa Ds Da / As Aa Ds Da	As Aa Ds Da / As Aa Ds Da	As Aa Ds Da / As Aa Ds Da	
8		As Aa Ds Da / As Aa Ds Da	As Aa Ds Da / As Aa Ds Da	As Aa Ds Da / As Aa Ds Da	As Aa Ds Da / As Aa Ds Da	As Aa Ds Da / As Aa Ds Da	
9		As Aa Ds Da / As Aa Ds Da	As Aa Ds Da / As Aa Ds Da	As Aa Ds Da / As Aa Ds Da	As Aa Ds Da / As Aa Ds Da	As Aa Ds Da / As Aa Ds Da	
10		As Aa Ds Da / As Aa Ds Da	As Aa Ds Da / As Aa Ds Da	As Aa Ds Da / As Aa Ds Da	As Aa Ds Da / As Aa Ds Da	As Aa Ds Da / As Aa Ds Da	
11		As Aa Ds Da / As Aa Ds Da	As Aa Ds Da / As Aa Ds Da	As Aa Ds Da / As Aa Ds Da	As Aa Ds Da / As Aa Ds Da	As Aa Ds Da / As Aa Ds Da	
12		As Aa Ds Da / As Aa Ds Da	As Aa Ds Da / As Aa Ds Da	As Aa Ds Da / As Aa Ds Da	As Aa Ds Da / As Aa Ds Da	As Aa Ds Da / As Aa Ds Da	
13		As Aa Ds Da / As Aa Ds Da	As Aa Ds Da / As Aa Ds Da	As Aa Ds Da / As Aa Ds Da	As Aa Ds Da / As Aa Ds Da	As Aa Ds Da / As Aa Ds Da	
14		As Aa Ds Da / As Aa Ds Da	As Aa Ds Da / As Aa Ds Da	As Aa Ds Da / As Aa Ds Da	As Aa Ds Da / As Aa Ds Da	As Aa Ds Da / As Aa Ds Da	
15		As Aa Ds Da / As Aa Ds Da	As Aa Ds Da / As Aa Ds Da	As Aa Ds Da / As Aa Ds Da	As Aa Ds Da / As Aa Ds Da	As Aa Ds Da / As Aa Ds Da	

Reinforcement Summary

Social Reinforcement

Symbols	Total No. Observed	+	Total Intervals Observed	=	% Intervals Behavior Observed
As	= _____	÷	_____	=	_____ %
Ds	= _____	÷	_____	=	_____ %
(As)	= _____	÷	_____	=	_____ %
(Ds)	= _____	÷	_____	=	_____ %

Social Approval Ratio: $\dfrac{\text{As}}{\text{As} + \text{Ds} + \text{(As)} + \text{(Ds)}}$ = ___ %

Academic Reinforcement

Symbols	Total No. Observed	+	Total Intervals Observed	=	%Intervals Behavior Observed
Aa	= _____	÷	_____	=	_____ %
Da	= _____	÷	_____	=	_____ %
(Aa)	= _____	÷	_____	=	_____ %
(Da)	= _____	÷	_____	=	_____ %

Academic Approval Ratio: $\dfrac{\text{Aa}}{\text{Aa} + \text{Da} + \text{(Aa)} + \text{(Da)}}$ = ___ %

RELIABILITY = $\dfrac{\text{Total Agree}}{\text{Total Agree} + \text{Total Disagree}}$ ___ %

Symbols	Number Observed		Same Symbol in Same Interval	
	Observer I	Reliability Observer	Agree	Disagree
As	___	___	___	___
Ds	___	___	___	___
(As)	___	___	___	___
(Ds)	___	___	___	___
Aa	___	___	___	___
Da	___	___	___	___
(Aa)	___	___	___	___
(Da)	___	___	___	___
"No Behavior Observed" ___	___	___	___	
Total			___	___

The *third* code uses Roman numerals and indicates the specific student response that is expected:

I-Looking   II-Minor Motor (writing)   III-Talking   IV-Listening
V-Major Motor (jumping, walking)   VI-Resting

Categories may be expanded by multiple designations or notes in the Comments section.

Teacher observation (Form A)

Learning Activities always start with Form A. During the first interval of each time period (10-second observing and recording intervals have been found to be most useful), the observer should observe and mentally note the ongoing behavior. Observers *do not record the behavior observed at this time.* During the second interval, the behavior observed during the first interval is recorded (marked) on the data sheet. Comments regarding general classroom interaction and/or descriptions of behavior should also be recorded during this time. No observation of behavior occurs during the second interval as this time period is devoted to recording. Observations are continued during the third interval, but are not recorded until the fourth. The same procedure is followed with the fifth and sixth intervals. Thus behavior is observed during the first, third, and fifth intervals and is recorded during the second, fourth, and sixth. Two or more *different* behaviors may be recorded during any one 10-second interval, but, unless specific directions are given to the contrary, only one symbol of the same behavior should appear in each interval box. After observation expertise has progressed (to .80 reliability), behaviors occurring twice during the same interval can be recorded for the appropriate symbol by using numbers or additional marks. All occurrences should be checked or marked in a conspicuous manner. Colored pencils are excellent for this.

Teacher observation (Form B)

Observe and record the behaviors continuously during the first five intervals of each time fine (10-second intervals have been found effective) and record comments or rest during the last interval.

RECORDING TEACHER BEHAVIOR

Teacher behavior as well as student behavior is rated with reference to the rules of the classroom. Always attempt to know the general rules for the class and the specific rules for the activity underway.

The ratings of teacher behaviors can perhaps be best conceptualized according to the following scheme, which is essentially the same chart as on page 64 but with two contingencies (withholding approval and threat of disapproval) excluded. Ignoring is also excluded because it cannot be observed.

In demonstrating the reinforcing function of approving and disapproving teacher behavior, a brief review is advisable. Reinforcement must follow student behavior—behavior is a result of its consequences—or there will be no effect upon student behavior. Reinforcement either increases or decreases behavior. When no effect is demonstrated, then no reinforcement has occurred. For example, the attempts of most teachers to elicit student responses by using interest-provoking questions are to be commended; however, for a behavior to be reinforced, the reinforcement must follow the behavior. The behavioral categories are designed to analyze teacher behaviors following responses from students.

When a teacher follows a behavior with approval, this may serve to reinforce the appropriate behavior (Box 1: When you do good things, good things happen to you). When a teacher gives approval following inappropriate behavior, this is regarded as a reinforcement mistake which may increase the rate of inappropriate behavior! This is called an *approval mistake* (Box 3: When you do bad things, good things happen to you).

Disapproval when properly used generally serves to stop or decrease the rate of the disapproved behavior (Box 4: When you do bad things, bad things happen to you). Therefore, the teacher may be making a mistake if

Behavioral Contingency Interactions: Table 8-2

		TEACHER BEHAVIOR	
		Approval	Disapproval
STUDENT BEHAVIOR	APPROPRIATE (Social and Academic)	As Aa (1)	(Ds) (Da) (Mistakes) (2)
	INAPPROPRIATE (Social and Academic)	(As) (Aa) (Mistakes) (3)	Ds Da (4)

disapproval follows appropriate behavior. This is called a *disapproval mistake* (Box 2: When you do good things, bad things happen to you).

Disapproval following inappropriate behavior is intended to decrease the inappropriate behavior (Box 4). But, if the student has learned an improper association, the disapproval may function in a different way, depending upon the reinforcement history of the student. Teacher attention may also be reinforcing, and students may work for whatever attention is forthcoming—even disapproval. Disapproving behavior alone without approval for appropriate behavior will often increase the very behavior that the teacher wishes to eliminate. In the lower half of Box 4, (Table 8-1) the attention serves as a payoff. The upper half of Box 4 shows occasional disapproval is strong enough to stop inappropriate behavior. (When you do bad things, bad things happen to you.) The effects of disapproval following any student behavior probably depend upon the amount of approval to appropriate behavior (Box 1) in relation to the amount of disapproval to inappropriate behavior (Box 4). When the teacher uses more approval to appropriate behavior than disapproval to inappropriate, then both are generally more effective. The contrast between approval and disapproval also serves to enhance the effect of both. When the teacher uses only approval, then students learn that no matter what one does, "good things" happen. When the teacher uses only disapproval, the students learn that no matter what they do "bad things" happen to them.

Approving and disapproving behaviors are not confined to verbal behavior. As human beings we communicate in a variety of ways by touch, by gesture, by facial expression. Therefore the teacher must be consistent within her/himself as well as with the rules for the particular activity. When the teacher smiles at a student and also verbally disapproves, the teacher is making either a disapproval or an approval mistake. When the teacher frowns while giving verbal approval, the teacher is also making a reinforcement mistake.

Responses available to the teacher to express approval or disapproval are classified in five categories:

1. Words (spoken or written)
2. Physical expressions (facial or bodily)
3. Closeness (nearness or touching)
4. Activities (social or individual)
5. Things (materials, food, awards, or tokens)

The observer should have these categories memorized and analyze teacher behaviors in terms of the responses available. Should the teacher dispense facial approval while hitting, shaking, or forcibly restraining a child, then all applicable categories should be checked depending upon the immediately preceding student behavior. Observers should study in detail the examples of approval and disapproval in Chapter 7.

Academic and social definitions

Approval for academic behavior is easily understood. This category includes what most teachers generally label feedback concerning the correctness of a student's academic response whether oral or written. Academic. approval concerns only the correctness of the answer to curricular materials and does not include approval for "working hard" or "trying hard" or getting out materials. Of course, any behavior may be academic if the teacher's goals are to teach the behavior as subject matter. Disapproval for academic behavior involves any means, verbal or physical, of indicating to the student that his answer to the specific activity or question is in error.

Approval for social behavior involves giving approval following any aspect of the student's behavior that gets or maintains the student on-task. This category includes reinforcement for appropriate interaction patterns with either the curriculum materials or other individuals. It does not pertain to the correctness or incorrectness of an academic response.

Disapproval of inappropriate social behavior involves disapproval following a discriminated aspect of the student's behavior that either interrupts or disturbs the learning environment for himself or another person. This is off-task behavior (see Glossary).

It is possible to approve the student's attempts to complete assignments (social behavior) while at the same time disapprove an incorrect academic response— "You are working hard; six responses are not correct." The student may be helped to understand the differences among learning how to "work hard," following instructions, and attempting academic material, even though the product is not as expert as it may become with continued effort. Alternately, some students may have many correct responses but still engage in inappropriate social behavior—"Johnny, all your answers are correct, but you should learn to stay on-task and quit disrupting during seatwork."

Teacher Observation Categories

Aa   Approval for academic behavior is recorded if the teacher indicates the academic work is correct. Academic approval usually involves words, spoken or written. The observer should watch carefully to determine if physical expressions, closeness, activities, or things (see Chapter 7) are specifically paired with correct answers, indicating attention or commendation for the correct answer rather than the "working" itself. Care should be exercised in discriminating between approval directed toward academic work and approval for correct social behavior.

As   Approval for social behavior is recorded if the teacher gives any approving response paired specifically with appropriate social behavior. This category includes words, physical expressions, closeness, activities, and things directed toward any social behavior (following rules, working, cooperating, getting on-task).

Da   Disapproval for academic behavior includes any disapproval indicating that a student's response to the curriculum materials was incorrect. Disapproval in classrooms generally involves words, spoken or written (grades), but one should not overlook physical expression, closeness (hitting, grabbing, forcibly holding, putting out of group), or deprivation of activities or things.

Ds   Disapproval for social behavior given by the teacher follows any disruption of the learning environment that interferes with learning. Disapproval includes words, spoken or written, that reprimand. Disapproval may be of either high or low intensity and includes yelling, scolding, threats, and threatening comments concerning later consequences. Disapproval also includes bodily expressions such as frowning, grimacing, or shaking a fist, closeness such as hitting, slapping, paddling, or other means of corporal punishment, and deprivation of activities or things.

(Aa)   An approval mistake of reinforcement following academic behavior occurs when the teacher indicates the academic response is correct when, in fact, the answer is incorrect.

(As)   An approval mistake of reinforcement following social behavior involves giving approval to inappropriate social behavior. For example, a teacher may touch a student "gently" during or following a misbehavior (closeness) or may reinforce the misbehavior through words, bodily expressions, activities, or things. An approval mistake is recorded when the teacher follows a student's breaking of classroom rules with an approval response (inconsistency). The teacher may verbally recognize a student who is walking around when he is supposed to be in his seat, or the teacher may recognize a student who blurts out an answer (whether correct or incorrect) although the student is supposed to raise his hand for recognition. An approval mistake could also occur if the teacher uses words to dispense group verbal approval (praise) when one or more of the students in the group is off-task.

(Da)   A disapproval mistake of reinforcement following academic behavior is recorded when the teacher indicates the student's academic answer was incorrect when the answer was, in fact, correct.

A disapproval mistake of reinforcement following social behavior is recorded if the teacher uses disapproval when the social behavior was indeed appropriate to the classroom situation. This occurs most frequently when the teacher gives group disapproval and one or more of the students are, in fact, on-task. A disapproval mistake may also occur when the teacher interrupts his work with one student in order to attend another student. Interruptions may lead to a disapproval mistake of reinforcement if the student behavior is disapproved in the process. Disapproval mistakes also occur when the teacher delays too long in using disapproval for inappropriate behavior. For example, a student engages in inappropriate behavior, stops the inappropriate behavior, is working appropriately, and then the teacher disapproves.

Nonreinforcement categories

Any response from the teacher that gives specific directions and requires a response from one or more students in the class is not recorded as either approval or disapproval. Academic instructions pertaining to the academic curriculum that do not require a response from the students are not considered as reinforcement.

Attempts by the teacher to stimulate behavioral responses are extremely common. Often these techniques elicit responses from students that can be reinforced. Questioning, probing, cueing, prompts, illustrations, modeling correct procedures, and so on, seem to be tools of most effective teachers, yet these procedures do not necessarily reinforce behavior. While eliciting techniques may increase reinforcement possibilities for some students, elicitation techniques are less effective with students who lack experience or the ability to stay on-task. Observations concerning reinforcements focus only on behaviors which follow a student's response. The individual teacher must establish goals and ascertain the most effective strategies of presentation to elicit responses that then can be reinforced. This is true especially for those individuals whose reinforcement histories do not include enough background for the academic materials to be self-reinforcing.

Student observation (Form C and Form D)

Classroom behavioral observation focusing on the student is concerned with two major behaviors: (1) on-task or appropriate behavior and (2) off-task or inappropriate behavior. Students' behaviors can be appropriate or inappropriate only with reference to classroom rules and/or the teacher's objectives. Therefore, observers must know the rules of each classroom and differing rules for specific situations before reliable observations can be recorded. It is sometimes necessary to ask teachers what their rules are, since some teachers permit students to stand up, sit on the floor, talk during certain activities, or leave their seats without permission.

Form C:Student Observation

Observer _____ Student _____

Reliability Observer _____ Teacher _____

No. in class or group _____ Grade or Subject _____ Date _____

General Activity _____ Time: Start _____ End _____

Observation Interval _____ Page _____ of _____

         (seconds)   Record Interval _____

                            (seconds)

TIME	ACTIVITY CODE	(1)	2 - RECORD	(3)	4 - RECORD	(5)	6 - RECORD	COMMENTS
1			+ N M O		+ N M O		+ N M O	
2			+ N M O		+ N M O		+ N M O	
3		OBSERVE NOW	+ N M O	OBSERVE NOW	+ N M O	OBSERVE NOW	+ N M O	
4			+ N M O		+ N M O		+ N M O	
5			+ N M O		+ N M O		+ N M O	
6			+ N M O		+ N M O		+ N M O	
7			+ N M O		+ N M O		+ N M O	
8			+ N M O		+ N M O		+ N M O	
9			+ N M O		+ N M O		+ N M O	
10			+ N M O		+ N M O		+ N M O	
11			+ N M O		+ N M O	OBSERVE NOW	+ N M O	
12		OBSERVE NOW	+ N M O	OBSERVE NOW	+ N M O		+ N M O	
13			+ N M O		+ N M O		+ N M O	
14			+ N M O		+ N M O		+ N M O	
15			+ N M O		+ N M O		+ N M O	
16			+ N M O		+ N M O		+ N M O	
17			+ N M O		+ N M O			

% On - task = _____ (+ %)

% Off - task = 100 - (% On - task) = _____

Intervals Observed

Totals: + = ____ - ____ = ____ %

N = ____ - ____ = ____ %

M = ____ - ____ = ____ %

O = ____ - ____ = ____ %

Child Categories

On-Task   This category includes verbal and motor behavior that follows the class-

+   room rules and is appropriate to the learning situation. On-task behavior is defined with reference to both the rules of the classroom and the
teacher-designated academic activity. If a student is working on the
appropriate academic activity and is obeying the rules of the classroom,
then the student's behavior is recorded as being on-task. Examples of
on-task behavior might include sitting at desk while working, engaging
in group games when appropriate, responding to teacher questions
(whether or not the answer is correct or incorrect), walking to chalkboard when asked, demonstrating activities to others when expected,
talking during class discussions, or participating actively in physical
education class.

Form D: Student Observation

Observer _____ Student _____
Reliability Observer _____ Teacher _____
No. in Class or Group _____ Grade or Subject ____ Date _____
General Activity _____ Time: Start _____ End _____
Observation Interval _____ Page _____ of _____
                    (seconds)   Record Interval _____
                                            (seconds)

TIME	ACTIVITY CODE	INTERVALS					COMMENTS
		1	2	3	4	5	
1		+NMO	+NMO	+NMO	+NMO	+NMO	
2		+NMO	+NMO	+NMO	+NMO	+NMO	
3		+NMO	+NMO	+NMO	+NMO	+NMO	
4		+NMO	+NMO	+NMO	+NMO	+NMO	
5		+NMO	+NMO	+NMO	+NMO	+NMO	
6		+NMO	+NMO	+NMO	+NMO	+NMO	
7		+NMO	+NMO	+NMO	+NMO	+NMO	
8		+NMO	+NMO	+NMO	+NMO	+NMO	
9		+NMO	+NMO	+NMO	+NMO	+NMO	
10		+NMO	+NMO	+NMO	+NMO	+NMO	
11		+NMO	+NMO	+NMO	+NMO	+NMO	
12		+NMO	+NMO	+NMO	+NMO	+NMO	
13		+NMO	+NMO	+NMO	+NMO	+NMO	
14		+NMO	+NMO	+NMO	+NMO	+NMO	
15		+NMO	+NMO	+NMO	+NMO	+NMO	

% On - Task = _____ (+%)

% Off - Task = 100 − (% On - Task) = _____ %

TOTALS INTERVALS PERCENT
OBSERVED

+ = _____ ÷ _____ = _____ %

N = _____ ÷ _____ = _____ %

M = _____ ÷ _____ = _____ %

O = _____ ÷ _____ = _____ %

Verbal Noise

Off-
task
N
Verbal noise is any oral response that breaks the class rules and/or interrupts the learning situation. This category may include inappropriate talking, yelling, blurting out, whistling, humming, screaming, singing, and laughing. The verbalization must be heard for it to be recorded. Simply seeing the student's lips move is not enough. If a child responds to a teacher's question or instruction, then the student is on-task. Further examples of verbal off-task behavior include blurting out an answer instead of raising hand, talking to a neighbor instead of working on materials, and singing during discussion.

Object Noise
Object noise is any audible noise resulting from any behavior on the part of the child that may cause other children to be off-task, such as slamming books, kicking furniture, or rapping a desk.

Motor
M   Motor off-task is any motor response (gross or minor) that breaks the class rules and/or interrupts the learning situation. Some motor behaviors are inappropriate during certain classroom periods but not always at others.

V or I   Should it be important to record differences between gross versus minor motor or verbal noise versus object noise, merely use a different check for each.

Gross Motor
Gross motor behaviors may include getting out of one's seat, turning around at least 90°, running, turning cartwheels, walking around the room, waving arms. Another area of inappropriate gross motor behavior includes behaviors generally labeled "aggressive"—hitting, kicking, pushing, pinching, slapping, striking another person with objects, grabbing another's property, and throwing.

Minor Motor
Minor motor behaviors are only recorded when attention is not directed toward the student's work. If the student is engaged in appropriate activities while he exhibits these small motor behaviors, then his behavior is recorded as being on-task with a check mark on "M" and mention is made of these motor activities in the comment section. Examples of minor motor behaviors include thumbsucking, fingernail biting, fiddling with hair, finger twiddling, chewing on a pencil or other object, and playing with academic materials when not appropriate.

Other or Passive Off-Task
O   The student is involved in no interaction or is doing nothing when expected to be involved. Behaviors recorded in this category include daydreaming and staring into space. The students must be engaged in no motor or verbal activity for this category to be recorded. It is important to remember that there are times when doing nothing is not inappropriate, for example, when an assignment is completed and nothing has been assigned. This is very rare as most teachers have activities for all students when one assignment is completed.

Student-teacher interactions (Form E and Form F)

Behavioral studies during the past few years have indicated that the response of the teacher to student behavior maintains a great deal both of appropriate, on-task behavior and inappropriate, off-task behavior (see Part II).

Form E: Student-Teacher

Observer _____ Student _____

Reliability Observer _____ Teacher _____

No. in class or group _____ Grade or Subject _____ Date _____

General Activity _____ Time: Start _____ End _____

Observation Interval _____ Page _____ of _____
(seconds)

Record Interval _____ (seconds)

TIME	NAME(S)	ACTIVITY CODE	(1)	2 - RECORD	(3)	4 - RECORD	(5)	6 - RECORD	COMMENTS
1	Teacher		OBSERVE NOW	+ N M O / Aa As Da Ds / Aa As Da Ds	OBSERVE NOW	+ N M O / Aa As Da Ds / Aa As Da Ds	OBSERVE NOW	+ N M O / Aa As Da Ds / Aa As Da Ds	
2	Teacher			+ N M O / Aa As Da Ds / Aa As Da Ds		+ N M O / Aa As Da Ds / Aa As Da Ds		+ N M O / Aa As Da Ds / Aa As Da Ds	
3	Teacher			+ N M O / Aa As Da Ds / Aa As Da Ds		+ N M O / Aa As Da Ds / Aa As Da Ds		+ N M O / Aa As Da Ds / Aa As Da Ds	
4	Teacher			+ N M O / Aa As Da Ds / Aa As Da Ds		+ N M O / Aa As Da Ds / Aa As Da Ds		+ N M O / Aa As Da Ds / Aa As Da Ds	
5	Teacher			+ N M O / Aa As Da Ds / Aa As Da Ds		+ N M O / Aa As Da Ds / Aa As Da Ds		+ N M O / Aa As Da Ds / Aa As Da Ds	
6	Teacher			+ N M O / Aa As Da Ds / Aa As Da Ds		+ N M O / Aa As Da Ds / Aa As Da Ds		+ N M O / Aa As Da Ds / Aa As Da Ds	
7	Teacher		OBSERVE NOW	+ N M O / Aa As Da Ds / Aa As Da Ds	OBSERVE NOW	+ N M O / Aa As Da Ds / Aa As Da Ds	OBSERVE NOW	+ N M O / Aa As Da Ds / Aa As Da Ds	
8	Teacher			+ N M O / Aa As Da Ds / Aa As Da Ds		+ N M O / Aa As Da Ds / Aa As Da Ds		+ N M O / Aa As Da Ds / Aa As Da Ds	
9	Teacher			+ N M O / Aa As Da Ds / Aa As Da Ds		+ N M O / Aa As Da Ds / Aa As Da Ds		+ N M O / Aa As Da Ds / Aa As Da Ds	
10	Teacher			+ N M O / Aa As Da Ds / Aa As Da Ds		+ N M O / Aa As Da Ds / Aa As Da Ds		+ N M O / Aa As Da Ds / Aa As Da Ds	
11	Teacher			+ N M O / Aa As Da Ds / Aa As Da Ds		+ N M O / Aa As Da Ds / Aa As Da Ds		+ N M O / Aa As Da Ds / Aa As Da Ds	
12	Teacher		OBSERVE NOW	+ N M O / Aa As Da Ds / Aa As Da Ds		+ N M O / Aa As Da Ds / Aa As Da Ds		+ N M O / Aa As Da Ds / Aa As Da Ds	
13	Teacher			+ N M O / Aa As Da Ds / Aa As Da Ds					

Totals :

+ = _____ Aa _____ As _____

N = _____ Da _____ Ds _____

M = _____ Aa _____ As _____

O = _____ Da _____ Ds _____

Observer _____
Reliability Observer _____
No. in Class or Group _____
General Activity _____
Observation Interval _____ (seconds)

STUDENT _____
Teacher _____
Grade or Subject _____
Time: Start _____ End _____
Page _____ of _____
Record Interval _____ (seconds) _____ Date _____

TIME	NAME(S)	ACTIVITY CODE	INTERVAL 1	INTERVAL 2	INTERVAL 3	INTERVAL 4	INTERVAL 5	COMMENTS
1	Teacher		+ N M O / Aa As Da Ds / Aa As Da Ds	+ N M O / Aa As Da Ds / Aa As Da Ds	+ N M O / Aa As Da Ds / Aa As Da Ds	+ N M O / Aa As Da Ds / Aa As Da Ds	+ N M O / Aa As Da Ds / Aa As Da Ds	
2	Teacher		+ N M O / Aa As Da Ds / Aa As Da Ds	+ N M O / Aa As Da Ds / Aa As Da Ds	+ N M O / Aa As Da Ds / Aa As Da Ds	+ N M O / Aa As Da Ds / Aa As Da Ds	+ N M O / Aa As Da Ds / Aa As Da Ds	
3	Teacher		+ N M O / Aa As Da Ds / Aa As Da Ds	+ N M O / Aa As Da Ds / Aa As Da Ds	+ N M O / Aa As Da Ds / Aa As Da Ds	+ N M O / Aa As Da Ds / Aa As Da Ds	+ N M O / Aa As Da Ds / Aa As Da Ds	
4	Teacher		+ N M O / Aa As Da Ds / Aa As Da Ds	+ N M O / Aa As Da Ds / Aa As Da Ds	+ N M O / Aa As Da Ds / Aa As Da Ds	+ N M O / Aa As Da Ds / Aa As Da Ds	+ N M O / Aa As Da Ds / Aa As Da Ds	
5	Teacher		+ N M O / Aa As Da Ds / Aa As Da Ds	+ N M O / Aa As Da Ds / Aa As Da Ds	+ N M O / Aa As Da Ds / Aa As Da Ds	+ N M O / Aa As Da Ds / Aa As Da Ds	+ N M O / Aa As Da Ds / Aa As Da Ds	
6	Teacher		+ N M O / Aa As Da Ds / Aa As Da Ds	+ N M O / Aa As Da Ds / Aa As Da Ds	+ N M O / Aa As Da Ds / Aa As Da Ds	+ N M O / Aa As Da Ds / Aa As Da Ds	+ N M O / Aa As Da Ds / Aa As Da Ds	
7	Teacher		+ N M O / Aa As Da Ds / Aa As Da Ds	+ N M O / Aa As Da Ds / Aa As Da Ds	+ N M O / Aa As Da Ds / Aa As Da Ds	+ N M O / Aa As Da Ds / Aa As Da Ds	+ N M O / Aa As Da Ds / Aa As Da Ds	
8	Teacher		+ N M O / Aa As Da Ds / Aa As Da Ds	+ N M O / Aa As Da Ds / Aa As Da Ds	+ N M O / Aa As Da Ds / Aa As Da Ds	+ N M O / Aa As Da Ds / Aa As Da Ds	+ N M O / Aa As Da Ds / Aa As Da Ds	
9	Teacher		+ N M O / Aa As Da Ds / Aa As Da Ds	+ N M O / Aa As Da Ds / Aa As Da Ds	+ N M O / Aa As Da Ds / Aa As Da Ds	+ N M O / Aa As Da Ds / Aa As Da Ds	+ N M O / Aa As Da Ds / Aa As Da Ds	
10	Teacher		+ N M O / Aa As Da Ds / Aa As Da Ds	+ N M O / Aa As Da Ds / Aa As Da Ds	+ N M O / Aa As Da Ds / Aa As Da Ds	+ N M O / Aa As Da Ds / Aa As Da Ds	+ N M O / Aa As Da Ds / Aa As Da Ds	

Form F: Student-Teacher

Analysis Form: Student-Teacher Forms E and F

Symbols	Total Number Observed		Total Intervals Observed		Percentage Intervals in which Behavior Observed
+	= _____	÷	_____	=	_____ %
N	= _____	÷	_____	=	_____ %
M	= _____	÷	_____	=	_____ %
O	= _____	÷	_____	=	_____ %

On - Task Percentage (+) _____ %

Academic Assignment _____

Teacher Academic Reinforcement

Symbols	Total Number Observed		Total Intervals Observed		Percentage Intervals in which Behavior Observed
Aa	= _____	÷	_____	=	_____ %
Da	= _____	÷	_____	=	_____ %
ⓐⓐ	= _____	÷	_____	=	_____ %
ⓓⓐ	= _____	÷	_____	=	_____ %

Approval Ratio: $\dfrac{\text{Aa}}{\text{Aa} + \text{Da} + Ⓐⓐ + Ⓓⓐ}$ (Academic)   = _____   = _____ %

Social Reinforcement

Symbols	Total Number Observed		Total Intervals Observed		Percentage Intervals in which Behavior Observed
As	= _____	÷	_____	=	_____ %
Ds	= _____	÷	_____	=	_____ %
Ⓐⓢ	= _____	÷	_____	=	_____ %
Ⓓⓢ	= _____	÷	_____	=	_____ %

Approval Ratio = $\dfrac{\text{As}}{\text{As} + \text{Ds} + Ⓐⓢ + Ⓓⓢ}$ (Social)   = _____   = _____ %

A common question asked by teachers who refer specific children for counseling or other outside help is: How does the teacher respond to these particular students in the classroom? The Student-Teacher Form is designed to answer this question.

This form is a combination of Form A and the Form C given above. During each interval, the observer checks whether the student is on-task (+) or off-task (N for noise, M for motor, O for other, or Passive) and also indicates the response of the teacher to *this particular child.* Following a series of observations (we suggest at least five be completed during those class periods the teacher considers most troublesome), an analysis can be made of the teacher responses to the particular student. Should the teacher or observer desire to note the differences between the teacher's overall responses to the class and his responses to the particular student, then one mark (e.g., X) can be used for responses to other class members and a different mark (e.g., 1) for the individual in question.

Many studies have been conducted using this form in a variety of ways. It can be expanded to include more than one student by using the student's initial as the recording mark and placing the initial for each student in the appropriate squares over the symbol, using red pencils. The form may also be used to observe from two to five students by using a coded number as the recording mark and writing the actual number in each square. Additionally, the form may be used to observe one child during the first time period (three or five intervals), a second child during the next time period, and so on, then recycling across all children after all have been observed.

The basic form has also been expanded into a series of observation forms that include space for more than one student in each observation block (see Form G). On Form G, three students are observed simultaneously and the teacher's responses are also recorded. For this form, mistakes of reinforcement are recorded as approval mistakes (Am) and disapproval mistakes (Dm), with no distinction between academic as opposed to social mistakes. Should this information be required, a different mark can be used. Thus it is also possible with Form E or other adaptations of it to record precise student teacher interactions.

Group on-task/off-task teacher response (Form H)

The average number of students off-task and on-task, expressed as a ratio of students engaged in appropriate or inappropriate behavior compared to the total number of students in the classroom or group being observed, usually is important to most classroom teachers. Form H may be used to collect these data. As with all forms, the identification section is completed so that accurate reconstruction of the observational situation is possible.

Observer _____
Reliability Observer _____
Students: 1. _____
2. _____
3. _____

Teacher _____
Date _____
Time Start _____ Time End _____
Page _____ of _____
Observation Interval _____

TIME	S	INTERVAL 1		INTERVAL 2		INTERVAL 3		INTERVAL 4		INTERVAL 5		COMMENT
1	1	X N M O	Aa Da	X N M O	Aa Da	X N M O	Aa Da	X N M O	Aa Da	X N M O	Aa Da	
	2	X N M O	As Ds	X N M O	As Ds	X N M O	As Ds	X N M O	As Ds	X N M O	As Ds	
	3	X N M O	Am Dm	X N M O	Am Dm	X N M O	Am Dm	X N M O	Am Dm	X N M O	Am Dm	
2	1	X N M O	Aa Da	X N M O	Aa Da	X N M O	Aa Da	X N M O	Aa Da	X N M O	Aa Da	
	2	X N M O	As Ds	X N M O	As Ds	X N M O	As Ds	X N M O	As Ds	X N M O	As Ds	
	3	X N M O	Am Dm	X N M O	Am Dm	X N M O	Am Dm	X N M O	Am Dm	X N M O	Am Dm	
3	1	X N M O	Aa Da	X N M O	Aa Da	X N M O	Aa Da	X N M O	Aa Da	X N M O	Aa Da	
	2	X N M O	As Ds	X N M O	As Ds	X N M O	As Ds	X N M O	As Ds	X N M O	As Ds	
	3	X N M O	Am Dm	X N M O	Am Dm	X N M O	Am Dm	X N M O	Am Dm	X N M O	Am Dm	
4	1	X N M O	Aa Da	X N M O	Aa Da	X N M O	Aa Da	X N M O	Aa Da	X N M O	Aa Da	
	2	X N M O	As Ds	X N M O	As Ds	X N M O	As Ds	X N M O	As Ds	X N M O	As Ds	
	3	X N M O	Am Dm	X N M O	Am Dm	X N M O	Am Dm	X N M O	Am Dm	X N M O	Am Dm	
5	1	X N M O	Aa Da	X N M O	Aa Da	X N M O	Aa Da	X N M O	Aa Da	X N M O	Aa Da	
	2	X N M O	As Ds	X N M O	As Ds	X N M O	As Ds	X N M O	As Ds	X N M O	As Ds	
	3	X N M O	Am Dm	X N M O	Am Dm	X N M O	Am Dm	X N M O	Am Dm	X N M O	Am Dm	
6	1	X N M O	Aa Da	X N M O	Aa Da	X N M O	Aa Da	X N M O	Aa Da	X N M O	Aa Da	
	2	X N M O	As Ds	X N M O	As Ds	X N M O	As Ds	X N M O	As Ds	X N M O	As Ds	
	3	X N M O	Am Dm	X N M O	Am Dm	X N M O	Am Dm	X N M O	Am Dm	X N M O	Am Dm	
7	1	X N M O	Aa Da	X N M O	Aa Da	X N M O	Aa Da	X N M O	Aa Da	X N M O	Aa Da	
	2	X N M O	As Ds	X N M O	As Ds	X N M O	As Ds	X N M O	As Ds	X N M O	As Ds	
	3	X N M O	Am Dm	X N M O	Am Dm	X N M O	Am Dm	X N M O	Am Dm	X N M O	Am Dm	
8	1	X N M O	Aa Da	X N M O	Aa Da	X N M O	Aa Da	X N M O	Aa Da	X N M O	Aa Da	
	2	X N M O	As Ds	X N M O	As Ds	X N M O	As Ds	X N M O	As Ds	X N M O	As Ds	
	3	X N M O	Am Dm	X N M O	Am Dm	X N M O	Am Dm	X N M O	Am Dm	X N M O	Am Dm	
9	1	X N M O	Aa Da	X N M O	Aa Da	X N M O	Aa Da	X N M O	Aa Da	X N M O	Aa Da	
	2	X N M O	As Ds	X N M O	As Ds	X N M O	As Ds	X N M O	As Ds	X N M O	As Ds	
	3	X N M O	Am Dm	X N M O	Am Dm	X N M O	Am Dm	X N M O	Am Dm	X N M O	Am Dm	
10	1	X N M O	Aa Da	X N M O	Aa Da	X N M O	Aa Da	X N M O	Aa Da	X N M O	Aa Da	
	2	X N M O	As Ds	X N M O	As Ds	X N M O	As Ds	X N M O	As Ds	X N M O	As Ds	
	3	X N M O	Am Dm	X N M O	Am Dm	X N M O	Am Dm	X N M O	Am Dm	X N M O	Am Dm	

Form G: Student (S)—Teacher

Form H: Group On-Task/Off-Task Teacher Response

Observer_____ Teacher_____
Reliability Observer_____ Grade or Subject _____ Date _____
No. in class or group_____ Time: Start_____End _____
General Activity_____ Page_____ of _____
Observation Interval_____ Record Interval _____
　　　　　　　　　　(seconds)　　　　　　　　　　　(seconds)

TIME	ACTIVITY CODE	NO. STUDENTS	INTERVALS							OFF-TASK RATIO		
			(1)	2 - RECORD	(3)	4 - RECORD	(5)	6 - RECORD		INTERVALS		
				No. Off- + or − Task　Students		No. Off- + or − Task　Students		No. Off- + or − Task　Students		2	4	6
1			OBSERVE NOW	As Aa Ds Da As Aa Ds Da	OBSERVE NOW	As Aa Ds Da As Aa Ds Da	OBSERVE NOW	As Aa Ds Da As Aa Ds Da				
2				As Aa Ds Da As Aa Ds Da		As Aa Ds Da As Aa Ds Da		As Aa Ds Da As Aa Ds Da				
3			OBSERVE NOW	As Aa Ds Da As Aa Ds Da	OBSERVE NOW	As Aa Ds Da As Aa Ds Da	OBSERVE NOW	As Aa Ds Da As Aa Ds Da				
4				As Aa Ds Da As Aa Ds Da		As Aa Ds Da As Aa Ds Da		As Aa Ds Da As Aa Ds Da				
5			OBSERVE NOW	As Aa Ds Da As Aa Ds Da	OBSERVE NOW	As Aa Ds Da As Aa Ds Da	OBSERVE NOW	As Aa Ds Da As Aa Ds Da				
6				As Aa Ds Da As Aa Ds Da		As Aa Ds Da As Aa Ds Da		As Aa Ds Da As Aa Ds Da				
7			OBSERVE NOW	As Aa Ds Da As Aa Ds Da	OBSERVE NOW	As Aa Ds Da As Aa Ds Da	OBSERVE NOW	As Aa Ds Da As Aa Ds Da				
8				As Aa Ds Da As Aa Ds Da		As Aa Ds Da As Aa Ds Da		As Aa Ds Da As Aa Ds Da				
9				As Aa Ds Da As Aa Ds Da								

TOTALS:

As _____ Aa _____ Cumulative Students Off-Task = _____(A)
Ds _____ Da _____ Cumulative Students Observed = _____(B)
(As) _____ (Aa) _____ $\frac{A}{B}$ = Percent Off-Task = _____
(Ds) _____ (Da) _____

The activity for the class or group is recorded for each time period, numbered down the left side of the page. The observer then records the number of students in the group who are being observed. This is necessary as the ratio of off-task to on-task students will change depending upon the number being observed. Five students recorded as off-task when a group of five is being observed is 100 off-task (0.0 percent on-task), whereas five off-task when twenty are being observed is 25 percent off-task (75 percent on-task). Therefore it is important to record the number of students present for each time interval. Within the record boxes, the upper half is for recording the total number of students off-task and the lower portion is for recording teacher responses.

During interval number 1, the observer scans the group or class and then records the number of students off-task by writing the number in the square under No. Off-Task. In most classrooms the number off-task is less than the number on-task, but if a very disruptive class is being observed, it may be easier to record the number on-task. During the recording interval, the observer also listens carefully to the teacher and mentally notes all teacher responses to the entire class. Then, following the recording of students off-task, the observer marks the teacher symbols in the lower portion of the interval. If, for example, the teacher had given approval for appropriate social behavior, the observer would check As in the lower portion under the number of students who were recorded as off-task. Immediately following the recording of teacher behavior and prior to the next observation interval, the observer records whether any students were added or subtracted from the group being observed during the preceding interval. If any change has occurred, the observer records the number under + or – students.

The observer then proceeds to the next interval and repeats the observational procedure, using exactly the same procedure as during the first interval and making certain to record the number of students in the group being observed who are off-task. When total observations have been completed, the Off-Task Ratios are subsequently recorded for all observation intervals. The area above the diagonal line is used to record the number of students off-task in each observed interval and the portion below the diagonal line to record the number of all students observed during that single interval.

Analysis of the percentage of students off-task represents an average of the percentage off-task during all observed intervals. This is computed by adding each individual fraction from the off-task ratios section and completing the division. If six intervals (two time lines) were observed with the following ratios:

Second interval (No. Students = 20, 5 off-task = 5/20), 3 students left (-3)

Fourth interval (20 – 3 = 17 Students, 4 off-task = 4/17), 10 students came in (+ 10)

Sixth interval (17 + 10 = 27 students, 8 off-task = 8/27), four students were taken out (No. Students, Line 2, 27 - 4 = 23)

Second interval (10 off-task = 10/23), number of students remained the same (± 0)

Fourth interval ($23 + 0 = 23$, 6 off-task = 6/23), two students came in (+ 2),

Sixth interval ($23 + 2 + 25$, 3 off-task = 3/25)

the average percent off-task would be computed as follows:

$5/20 + 4/17 + 8/27 + 10/23 + 6/23 + 3/25 =$
$.25 + .235 + .296 + .435 + .26 + .12 = 1.596/6 = .266 =$
27 percent average off-task.

Calculating on the form (Note that cumulative off-task is different from average off-task):

Cumulative Students Off-task (A) = $5 + 4 + 8 + 10 + 6 + 3 = 36$.

Cumulative Students Observed (B) = $20 + 17 + 27 + 23 + 23 + 25 = 135$.

A/B = $36/135 = .266 = 27$ percent off-task.

The analysis of teacher responses takes place in exactly the same way as when using the Teacher Observation Form. The result is an indication of the average classroom off-task behavior and at the same time shows how the teacher reinforcement for both academic and social behavior may be maintaining the on- or off-task behavior. An interval by interval analysis of the data in terms of increase and decrease across specific intervals can be used in examining results with teachers who desire to become more competent in the application of reinforcement principles in the classroom.

INTERPERSONAL OBSERVATION

Interpersonal observation (Form J)

Sometimes interpersonal behaviors between students need to be observed. This is especially pertinent in newly integrated situations regardless of mode of integration: race, sex, academic ability, schools, aggression, passivity, or other relationships between one, two, or any group of people.

Interpersonal behaviors are most frequently expressed by means of verbal or motor expression. Verbal behaviors include any oral response of either an approving or disapproving nature by the person being observed, directed toward any designated person(s). Verbal responses primarily include words spoken, but also comprise yelling, whistling, humming, screaming, and laughing. Verbalizations must be heard for the observer to record the behavior.

Form J: Interpersonal Observation

Person (s)_____ Teacher_____
Observed_____ Grade or Subject_____ Date_____
Observer I_____ Activity_____
Reliability Observer_____ Time Start_____ Time End_____

TIME	ACTIVITY	Interval 1				Interval 3				Interval 5				Analysis
		V	V	M	M	V	V	M	M	V	V	M	M	COMMENTS SYMBOL FREQ. %
		x ↓ o	o ↓ x	x ↓ o	o ↓ x	x ↓ o	o ↓ x	x ↓ o	o ↓ x	x ↓ o	o ↓ x	x ↓ o	o ↓ x	Vx → o$_a$ ____ ____
														Vx → o$_d$ ____ ____
1														Vo → x$_a$ ____ ____
2														Vo → x$_d$ ____ ____
3														Mx → o$_a$ ____ ____
4														Mx → o$_d$ ____ ____
5														Mo → x$_a$ ____ ____
6														Mo → x$_d$ ____ ____
7														
8														Reliability
9														Agree Disagree
10														x → o$_a$ ____ ____
11														x → o$_d$ ____ ____
12														o → x$_a$ ____ ____
13														o → x$_d$ ____ ____
14														Total ____ ____
15														
16														Total Agree _____
17														

$$\frac{\text{Total Agree}}{\text{Total Agree + Total Disagree}} =$$

REACTION_____

Motor behavior includes both gross and minor motor behaviors as well as bodily and facial expressions. Touching, hitting, pushing, slapping, and striking with objects are motor behaviors, as well as patting and tapping. Bodily expressions such as raising hands or holding fists may also be included.

This observation form provides two basic designations for persons being observed (X and 0) and a method of recordings the direction of the behavior (X toward 0 or 0 toward X). These X and 0 symbols may designate any individual or number of individuals.

Interpersonal Categories

Vx o_a　Any verbal behavior (words spoken) initiated by the student designated by the X subsymbol (white-black, male-female, friend-protagonist), directed toward the student designated by the 0 subsymbol, and defined as approval. (See teacher approval category.)

Vo x_a　Any verbal behavior (words spoken) initiated by the student designated by the 0 subsymbol, directed toward the student designated by the X subsymbol, and defined as approval. (See teacher approval category.)

Vx o_d　Any verbal behavior (words spoken) initiated by the student designated by the X subsymbol, directed toward the student designated by the 0 subsymbol, and defined as disapproval. (See teacher disapproval category.)

Vo x_d　Any verbal behavior (words spoken) initiated by the student designated by the 0 subsymbol, directed toward the student designated by the X subsymbol, and defined as disapproval. (See teacher disapproval category.)

Mx o_a　Any motor (definition of student categories) behavior (bodily expression or closeness) initiated by the student designated by the X subsymbol, directed toward the student designated by the 0 subsymbol, and defined as approval. (See teacher approval category.)

Mo x_a　Any motor (definition of student categories) behavior (bodily expressions or closeness) initiated by the student designated by the 0 subsymbol, directed toward the student designated by the X subsymbol, and defined as approval. (See teacher approval category.)

Mx o_d　Any motor (definition of student categories) behavior (bodily expressions or closeness) initiated by the student designated by the X subsymbol, directed toward the student designated by the 0 subsymbol, and defined as approval. (See teacher disapproval category.)

Mo x_d　Any motor (definition of student categories) behavior response (bodily expressions or closeness) initiated by the student designated by the 0 subsymbol, directed toward the student designated by the X subsymbol, and defined as disapproval. (See teacher disapproval category.)

If we assume that a teacher desires to observe the approval and disapproval behaviors directed toward a particular pupil who does not appear to respond to interpersonal contingencies, the observer could designate this child as X and all other children as 0. Observations are then recorded in the appropriate squares underneath the symbols by placing either an A (approval) or D (disapproval) in the square and a number to indicate the number of children who received or dispensed the particular behavior. Suppose that three children stuck out their tongues at a retarded student. The observer would record a D in the first interval under $M_{0 \to x}$ and following the D write a small "3." Should the observer desire to record the particular response the word "tongue" could be written under the comments section. Anyone analyzing the report would then know that three children engaged in motor disapproval toward the particular pupil.

It is thus possible to observe one or more students at any time. In a newly integrated high school class, for instance, the teacher wished to know the number of approving and disapproving responses directed toward members of each group by all members of the group. In this case, the X would be one group and the 0 would designate the other group. The observer would record the number of responses in each square as well as the symbol A or D. This particular example of recording would indicate the total number of approval or disapproval responses, whether motor or verbal or both, of an entire group in each interval. Similar procedures can be used for any number of questions involving interpersonal responses in classrooms, recreation areas, cafeterias, playgrounds, and so on.

The precise designation of persons being observed depends upon the questions of interest to the persons who are responsible for asking such questions. Should more than two groups or persons be of interest, it is necessary to attach a subsymbol to the A and D. For example, the responses of male and female faculty (two groups) toward male and female students could be of interest. In this case, the A receives a subscript. Thus X represents faculty and 0 represents students. Responses of an approving nature by males is recorded A_m and by females A_f. These kinds of distinctions may, of course, be expanded, but it is suggested that no more than four groups be observed at any one time as it becomes much more difficult with each additional subscript.

Interpersonal observation (Form K)

Precise observations of group interactions are possible with the use of Form K: Interpersonal Observation. Through the analysis of the categories, group totals, individual reactions, and individual or group reactions to a teacher or group leader may be analyzed.

Categories include Verbal, Contact, and Expressions of an approving nature; Verbal, Contact, and Expressions of a disapproving nature; and Neutral interactions.

Observer Name _____ Date _____ Time _____ End _____

Activity _____ Location _____ Reliability Observer _____ Number in Group _____

Page _____ Of _____ Subject Name _____ Subject Number _____

Observation Interval _____ Record Interval _____

	Record A												Record B												Record C												Line Totals											
	APR		NEU		DISAPR			APR		NEU		DISAPR			APR		NEU		DISAPR			APR		NEU		DISAPR	
	V	C	E	V	C	O	V	C	E	V	C	E	V	C	O	V	C	E	V	C	E	V	C	O	V	C	E	V	C	E	V	C	O	V	C	E
1																																				
2																																				
3																																				
4																																				
5																																				
6																																				
7																																				
8																																				
9																																				
10																																				

Page Totals

Form K: Interpersonal Observation

It is recommended for this type of recording that one observer record each participant and indicate the direction of the recorded behavior. For example, if there were eight participants, all would be numbered and the observer watching No. 4 would record each behavior and indicate whether it was directed toward any other participant by recording the other participants' number(s) under the appropriate symbol. Recording in this manner requires a great deal more time for reliability training than the more simple observation codes (twelve to eighteen hours of training).

Should one desire to reconstruct a precise matrix of behavioral interactions, it is necessary to employ some mechanical means of keeping all observers in the same interval at the same time. A prerecorded tape may be used for this purpose. The taped voice begins by warning the observers prior to the first observation and then states "Get ready. . . . Line one. . . . Observe." This is followed by fifteen seconds of blank tape whereupon the taped voice continues; "Record." The recording interval usually constitutes five seconds of blank tape and the recorded voice then continues, "Observe," with fifteen seconds of blank tape, and "Record," with five seconds of blank tape, until four intervals have been recorded. The recorded voice will then state, "Line Two . . . Observe." The taped voice takes little time to prerecord and keeps all observers on-task while reducing unreliability when observers lose their place. Thus these time indicators given every minute allow few problems with observers and eliminate recording in the wrong interval.

Behavioral Definitions

The following behavioral definitions used in analysis of a series of "encounter and personal growth groups" indicate that the categories of Approval, Disapproval, and Neutral are sufficient for almost all interpersonal interactions.

Symbol

V   Verbal: One continuous, audible, meaningful phrase or idea.

Approving Verbal. Verbal communication that indicates either a compliment or caring, correctness, acceptance, or agreement that is unbroken by a different thought or idea.

Examples: Words

yes	fantastic
good	terrific
nice	swell
great	marvelous
fascinating	exactly

	charming	of course
	commendable	cool
	delightful	great
	brilliant	likeable
	fine	wonderful
	uh-huh	outstanding
Apr	positively	exciting
V	go ahead	interesting
	yeah	pleasant
	all right	delicious
	correct	fabulous
	excellent	splendid
	that's right	thoughtful
	perfect	remarkable
	satisfactory	cheerful
	absolutely	friendly
	keep going	elegant
	beautiful	well thought out
	wonderful	

Examples: Sentences

I like you.	You are very friendly.
I respect you for that.	You have a nice
I agree.	That's interesting.
I approve.	Show us how.
I'm glad you're here.	You're doing better.
You make us happy.	That's very good.
That shows thought.	I'm proud of you.
How charming.	That's logical.
We think a lot of you.	You're polite, nice courteous, etc.
You're very pleasant.	You have (a) nice eyes, smile,
You're so outgoing.	personality, etc.
Yes, please continue.	I like your clothes.
A good way of putting it.	

Disapr
V
    Disapproving Verbal. Audible communication of disagreement, dislike, disinterest, nonacceptance, or incorrectness that is unbroken by a different thought or idea

Examples:

Impractical	That's ridiculous, meaningless,
Work faster	absurd, bad, nonsense.
Try to understand.	Too vague
Do your best.	Try harder.
Unclear explanation	That's not right.
Don't you want to do things	Incorrect
right?	You should be ashamed.

It can't be that difficult.   That's not clear.
You're too slow.   I dislike you.
Stop talking.   I dislike that.
Pay attention.   Don't make excuses.
Don't   Listen to me.
Wrong   Leave her alone.
Stupid   You're dull.
Think for a change.   It's hopeless for you.
Use some thought.   You're worthless.
No, that's not what I said.   You're rude.
You don't understand because   Don't laugh at me.
    you don't listen.   That's childish.
You're gutless.   That wasn't the right thing to do.
You'd better get on the stick.   You haven't been paying attention.
You must be confused.   People never change
I don't see your point.   You know better than that.

Neutral Verbal. By exclusion, all other verbal behavior.

Examples:

Neu
V

I went to the store today.   I have two kids.
It sure is hot and humid   It sure is pretty today.
    outside.   I went home yesterday.
It is going to rain.

E

Expressions: Muscular movements of the face or body that express interpersonal meaning.

Approving Expression. Communication by movement of caring, correctness, acceptance, or agreement directed toward some person(s).

Examples: Facial

Apr
E

smiling   widening eyes
winking   wrinkling nose
nodding   blinking rapidly
raising eyebrows   giggling
fawning kiss   whistles
opening eyes   cheering
slowly closing eyes   licking lips
laughing   smacking lips
chucking   rolling eyes

Examples: Bodily

clapping hands   shaking head
raising arms   shrugging shoulders
grabbing   expansive movement of hands
bouncing   taking a fast breath

signaling OK.	opening hands
cocking head	embracing hand or finger to face,
rubbing stomach	hair, head
thumbs up	"right-on" sign

Disapr
E

Disapproving Expression. Communication by movement of dislike, disinterest, nonacceptance or incorrectness directed toward some person(s)

Examples: Expression

frowning	clicking tongue
curling lip	pointing finger
furrowing brows	putting hand behind ear
lowering eyebrows	grimacing
shaking finger or fist	sniffing
squinting eyes	tightening jaw
wrinkling forehead	sticking out tongue
puckering lips	snickering
pounding fist	turning head away
laughing at	letting out breath
shaking head	kissing
turning away	fingers in front of lips
gritting teeth	shaking head no
biting lips	showing teeth
closing eyes	pulling in bottom lip

None   Neutral Expression. Not recorded

Contact: The touching of any parts of the bodies of two or more people

Apr
C

Approving Contact: The touching of another person that expresses caring, correctness, acceptance, or agreement. Examples:

hugging	nudging
patting	holding
kissing	leaning against
touching	caressing

Disapr
C

Disapproving Contact: The touching of another person that expresses dislike, disinterest, nonacceptance, incorrectness (determined by intensity). Examples:

hitting	restraining
grabbing	kicking
pushing	shoving

Neu
O

Neutral contact. Recorded as neutral other. Unintentional contact or passive behavior.

General Instructions: All behaviors should be recorded even if they occur simultaneously. If a person being observed makes a comment, smiles, and touches someone else, then a mark would be placed under verbal, expression, and contact. In addition, all behaviors should be recorded even if they are contradictory. A smile is always recorded as an approval. Sarcasm when it can be recorded is disapproving.

If a behavior begins prior to the record time and its meaning cannot be determined, then record the behavior as neutral. Two or more unbroken statements of the same type (either approving, neutral, or disapproving) are recorded as one unit of behavior. A broken statement is one which is interrupted; a pause is not considered as a break.

The direction of the behavior (toward another member of the group) is sometimes difficult to assess and observe correctly. If the direction of the behavior is unknown, record the behavior under the appropriate symbol by using a question mark. When the behavior is directed toward the group (four or more persons is considered as the group), a G should be used in the appropriate box.

During each observation interval, the observer should be prepared to answer the following questions with recorded data:

Did a vocalization (verbal behavior) occur? If the answer is yes, determine whether it was approving, disapproving, or neutral.
Was there an expression other than neutral? If so, then determine whether it was approving or disapproving.
Was there physical contact? If yes, then determine whether it was approving, disapproving, or neutral.

Should behaviors occur that do not fit any of the category definitions, implied by the above questions during the observation interval, put an X in the Neutral Other category.

General observation (Form L)

Form L: General Observation is an overall model for record keeping. As most teachers realize, behavioral principles are of little use unless accurate records are kept. Behaviors are defined (pinpointed) in precise behavioral terms and then observed by checking occurrences of the defined behavior during the planned recording interval. Consequences are applied systematically and recorded, then the behavior is again measured (recorded) in order to evaluate the effect of the consequences.

The specific behavior to be observed is determined and written on the pinpoint line. The person or persons to be observed are indicated together with the person who is going to do the observation (teacher,

Form L: General Observation

PINPOINT _____   Person(s) observed _____

Observer(s) _____   Location _____

Time of observation _____   Desire that behavior increase decrease _____

I (we) will conduct _____ observations per _____ every _____ for _____
          (number)   (min-hr-day)   (day-wk)   (day-wk)
before consequating takes place

Observation interval _____   Time between obs. _____
          (sec-min-hr-day)   (sec-min-hr-day)

RECORD Each occurrence of Pinpoint			CONSEQUATE Consequences following occurrence of behavior					EVALUATE Each occurrence of Pinpoint		
Date	Obs. Nos.		Date	Obs. Nos.	Approval	Dis-approval	Other	Date	Obs. Nos.	

Total = _____   Totals = _____   _____   Total = _____
No. Obs. = _____   When _____   When _____   No. Obs. = _____
Average = _____   Average = _____

                         (appropriate)   (inappropriate)
Comments _____   for _____   Then this   SUMMARY
_____   (time-times)   disapproval
_____   Then these approvals   will follow: Record total _____
_____   will follow: a. _____   Evaluate total _____
_____   a. _____   Record average _____
_____   b. _____   Evaluate average _____
_____   c. _____   Increase _____
_____   d. _____   Decrease _____

students, themselves, other pupils, teacher aides). The recording times for observations are determined, and whether the behavior is to be increased or decreased is noted by circling the appropriate word. Next the observer makes a contract with himself or the teacher to ensure that a sufficient number of observations (baseline recording) take place prior to the application of consequences.

The Record section includes dates, observation number(s) and a space for checking, or marking in any way, each occurrence of the behavior observed. It is recommended that observations take place over at least a five-day period and/or that ten observations be made to ensure that an accurate representative measure of the behavior has been achieved. The teacher then determines what consequences are to be applied (approval and/or disapproval) and fills in the lower portion of the consequate section. During the Record phase, the teacher has sufficient time to determine just what potential reinforcers are to be used and when these consequences are to be applied (schedule of reinforcement.) The observer records the number of approvals and/or disapprovals. A record of the pinpointed behavior is generally achieved automatically and this gives a preliminary check to see if the behavior is increasing, decreasing, or not changing. However, it is suggested that a teacher apply consequences for two weeks before taking additional observations to evaluate the effectiveness of the program.

Following the application of consequences for two weeks, the observer records in the Evaluate section using exactly the same procedure as was employed during the Record phase. The Summary indicates the effectiveness of the procedures by comparing the Record average with the Evaluate average.

Following completion of Form L, it is generally necessary to maintain the appropriate behavior through effective use of reinforcements. When the environment of the child changes, it is expected that the responses of the child will also change. Self-motivation (response to internal reinforcement) is achieved only after extensive structuring across many different situations. Continual reevaluation and application of appropriate contingencies is almost always necessary.

COMPUTERIZED OBSERVATIONAL INSTRUMENTS

With the advent of computer technology, observational instruments have gained a new perspective. Although any observation is in a sense time sampling, through new technologies sampling can be made, at least during any particular event, more complete. Observations can be done with videotapes of events, and video recorders are commonplace in most institutional settings. Furthermore, computer technology has made observation by taking continuous data, and not needing to stop the observational process to record observations. Three such observational tools are described in this section.

One of the problems with computerized observational tools is the computer itself. Often the computer can be too cumbersome to make it a practical on-site observational instrument. Even with laptop computers, observational attachments can make the process too intrusive to get an accurate observation of the events in a field setting. Most of the time computerized observational tools are best utilized with videotaped classes or sessions. However, with the rapid improvements in technology, the bulkiness of the computerized observational tools, as well as the distracting sounds that can accompany using these devices, may soon be eliminated.

Continuous Response Digital Interface

The Continuous Response Digital Interface (CRDI) makes possible the storage of continuous responses during an observation. The CRDI device connects a potentiometer dial directly to a computer that measures the dial position across a continuum. The dial is mounted on a 13' × 13' Plexiglas board that delineates an arc in which the dial may travel. Each degree of that arc translates to a different digitized number (0-255) which is sampled by the computer up to 10,000 times per second. The Plexiglas board can be labeled in such a way as to assign any meaning to degrees on the dial, and thus to the numerical readout that the observer delineates. This technology has proved useful in measuring responses during a variety of observational tasks. The reliability of this instrument has been established in many separate studies and has been very high.

SCRIBE

SCRIBE, Simple Computer Recording Interface for Behavioral Evaluation, developed by Robert Duke at the University of Texas-Austin in 1998, is a computer software program that allows for the timed recording of events. The user defines all behaviors to be observed and designs a simple computer screen with buttons for each event noted. Only the computer screen limits the number, size, and layout of the buttons. The observer then clicks a button to indicate the presence of a behavior, and all "clicks" are recorded through time. The output of this program presents a chronological record of computerized clicks.

ProBES

The Professional Behavior Evaluation System is a behavioral observation tool that solves most problems that exist with other observation programs. It runs on a pocket computer that is transportable. It allows for data collection over events, duration, and partial interval schedules. It saves templates and is easily customized. It allows for data collection on as many as six behaviors in four different treatment conditions. Obviously this is a very flexible instrument that can easily be adapted to many settings. However, in the effort to make it small enough to be transported, it must also be used for limited tasks.

OBSERVATIONAL ANALYSIS

Observational information should include all necessary identification as well as a complete summary. Observational forms include an analysis section (on the back or front) which should be completed.

Frequency: All discrete observational symbols recorded (marked or written) should be counted across all intervals and the total number written on the line opposite the appropriate symbol.

Percentages: After recording the frequency of various behaviors, the relative frequency with which each rated behavior has occurred should be computed. It may be desirable to express observational findings in terms of the percentage of observational intervals in which a given behavior was recorded, rather than dealing only with frequency.

The percentage of occurrences for each discrete symbol is found by dividing the total number of times a symbol was recorded by the total number of intervals over which observation was conducted. For example, let us assume that Aa is recorded four times in a 15 minute observation, three 10-second observations being made each minute. The numerator in this case is four. The denominator is found by multiplying the number of minutes in the observation period (IS minutes) by the number of observation periods per minute (three). In this example, the denominator is 45. When the necessary division is made, it is found that during .088 or .09 or 9 percent of the intervals observed, an approval for academic behavior was recorded. In the same manner, percentages may be obtained for all other symbols.

Percentages for any symbol or combination of symbols may be graphed across time intervals such as subject periods, times a day, days, or weeks. Such a graph will supply information as to whether the behavior(s) being observed is increasing, decreasing, or remaining the same. Applications of specific consequences may be indicated and changes in behavior noted.

Reliability Computation

Observer reliability concerns the amount of agreement/disagreement on the part of various observers when observing the same behaviors at the same time. In behavioral observation it is very important to determine the measure of agreement between two observers. This is expressed as a percentage

—how often do two observers watching the same behavior record it as the same behavior? In this way it is possible to check the accuracy of any classroom observation.

While it is important to assess interobserver reliability, it is also usually not practical to have two observers at all times. Reliability training can be conducted and then one may assume that reliable observation is achieved. Generally a reliability coefficient of .80 is considered a minimal average. After training, reliability should be assessed often to be certain there is not a systematic change in one or more observers. It has been determined that when reliability checks occur 20 percent of the total observation time with subsequent observer feedback, then observers remain reliable. Of course, some particular projects may require additional reliability checks.

When calculating observer reliability, each discrete symbol is listed separately. For computation, use the reliability section of the observer form and record the number of times observer 1 and the reliability observer agree for each symbol in the same time intervals. Thus, if As behavior has been checked on both forms in the third interval of the second time period and the first interval of the fourth time period, then two agreements would be recorded for the As category. Similarly, if Da behavior occurred in the second interval of the first time period, the third interval of the tenth time period, and the first interval of the fifteenth time period on both observer forms, then three agreements would be recorded for the Da symbol. To compute reliability, systematically check each symbol on both forms in every interval for agreements.

The next stage is to record the number of times both observers disagree for each symbol. When each observer has a different symbol checked in the same interval, disagreement is recorded under both symbols. For example, if a Ds behavior occurred on one observation sheet and a Da behavior occurred on the other sheet, both in the first interval of the third time period, then a disagreement would be recorded for each symbol (Ds and Da). This procedure is continued across the entire observation with the total number of agreements and disagreements being recorded for each symbol.

Nothing is also a category and can be recorded with a horizontal line through the interval. This category may be included in reliability calculations. However it is better that reliability approaches .80 using defined categories only.

In the final stage, sum the total number of agreements and total number of disagreements for all symbols. Next, divide the sum of the total number of agreements by the sum of total agreements plus total disagreements in order to obtain a percentage of reliability, as shown:

$$\frac{\text{Total Number Agreements}}{\text{Total Number Agreements plus Disagreements}} = \begin{array}{l}\text{Percentage} \\ \text{Reliability}\end{array}$$

While there are many different formulas to compute reliability, the above is both stringent and manageable enough to be used with all observers.

Observer reliability for group off-task student behavior uses the same basic rationale and is calculated as follows:

$$\frac{\dfrac{(N - [n_1 - n_2]) + \ldots + (N - [n_1 - n_2])}{N} \qquad \dfrac{(N - [n_1 - n_2])}{N}}{100} = \frac{}{} \%$$

where N = total number of students under observation in each interval, and

n_1 = number of students observed off-task by the first observer.
n_2 = number of students observed off-task by the second observer.

Observational Summary

Accurate recording, assessment of social behavior, and subsequent remediation seem to be the most important considerations when students are referred for inappropriate behavior. Unfortunately, when many students are referred, they are taken out of the environment where the problem is occurring (the classroom) and are administered tests by a professional who only rarely observes the child in the classroom. The use of a combination of observational procedures (including tests), when analyzed properly, are generally more beneficial to teachers. However, cursory nonsystematic observation does not appear to be any better than other types of nonspecific evaluation. The environmental situation must be carefully analyzed (baseline) by rigorous observation, and a specific plan designated for implementation. Discussions may then be held with appropriate personnel and procedures determined to alter the student's inappropriate responses. Diagnostic evaluation, whether by tests or observation, seems limited unless remedial steps are planned and implemented in the classroom where the maladaptive behaviors occur.

Complete analysis of a child's problem requires that the person who is to interpret the results knows the implications of the results. If a teacher is told that a child who was referred for observation engages in 50 percent inappropriate behavior, what conclusion can be drawn? Obviously the conclusion must be based upon answers to some of the following questions: Were the inappropriate behaviors of a passive variety or active interference with other children? What behaviors of the teacher or peers served to maintain or reinforce the inappropriate behavior? Was the activity during which the student was observed of such a nature that the whole class was approaching 50 percent off-task behavior? What constitutes the baseline of appropriate behavior for this class during these particular activities? How many observations of other members of the class have been taken under similar circumstances? Were the behaviors of an interpersonal nature? What is the academic achievement level of the student during this activity? Is the academic material geared to the student's level? What is the level of off-task behavior in other activities with the same teacher? Different teachers? What reinforcers are important to the particular student? Does the teacher use appropriate rewards for this student as well for others?

An analysis of answers to these and similar questions is generally necessary if the student is to be helped to achieve his/her highest potential.

STUDY GUIDE FOR CHAPTER 8

Questions:

1. Explain why it is not possible to observe ignoring.

2. What observation form would be most useful in observing student/teacher interactions? Why?

3. What would you expect within a classroom if the teacher gives an extremely high amount of approval to appropriate academic behavior but makes approval social mistakes?

4. What would you expect within a classroom where the teacher pays a great deal of attention to appropriate social behavior but ignores most academic behavior?

5. Why is it necessary to observe in small amounts of time if one is observing interpersonal and very subtle interactions?

6. Do you believe that it is more damaging (in the long run) for the teacher to make approval mistakes or disapproval mistakes? Why?

7. Why is it necessary to observe a student if the teacher can already tell what the student's problem is?

8. Why is it necessary to compute reliability? How valid are observations without some reliability check?

9. What would you list (from your own observations) as the most important positive aspect of the teaching/learning situation? What was the most negative aspect?

10. Is it possible from your observation to ascertain why some children are "liked" more by some teachers? Is it because the children are "nice"? Is it because teachers treat them with approval and therefore they become that way?

LEARNING ACTIVITY 15— OBSERVATIONAL EVALUATION

Instruction:

Study carefully Chapter 8, paying special attention to the definitional categories. Complete all answers on the Observational Evaluation. Small discussion groups provide an excellent method to check the accuracy of the test responses and in addition develop a general competency in the application of observational rules prior to actual classroom observation.

Part I: For each category listed below, please put the appropriate symbol to the right of the category.

Teacher reinforcement categories

1. Approval Mistake (Social) _____

2. Disapproval (Academic) _____

3. Approval (Social) _____

4. Approval Mistake (Academic) _____

5. Disapproval Mistake (Social) _____

6. Instructions _____

Student categories

7. Verbal (Noise) Off-Task _____

8. Motor Off-Task _____

9. On-Task _____

10. Passive Off-Task _____

Part II: Below are listed the rules for Mrs. Jones' classroom. Using these rules, check the appropriate space(s) as to how the specific behaviors should be categorized.

Rules for specific activity

1. Work quietly (no talking).

2. During this period work individually on math in your seat.

3. Raise your hand to receive help.

4. You may get materials without permission.

5. Sign in and out on the list for going to the restroom without asking permission.

Part II A. You are observing the students. Record behaviors using the observational code:

	On-Task	Off-Task	None Apply
	N	M	O

11. One student is talking to his neighbor.

12. Student is quietly writing spelling words.

13. Student is staring out the window while chewing on his pencil.

14. Student is working in seat on math.

15. Student lies on floor working on math.

16. Student is staring out of window.

17. Student signs list to go to restroom, but does not ask teacher's permission.

18. You can see the student talking to his neighbor, but you cannot hear him.

19. Student is turned 45 degrees in his seat.

20. Student turns around 90 degrees and talks to her neighbor.

21. Student hits his neighbor.

22. Student calls out to teacher.

23. Student staring at floor.

	On- Task N	Off- Task M	None Apply O
24. Teacher asks student a question and student responds with an incorrect answer.			
25. Student gets up to get materials.			
26. On the way back from getting materials, the student stops and talks with another student.			
27. A child puts up his hand and looks around the room.			
28. A student is talking to himself.			
29. A student is gently drumming his desk while working on math.			
30. A student is asking a fellow student about an assignment.			

Part II B: Teacher Behaviors
        Record teacher behaviors using the following code:

Aa	Approval-Academic	As	Approval-Social
Da	Disapproval-Academic	N	Disapproval-Social
(As)	Approval Mistake-Academic	(As)	Approval Mistake-Social
(Da)	Disapproval Mistake-Academic	(Ds)	Disapproval Mistake-Social
		–	No Behavior Rated

If more than one code applies, use the following order of importance:

1. Mistakes of Reinforcement
2. Approval
3. Disapproval

31. "That's a correct answer but sit down while working." _____

32. "That's good; you raised your hand for help." _____

33. Teacher asks student to respond.   _____

34. "Sit up straight. You look sloppy."   _____

35. Teacher gently places hand on student while telling
    him to sit down.   _____

36. "The whole class is doing well."
    (Two students off-task)   _____

37. Student blurts out answer and teacher says,
    "That's correct, Jimmy."   _____

38. "I don't want to hear another word for the
    next ten minutes."   _____

39. Teacher calls on student who is quiet but
    does not have hand up. (Student behaving
    appropriately except that his hand is not up.)   _____

40. Student is out of his seat and taps teacher
    on shoulder. Teacher says, "Sit down, Johnny.
    I will not talk to you unless you raise your hand."   _____

41. Student is out of seat and touches teacher.
    The teacher puts his arm on shoulder and says,
    "Sit down. I will not talk to you unless your hand
    is raised."   _____

42. "No, Johnny. That is not the right answer."   _____

43. "This class is just not working."
    (Two students are working.)   _____

44. "Except for Linda and Jane, who are working
    very nicely, the rest of you are behaving abominably.
    Sit down and stop talking."   _____

45. The teacher responds to a student's answer to
    a question by repeating the student's answer.   _____

46. The teacher inadvertently marks a correct
    answer as incorrect.   _____

47. "Johnny, you're always raising your hand
    to answer. Let someone else answer for a change."   _____

48. "Johnny, stop copying Jimmy's paper."   _____

49. "That's almost right."   _____

50. The teacher puts her arm around a student and says,
    "These problems are all correct," when in fact,
    two are incorrect.   _____

LEARNING ACTIVITY 16—CLASSROOM OR ROLE-PLAYING OBSERVATIONS

Participants should be separated into small groups of approximately four to six and will discuss human relations problems while keeping records of group interactions.* Prior to discussion, the group should determine the period of time that each record keeper will maintain the record, list each participant's name on the form, decide upon topics to discuss, set the timer, and begin discussions. Following each discussion period, the record keeper should tally the number of positive and negative comments and approving and disapproving bodily expressions and report totals for all group members prior to beginning the next discussion session. The same procedure should be repeated either until the time is used or until all members of the group have had the opportunity to be recorders.

The previous form is an indication of how the record will look after each recording session.

Note: An extension of this activity has proved to be very effective in reducing negative comments in teachers' lounges, principals' offices, homes, and work areas. Construct a large chart with the name of each person written down the side of the chart and whenever any other person in the vicinity hears either a positive or negative word or comment from any other member of the group that person goes to the chart and puts a mark under either the positive or negative half of the sheet. This procedure has increased approving statements and decreased disapproving statements.

*Rotate record keeper approximately every five minutes. A kitchen timer with a bell is most effective as it reminds the group to stay on-task as well as indicates the time to change record keepers.

INTERACTION ANALYSIS FOR GROUP DISCUSSIONS

Date _____

General Topic _____ (Time: Start _____ End _____

Number in Group _____ Observation Interval _____

Names of Participants	APPROVAL		DISAPPROVAL	
	Words*	Expressions**	Words†	Expressions††
Bob *Complainer*			卌 卌 /	卌 ///
Jane *Ambivalent*	卌 /	///	卌 /	///
Sam *Kindly*	卌 卌 卌 卌	卌 卌 ////		
Suzy *Average*	////	/	卌 /	//

*Words-Approval are positive comments, defined as specified solutions to specific problems

**Expressions-Approval are bodily or facial expressions of an approving nature

†Words-Disapproval are negative comments, defined as the statement of problems with no specified solutions

††Expressions-Disapproval are bodily or facial expressions of a disapproving nature

Techniques for Consequating Behavior

Behavior is constantly being modified. As societal agents, either we modify the behavior of our students/clients purposefully, or it happens by chance. Only through careful observation can we understand the elements of behavioral change. Behavior is usually the result of some **antecedent** environmental event. The **behavior** is a sequential result and is followed by some **consequence**, which is perceived by the subject as good. If the consequence to that behavior is not "good," when presented with the same antecedent events a different behavior will likely occur. However, that is only if the student/client has another behavior in his/her repertoire of behaviors. It is the task of the societal agent to understand both the antecedent event and the reinforcements operating in the subject's environment. Furthermore, the societal agent has the responsibility to control the environment such that the person's behavioral choices include positive options that can be appropriately reinforced.

STRATEGIES FOR TEACHING NEW BEHAVIOR

Most strategies for teaching new behaviors do not include specific reinforcement as much as they set an environmental antecedent event that will encourage an appropriate behavioral response. Once the student has responded, it is critical that reinforcement accompanies the resulting appropriate behavior.

Task Analysis

Possibly one of the most important and difficult aspects of teaching any new skill is to analyze all of the steps that contribute to successful completion of the task. A task analysis is the process of breaking down any complex behavior into its smallest component parts. A task analysis requires the societal agent to determine every step, link, or component of an activity, and to order and arrange them such that the student can complete the task correctly. This activity is closely related to errorless learning, chaining, shaping, and modeling. Teachers can apply task analysis to behaviors as simple as drinking from a cup, or as complex as writing a thesis.

The process of task analysis includes a starting point, an end goal, the necessary materials, and a systematic procedure for teaching the task. An example of a hand washing task analysis might be:

Assemble: soap, soap dish, running water, paper towels, and waste can.
1. Put one paper towel in hand.
2. With paper towel held between the hand and faucet, turn on the faucet.
3. Adjust water temperature.
4. Dispose of paper towel in waste can.
5. Wet hands with the fingertips pointed downward.
6. Pick up soap.
7. Lather hands well.
8. Rinse soap off.
9. Replace soap in soap dish.
10. Rub hands together in circular motion and by interlacing fingers.
11. Clean fingernails.
12. Pick up soap again.
13. Lather hands well.
14. Rinse soap.
15. Replace soap in soap dish.
16. Rub hands together in circular motion and by interlacing fingers.
17. Rinse hands, fingertips down.
18. Dry hands thoroughly with paper towels.
19. Dispose of paper towels in waste can.
20. Put one paper towel in hand.
21. With paper towel held between hand and faucet, turn off the faucet.
22. Dispose of paper towel in waste can.

If a student/client has already acquired many of the prerequisite skills, it may be possible to skip several steps in this analysis. However, if the student/client is in need of additional help, it may be necessary to add some steps. This is especially important if the student/client makes any mistakes in completing the task. If that occurs, we misestimated and did not break down the task into enough component parts in the first place. This error in judgement will likely teach a mistake, which the student/client must unlearn and replace with a correct response. Task analysis is a difficult skill to learn, but once learned, is one of the most important skills anyone can master, and may be a key behavior in what determines the difference between an average teacher/therapist and a truly exceptional one.

Prompts

A prompt is the most basic building block for aiding a person to respond correctly. It is simply an additional stimulus that increases the probability of a desired response. Most people have had the occasion of seeing a toddler make a demand on a parent without saying "please." The parent may then prompt appropriate manners by asking what word was left out (verbal), or by looking at the child inquisitively until the child responds with the word "please" (visual). Prompts can be discarded when no longer needed.

The effective use of prompts requires the societal agent to attend to several influences. Among those influences are issues concerning focusing subjects' attention while not distracting from the task at hand. Distractions can occur in any number of ways, not the least of which might be an over-illustration or an interruption of the thought process while the student is formulating a response. Prompts should be as non-intrusive as possible, yet still result in the desired behavior. If a prompt is too strong, learning may be replaced with frustration.

There are three types of prompts. The least intrusive type of prompt is a *visual* prompt. Examples of visual cues include touching a forefinger to lips in order to signal for silence, or reminding a student/client of the class rules by raising one's own hand when they respond without raising theirs. Other types of visual cues can include writing rules on the board as a reminder of classroom rules, or the use of a bulletin board to post notices. Most teachers/therapists give many visual cues to remind students/clients of appropriate behavior; it is important that they perceive these visual prompts in the manner intended.

The second type of prompt is *verbal*. A verbal prompt can be simply presenting an additional question to a student/client, or giving an additional direction. A verbal prompt is meant to provide a cue for the student/client to engage in an appropriate behavior. For example, a grade school teacher tells a class to line up "quietly." "Lining up" is the instruction, but "quietly" functions as a prompt designed to increase the probability of *correctly* lining up. Students perceive verbal prompts aurally.

The final type of prompt is *physical guidance*. This type of prompt is generally more intrusive than the other types. It includes physical contact with the student/client in order to cue or guide a manual skill. It is often accompanied with verbal instruction. One critical aspect of physical guidance is that the implementation of this prompt must not be restraining or perceived as negative by the student/client. When engaging in this activity, the teacher/therapist must be sure that the student/client is not resistant. One must also be sure that the student/client does not perceive something other than the physical guidance prompt. Though this type of prompt is often thought of as being used with persons with disabilities in order to teach certain motor skills, it is also often used when students/clients are beginning to write, color, or when students are beginning to play a musical instrument. The subject perceives physical guidance prompts in a tactile manner. It is important when using physical prompts that no inappropriate behaviors are being given by the teacher/therapist or cued by the student.

Fading

The process of *fading prompts* is very similar to the process of *thinning reinforcement*. Eventually all prompts must be eliminated if the student/client is to be independent. The goal is to ensure that the least intrusive directions will elicit appropriate responses, and that the behaviors themselves will eventually become reinforcing. However, there are two problems with fading: (a) if fading occurs too quickly, the behavior will discontinue; alternately, (b) if fading occurs too slowly, students may become dependent upon the prompt. Either way, fading prompts should be done thoughtfully and not haphazardly. If not done correctly, over time, behavioral responses might not develop as expected.

Errorless Learning

Errorless learning is a procedure using prompts to establish accurate learning as rapidly as possible without making *any* mistakes. Once a mistake is made, a person is likely to repeat it. A step by step plan to prompt only correct responses allows a person to complete a task without learning mistakes, and therefore, not having problems to correct. The task is then repeated while the prompts are faded as a new skill develops accurately.

An example of errorless learning could include a "programmed text" or any other approach that ensures errorless learning. The teacher/therapist begins by presenting material that includes the correct answer. An example of this might be in teaching children the capitol cities for each state. For example, the instructor might begin by saying: "The capitol of Utah is Salt Lake City; Salt Lake City is the capitol of Utah." "Brandon, the capitol city of Utah is Salt Lake ____?" The teacher waits for the correct response making sure that the student responds correctly, and so on.

An example of fading could come when the instructor first quizzes the students on state capitols, where both the states and capitol cities are evident on the chalkboard. However, as the days pass, the teacher ever so slightly erases the answers so that they become lighter and lighter on the board. Eventually the board is so clean that the answers are no longer discernible.

Such a procedure has its advantages and disadvantages. Advantages include learning only correct information and not having to re-learn because material was learned incorrectly as would probably be the case if new learning began with the teacher saying: "Children, I want someone to guess what the capitol of Kentucky is." One disadvantage to errorless discrimination learning is that students might not acquire certain problem solving skills if never presented with the frustrating task of trial and error learning. Furthermore, outside of the classroom, students must solve different types of problems, sometimes without appropriate reinforcement. While it may be possible to teach problem solving skills in an environment using errorless learning techniques, it is still the subject of debate.

Many teachers use both errorless learning and trial and error learning by making a distinction between *facts*, which are taught with errorless learning, as facts ought not to be debatable. Yet concerning *value judgements* (which by definition are not facts and are often debatable) teachers use a questioning format by asking each student what the individual student thinks or believes. For example, "Brandon, if you lived in Utah, do you think that you would like to live in Salt Lake City, or would you rather live in a smaller Utah town?"

Chaining

Sequences of behaviors that combine to make up a complex task are called behavioral chains. If a nursery school teacher were to instruct students to stand in a circle, children might attempt the task, but it could be chaotic and would not likely result in a good circle for quite some time. However, if that same teacher did the necessary task analysis for standing in a circle, the instructions might resemble:

Minding everyone's personal space (prompt), slowly (prompt) walk up to the front of the room.

Minding everyone's personal space (repeated prompt), hold your right hand straight out in front of you.

Slowly (prompt) move until everyone's right hand is touching everybody else's right hand in the center.

Everyone, drop your hands to your sides.

Take one step back.

Result: students standing in a circle. After the students practice the chain a few times, it is likely that each step would become a cue for the next step. The teacher could truncate the steps over time until at the instruction to form a circle, the students would comply successfully.

Forward Chaining

When using forward chaining, the teacher/therapist begins with the first task in the chain and teaches it. Once that is mastered, the next behavior in the sequence is added. Teaching a student/client to spell his or her name using forward chaining would begin with teaching the first letter, then the first and second letter, and so forth until the student could spell the whole name without prompting.

This might be scripted as follows:

> Teacher (T): M
> Student (S): M
> T: M – i
> S: M – i
> T: M – i – k
> S: M – i – k
> T: M – i – k – e
> S: M – i – k – e
> T: Spell your name
> S: M – i – k – e

Backward Chaining

When employing backward chaining, students/clients acquire components of the behavioral sequence in reverse order. When the student/client masters one link, the teacher/therapist removes another. If one were to teach someone to spell his/her name using backward chaining techniques, the teacher/therapist would spell out the entire name. Then the name would be spelled again leaving out the last letter and having the student/client say the missing letter. This would continue until the student/client could spell the whole word and the teacher/therapist would simply prompt the beginning of spelling.

This might be scripted as follows:

> Therapist (T) & Student (S): M – i – k – e
> T & S: M – i – k
> S: e
> T & S: M – i
> S: k – e
> T & S: M
> S: i – k – e
> T & S: M
> S: M – i – k – e
> T: Spell your name
> S: M – i – k – e

Shaping

Shaping represents differential reinforcement of successive approximations toward a specified target behavior. One must understand several aspects of this technique to be successful. Shaping starts with an existing behavior and modifies it toward a new target behavior through reinforcing each successive approximation toward the final goal. In order for shaping to occur, there must be some current behavior on which to build; otherwise, a new behavior must be taught before shaping can occur. There is an infinite difference between no behavior and the first behavior. Beginning at the student's/client's initial level of competence and setting small increments for improvement are necessary in order that the student/client comes in contact with the reinforcers. A shaping project for academic achievement might be as follows:

Current behavior: The student comes to class almost every day with a pencil and paper. In the process of taking vocabulary tests, the student usually does not spell or use any words correctly.

Target behavior: Student spells and uses all words on the vocabulary test correctly.

Successive approximations to the goal receiving reinforcement might include:

1. Coming to class with pencil and paper.
2. (Teacher gives the student one word for the test) Writing down the vocabulary word spelled correctly.
3. Student writes down the vocabulary word correctly several times.
4. Student writes the vocabulary word with the definition.
5. Student writes and uses the vocabulary word correctly on a one-word test.
6. Teacher repeats the process with two words, and so on.

Modeling

Modeling is one of the strongest techniques for teaching new behaviors. Studies have shown that people are constantly reinforced for imitating others. From the very earliest stages of infancy, parents reinforce children for acting like the parents. Children reinforce each other for "doing it like me," and many children's games are structured on this premise (e.g., follow the leader). Imitating positive models is, most often, a good thing. However, children and adults may also choose to imitate models that do not exhibit desirable behaviors. Furthermore, just as teachers/therapists model with purpose, inadvertent modeling occurs constantly. The cliché "do as I say, not as I do" makes this point. It should be a primary goal for teachers/therapists to model exactly what they want their students/clients to do, and avoid "working against themselves" by modeling inappropriate behaviors or responses.

STRATEGIES FOR INCREASING BEHAVIORS

Positive Reinforcement

Positive reinforcement is the contingent presentation of a stimulus following a response that increases the future probability of that response. The three key words in this definition are presentation, contingent, and increases. The positive aspect of positive reinforcement refers to the *presentation* of a stimulus, as opposed to the removal of one. The last word refers to an increase in behavior, which is the operational definition of reinforcement. The final operative word is *contingent*. If positive reinforcement is to function as intended, it must be delivered only as the result of appropriate behavior; only then is the target behavior likely to reoccur.

Reinforcers must be chosen with specific individuals in mind because a positive reinforcer (by definition) must result in an increase in behavior—it is the function, not the intention that matters. Something that functions as a reinforcer for one student may not necessarily function for another. It is therefore not enough to choose a reinforcer for a class and expect it to function for everyone. Reinforcers must be individualized as well as contingent. There are many different types of reinforcers, and an infinite number of variations for each type (See Chapter 7).

Primary Reinforcers

Primary reinforcers are stimuli that have a direct biological (survival) connection to the individual. These reinforcers are generally considered natural, unlearned, and hence, unconditioned. Examples of primary reinforcers include food, liquid, sleep, some types of touching, and shelter. *Caution:* While primary reinforcers are extremely effective, most often they should not be used contingently except within regulated strict guidelines. Often institutional policies prohibit any use of primary reinforcers.

In order for the chosen primary reinforcer to function, the subject must be in a state of deprivation. Using food to reinforce behavior right after the student/client has returned from lunch would most likely prove ineffective; however, using food as a reinforcer for appropriate behavior prior to lunch may serve as an excellent motivator for future behavior. This does not mean that a student/client must be starving for food to function. However, if the student/client is satiated, more food will likely not prove motivating.

Satiation is also a problem with any reinforcer, but seems principally applicable to primary reinforcers. If a raisin is given for each correct response, eventually raisins will lose their effectiveness. In most cases, students/clients get full, and certainly full of raisins. It may be necessary to modify the reinforcer so that a variety of foods are available. Thinning the reinforcement rate may also be appropriate. The student then might receive a raisin for every two or three correct responses. The use of primary reinforcers should be used with great caution. If used, the goal for teachers and therapists is to replace primary reinforcers with secondary reinforcers as quickly as possible.

Secondary Reinforcers

Secondary reinforcers are stimuli that have direct social implications for an individual. These reinforcers are generally considered to be learned, and hence, conditioned reinforcers. Secondary reinforcers include words of praise, positive social interactions, opportunities to engage in preferred activities, and tangible items.

Social Reinforcers

All *social reinforcers* are, by definition, secondary learned reinforcers. Almost everyone uses social reinforcers unwittingly. Indeed, social reinforcers are so ubiquitous that many people do not even consider them as reinforcers. The unfortunate aspect of this "natural" approach is that because it is often unwitting, it can also be accidental and mistakes can be made because of being off-task. There are an unlimited number of social reinforcers when the nuance of each behavior is considered, but most are categorized as words and expressions, or proximity and touching (See chapter 7).

Note that although social reinforcers often function as rewards for appropriate behavior, a student/client might interpret these responses negatively. A slight variation in nuance of expression, or subtle change in proximity, may alter the meaning of the interaction. Furthermore, touching intended to be positive can function either positively or negatively depending on the person touched. Even a pat on the back can be mistimed or unadvisable under certain conditions.

The second aspect of social reinforcers is that if delivered appropriately, they require that the teacher's/therapist's *attention* be directed toward the student/client. The cliché *All he wants is a little attention* probably applies to everyone. Indeed, many would say that this is all most humans of all ages want. This may be the reason why social reinforcers can have the ability to be so strong. Unlike many of the other secondary reinforcers, they provide one person with another person's attention. Attention is very reinforcing.

Tangible Reinforcers

Objects presented subsequent to the performance of a target behavior that increase the probability of that behavior being repeated is called a *tangible* reinforcer. Tangible reinforcers include small toys, trinkets, check marks, stickers, and a variety of things.

Activity Reinforcers (Premack principle)

The *Premack* principle states that if access to a high frequency behavior is made contingent on the completion of a low frequency behavioral task, then the low frequency behavior is likely to be completed. It has been hypothesized that high frequency behaviors can simply be identified through free operant observation. For example, "You may go play outside" (high frequency behavior) "when you have finished cleaning your room" (low frequency behavior).

Activity reinforcers might also be highly prized activities that do not necessarily represent high frequency activities. For instance, a class may not engage in CD parties often, but a teacher might use one as a reinforcer. For example, "We will have a CD music party" (preferred but not high frequency activity) "if everyone completes the mathematics assignment" (low frequency behavior). These examples may be considered as withholding approval.

Generalized Conditioned Reinforcers

A generalized conditioned reinforcer (*generalized reinforcer*) is one that provides access to other types of reinforcement. The other type of reinforcement can be either primary or any variety of secondary reinforcement. A clear example of this is money. Money, in and of itself, possesses little value, but it does allow a person access to many other things as well as activities. A second example of a generalized reinforcer would be a token. Again, while tokens, like money, have no inherent value, they allow the person possessing them to choose any reinforcing item from the options provided in the token economy (see below).

Pairing

The combined use of primary and secondary reinforcement is *pairing*. The task is to present the primary reinforcer with the secondary reinforcer consistently and contingently for appropriate behavior. Eventually the societal agent will begin to gradually thin the use of the primary reinforcer, while maintaining the delivery of the secondary reinforcer. The end goal is to remove the primary reinforcement while maintaining the secondary reinforcer, and for it to function as strongly as the primary reinforcer did at the beginning of the program. With persons for whom secondary reinforcers have no value, primary reinforcers may be necessary. However, as the goal is to have no one dependent on primary reinforcers, their use should always be in conjunction with secondary reinforcers.

Note that most students have a reinforcement history that includes several secondary reinforcers. Instead of ever choosing to use primary reinforcers, it might serve the teacher/therapist better to seek a wider range of secondary reinforcement options first. However, the student/client may be responding to less attractive secondary reinforcers, necessitating that the societal agent use pairing techniques in order to create a new set of functioning reinforcers. For example, a therapist might find that a client will work for stickers but not praise. The therapist may then provide stickers paired with praise to reinforce the student. Eventually presentation of stickers would diminish until praise alone would function to maintain the desired behavior.

Token Economy

Token economies have become widely used in schools. They require two components: tokens and back-up reinforcers. A token, by definition, does not have any inherent value, but is delivered to a person such that a person may use it to "buy something." The token may be poker chips, game pieces, pieces of construction paper, washers, check marks, or even holes punched in a special card. People exchange these tokens for a variety of back-up reinforcers. Back-up reinforcers can include both primary and secondary reinforcers such as food items, special privileges, special activities, toys, and even bolts to hold washer tokens. The selection of back-up reinforcers can be one of the most difficult aspects of a token economy. If the "menu" does not include a back-up reinforcer that reinforces every person, then individuals may well choose not to participate. This undermines the token economy system and it will not succeed. Furthermore, there must be a variety of back-up reinforcement levels, such that some people can save for big things, while others can spend tokens as soon as they get them (some people need more frequent or instant gratification).

Setting up the economy takes thorough planning regarding how the economy will function. There must be enough tokens in the economy to allow for saving. Furthermore, there must be a way to account for tokens. As with any economy, there is always the possibility of theft and forgery, which would devalue the economy and the behavior of the participants. There must also be parameters set with regard to delivery of tokens, their subsequent care, and how and when tokens may be exchanged for back-up reinforcers.

It is easily seen how a token economy system can become a monumental task. Token systems can also be very effective in teaching many behaviors. Probably the most consequential aspect of a token economy is also the most often overlooked. In the absence of an overall proliferating economy throughout the entire system the economy must eventually be eliminated. Any economy that is begun must have a starting and ending date. Furthermore, when the economy has been eliminated, another reinforcement system must take its place. The goal of the economy is not simply to encourage student/client participation, but also to get them to begin to be reinforced by more naturally occurring reinforcements. Before implementing a token economy, a plan for fading and hence eventual termination must be in place.

Contracting

The act of *contracting* places a contingency for reinforcement into a written document. The contract itself becomes a permanent record to which all can refer in order to answer questions or avoid uncertainties. Good contracts have many components that provide for simplicity, clarity, and reinforcement.

The contract must consider the student's/client's current behavior. If a person cannot sit for 3 minutes, it does little good to contract for 40.

The contract must specify the behavior and the criterion level.

The contract must include the type, amount, and method of delivery of the reinforcement.

The contract should specify its beginning and ending dates.

Contracts for large goal behaviors should include successive approximations toward long-term goals.

Contracts should be phrased positively. Rather than focus on inappropriate behaviors, the contract should specify desired behaviors and state the rewards available for goals met. If a contract focuses on specific undesirable behaviors, a student/client might engage in an infinite number of different behaviors that are as destructive as the original behaviors; however, if the contract is met, reinforcement must be forthcoming.

One should be aware that tangible, activity, and generalized reinforcers are commonly used in contracts. It is rare that social reinforcers are included in a contract. If the ultimate goal is behavior management through naturally occurring reinforcement, then one should carefully pair social reinforcement with the contracted rewards. Eventually the contracted contingency (as well as the contract) should become unnecessary.

Group Contingencies

Group contingencies can be a very strong means of managing behavior toward both positive and negative outcomes. Peer pressure plays an important role in most young people's lives as in the case of street gangs who engage in deviant behavior. Alternately, group contingencies can be used to facilitate positive outcomes. Although there are many varieties of group contingencies and methods for their implementation, the one most often used is when a reward for an entire class is made contingent on the behavior of every student. If one student does not achieve the target behavior, no reinforcement is forthcoming for anyone in the group. If used wisely, group contingencies can be a very effective management device. Furthermore, group contingencies can be excellent training for life outside of the classroom.

An example of this method might be "If everyone quietly works at their desks for the next 10 minutes, we will add 10 minutes to recess after lunch." As long as all students work quietly at their desks, everyone will receive an extended recess time. However, if any one person either makes noise or leaves her/his desk, the entire group is penalized. One problem with this system is that one person's indiscretion results in others not receiving extended recess. Though this may not be perceived as "fair" for those who behave appropriately, arguing the fairness of any system is generally unproductive, and being drawn into an argument of fairness is unwise. Fair might be that the contingency was set by the societal agent, and the fair thing to do is carry out the constructed paradigm. This situation is only serious when the teacher's contingency for reinforcement is set so high that there is the strong possibility that there are students in the group not capable of meeting the criterion. In this case, the teacher has erred.

If this type of contingency is setup, the teacher (in order to be fair) must not give any second chances regarding talking or out-of-seat behaviors. The first time a student violates a rule, the "reward" is removed (i.e., recess cannot be extended). As long as the teacher remains unemotional, students will likely blame the student who did not behave appropriately. Sometimes students engage in retaliation toward the offending person. This is a drawback of a group-oriented contingency; while it is intended to place the responsibility on all students, the punishment toward any wrong doer might "take on a life of its own." Teachers must plan for potential consequences.

Another caution is that if any student does not enjoy recess, he or she may sabotage the group by behaving inappropriately. Although this type of situation should be addressed on an individual basis, it is likely that peer pressure will outweigh the unpleasantness of an extended recess. (See essays *What Constitutes Reward* and *Is the World Fair?* Chapter 4).

Negative Reinforcement

Negative reinforcement is the contingent removal of an aversive stimulus following a behavior that increases the future probability of the response reoccurring. Whereas in positive reinforcement the societal agent presents a positive consequence, negative reinforcement involves the *removal* of an unpleasant condition.

An example of this might be, "Bill, you must stay at the table alone until you finish all of your broccoli." The aversive condition (staying at the table alone) will be removed when he has eaten his vegetables. Bill's vegetable eating behavior is expected to increase so that he may leave the table (escape), and may well increase tomorrow, so he that he can leave with everyone else (avoid).

Negative reinforcement often results in escape or avoidance behaviors. These are not considered positive, proactive behaviors. Taken to an extreme, children with whom negative reinforcement is used enough will avoid not only the particular setting (vegetables), but also the enforcer (dinner or mom and dad). Negative reinforcement can bring short-term success (eventually the child *will* eat the broccoli), but in the long term, we might be teaching undesirable behaviors.

Another unintended scenario might be as follows: "Lori, if you clean your room, then you may come out and watch TV with the rest of us." Lori then cleans her room, but she has a tantrum in the process and also does a sloppy job in order to get out of her room as quickly as possible. What has she learned? In all probability, she has learned to clean her room poorly (i.e., as quickly as possible) and possibly to even get mad about doing it. Undoubtedly she has *not* been taught to appreciate the advantages of cleanliness and orderliness. Teaching these desirable behaviors would probably take more time, and much more effort. The question becomes, what do we want taught?

Another way to view negative reinforcement might be if students whine (behavior) about a given assignment (aversive condition) and the teacher then removes the work task (negative reinforcement); whining is thereby reinforced and will most likely recur. In fact, the teacher may begin to alter assignments in order to avoid future whining (avoidance behavior). Often this same teacher does not understand how students are actually "taught" to whine and complain.

Natural Reinforcement

Structuring reinforcement in the classroom or therapeutic setting serves many important purposes. It allows the teacher/therapist to keep order as well as plan for success. In a positive and contingent environment, students learn about the cause-and-effect relationship between their behavior and their surroundings. However, because other environments often lack consistent and contingent reinforcement schedules, it becomes important to get students/clients "hooked on reinforcers" that occur naturally as consequences of their behavior. Though one might use tangibles to reward solving a math problem, and pair that with praise for completed math tasks, eventually the student must do math because it is reinforcing, or math behavior will cease at the conclusion of school. Of course, reinforcers that are natural outgrowths of specific behaviors are not only more effective than contrived reinforcers, but are longer lasting. It would seem that every societal agent should eventually have every student/client on a schedule of reinforcers that occur naturally, such that programmed reinforcers would not be necessary.

STRATEGIES FOR WEAKENING BEHAVIORS

When people complain about others, the topic often concerns misbehavior. The solution to this problem is often to punish everything that is wrong, supposedly leaving only the good. In fact, the use of punishment can become very reinforcing. The reasons for this are understandable; punishment takes very little time, it is easy, and it usually works immediately. Fortunately, punishment is not the only tool for weakening behavior. There are several other methods available. Unfortunately, most of them take more thought and are not as immediate in their results. It seems that if we are to eliminate behaviors we should consider what it is we want as an end product. This end product not only encompasses the individual behaviors of the student/client, but also the "whole person." If we choose a less intrusive manner to eliminate undesirable behavior, the inappropriate behavior might take longer to extinguish, but we might also teach an appropriate behavior to replace it. Also, one maintains a great deal more dignity if not punished into submission.

Differentiated Reinforcement

Differentiated reinforcement is probably the least intrusive method of behavior reduction. It also works more slowly than any of the other choices outlined in this section. Generally positive reinforcement is used to increase or encourage one specified target behavior while another targeted behavior is being reduced or eliminated.

Differential Reinforcement of Low Rates of Behavior (DRL)

Teachers/therapists use this schedule of reinforcement to decrease behaviors that, while acceptable or even appropriate on a limited basis, are inappropriate when their frequency or magnitude are too high. This technique requires the use of positive reinforcement for appropriate occurrences of the behavior, but when frequency or magnitude levels become inappropriate, the societal agent does not reinforce, or ignores the behavior.

A common example of a DRL schedule involves group participation. Group participation is generally a desirable behavior; however, when one person participates too much, that person begins to monopolize the discussion or activity. For example, once the teacher/therapist decides what is an appropriate number of times to contribute to a group discussion (e.g., two distanced responses per day), the teacher/therapist reinforces the student/client's initial participation. The teacher/therapist will then not call on that same person for 15 minutes. The next time the same person volunteers a second response (after 15 minutes has elapsed), the teacher/therapist calls on the person and again reinforces participation. The teacher will not call on that student again till the next day and must ignore all unsolicited responses. It is important that all other regular positive social reinforcers remain at constant levels, so that the person will learn appropriate discussion participation. In this manner, the student/client does not feel that the teacher/therapist "doesn't like me," but instead learns when and how to contribute to group discussions. The student/client will have also learned this without having received disapproval in front of peers.

Differential Reinforcement of Other Behavior (DRO)

This procedure is intended to result in a decrease of a specified behavior. Generally, it positively reinforces "non-behavior." If a specified behavior does *not* occur during a specified time frame, then the teacher/therapist delivers positive reinforcement. In its purest form, the positive is given if the behavior occurs zero times, no matter what else the student/client might do. In reality, the teacher/therapist may eliminate an inappropriate behavior, but other inappropriate behaviors could also result.

An example of a *DRO* schedule might involve the elimination of talking-out in class. Using this technique, the teacher may approach the student before social studies and say, "if you wait to be called on before speaking during social studies today, you may choose the song for the class to sing before lunch." One problem with a DRO schedule occurs when the student makes a mistake. If the time interval for reinforcement is the whole period, and the student engages in the undesired behavior early on, no contingency is left for the student. The student may then choose to re-engage in that behavior for the rest of the interval without any recourse.

One way of solving this problem might be to structure the reinforcement for every 10 minutes (or some other manageable amount of time). If the student reaches the 10-minute goal, the teacher delivers a reward. If the student makes a mistake, no reward occurs, but the teacher resets the timer for another 10 minutes. Using a system of smaller time increments, students have a greater opportunity to succeed and receive reinforcement for appropriate behavior. Time increments can then be extended until the student can behave appropriately for the balance of the class.

Differential Reinforcement of Incompatible or Alternative Behavior (DRI/DRA)

The third method of differential reinforcement is the reinforcement of either an *incompatible* or an *alternative* behavior. This method is usually preferable to a DRO schedule if at all possible. Instead of reinforcing the lack of a behavior, it reinforces a behavior that can replace the behavior targeted for weakening. In a DRI schedule, a behavior that is incompatible with the behavior targeted is reinforced. For example, if the teacher targets out-of-seat behavior for reduction, the teacher then reinforces in-seat behavior. One cannot physically engage in both behaviors at the same time, thus making the inappropriate behavior impossible and replacing it with an appropriate behavior.

DRA reinforces a behavior that is an alternative to the targeted behavior. However, with DRA, the targeted behavior is not physically impossible, but topographically dissimilar. For example, each time Mary begins to demand something, she is redirected to say "please"; she is reinforced for appropriate manners by receiving the requested item. Sometimes the act of redirection (a reminder) will function as a gentle punisher, however the predominance of the behavioral chain is reinforcing, while providing an alternate behavioral choice (a "please" request instead of a demand).

The most difficult aspect of a DRI or DRA schedule is choosing/finding an incompatible or alternative behavior within the student's/client's repertoire. If no clear choice is apparent, one might simply reinforce another positive behavior such that the student/client chooses to engage in the alternate behavior instead of the targeted behavior. Another possibility is to find an alternate behavior that is not in the person's repertoire, teach it, and then reinforce the new behavior as the alternative.

Extinction (terminating reinforcement)

Extinction is the abrupt withdrawal of positive reinforcement that is maintaining an inappropriate behavior. Extinction is used to decrease maladaptive behavior. For example, teachers/therapists use extinction when inappropriate behavior is maintained by the teacher's/therapist's attention.

In this case, one of the most difficult aspects of extinction is determining if attention is in fact reinforcing the inappropriate behavior. An outside observer recording or videotaping interactions within a class period or session may help clarify this. If the societal agent's attention causes an increase in the target behavior, then it can be assumed that the attention is functioning as reinforcement.

Before implementing extinction procedures, several issues must be considered. Among these are the following:

1) Can the predictable increase (escalation) of the targeted behavior be tolerated? The societal agent must expect an escalation of the behavior when the targeted behavior is ignored. The student/client is likely to do many things in order to get the teacher's/therapist's attention. It is not enough to ignore the original inappropriate behavior. The real question is, can the teacher/therapist ignore the escalation that follows? Remember that behaviors previously maintained by a partial reinforcement schedule usually escalate (sometimes in the extreme) before they are extinguished.

2) Are there alternative behaviors to reinforce? If one can find other behaviors to reinforce, thereby giving attention (reinforcement) for appropriate behavior, the student/client will be less likely to engage in inappro-

priate behavior for no attention. Furthermore, if appropriate behaviors can be found to reinforce that are within the current repertoire, the student/client might engage in self-shaping behavior.

3) Does the teacher/therapist have good distracters prepared? It would be absurd (as well as ineffective) to say, "I'm ignoring you." Additionally, any nonverbal indication that the student/client gets will probably function as attention (reinforcement). The teacher/therapist must have a plan of action in order to avoid being caught off-task.

Counterconditioning

A second approach to the modification of maladaptive behaviors employs the principle of *counterconditioning*: there are certain responses that do not "go together"—that are incompatible; if one occurs, the other will not. For example, one cannot experience intense "hate" and "love," or excitement and tranquility, at precisely the same time. The concept of structuring an incompatible response is employed by many behavior modifiers in treating conditioned respondents. In essence, counterconditioning is accomplished by selecting a response incompatible with fear, usually something pleasurable to the individual, and gradually introducing some aspect of the conditioned stimuli that no longer evokes the fear reaction. If both techniques are used, the combined forces of reconditioning and extinction at each step will eventually result in the elicitation of a pleasurable response, in place of fear, when the conditioned stimulus is presented.

Desensitization

Desensitization, aligned with counterconditioning, is a very popular technique employed by behavior modifiers. Desensitization is probably successful because of the principle of incompatible behavior; that is, if a response that prevents anxiety can be made to occur in the presence of the anxiety-evoking stimuli, new responses will then be learned. In systematic desensitization, the response that prevents anxiety is usually complete relaxation, and the "anxiety-evoking stimuli" are the fears and phobias that represent a part of or the essence of the maladaptive behaviors of the individual.

Desensitization consists of eliminating the fears and phobias through extinction, as well as reconditioning the former anxiety-stimuli to the response associated with complete relaxation. This process generally involves three basic operations: (1) training muscle relaxation, (2) the construction of anxiety hierarchies (specific stimuli arranged from least to most anxiety provoking), and (3) counter-posing relaxation and anxiety-evoking stimuli from the hierarchies.

Punishment

A punisher can only be defined in terms of its effect on the subsequent behavior. If a punisher is administered contingently and immediately following the occurrence of an inappropriate behavior, then the rate of that behavior will, in all probability, decrease. The last two sections (removal of desirable stimuli and presentation of aversive stimuli) discuss methods of punishment.

Removal of Desirable Stimuli

Response Cost

Response cost is a form of punishment in which the subject incurs a specific reduction of reinforcement (cost) for inappropriate behavior. This decreases the probability of a reoccurrence of the targeted behavior. Response cost is an attractive method of punishment for several reasons. First, it generally has a rapid effect on behavior. Second, it is easy to implement in most settings. Finally, it can exist alongside other systems such as various token economy systems.

Similar to other methods of behavioral management, there are several considerations one must examine before implementation. A response cost program will be most effective if implemented in an environment where a token economy is in place. This allows a person to lose tokens for inappropriate behavior, but also to earn them back for appropriate behavior. This encourages participation in the token system.

Another consideration is the severity of the cost for inappropriate behavior. If a person loses a whole day's worth of tokens for a relatively small mistake, that person is likely to get discouraged and "refuse to play." Additionally, one must consider what the societal agent would do if a person loses all tokens when *response cost* is the only method of punishment.

Probably the best example of this kind of system is a citation for a traffic violation. One usually does not lose *all* tokens for speeding, but a graduated scale aligns the number of tokens to the severity of the inappropriate driving behavior. Though driving is a very habituated behavior, at least for some time after receiving a citation, drivers generally modify their behavior. At least this is the case for a certain period of time (perhaps only minutes).

A second kind of response cost involves removing secondary reinforcers other than generalized conditioned reinforcers. Most people use this method much more often than formally withdrawing tokens, but most of the time it is used unwittingly. This occurs with the loss of a social reinforcer (positive words or touches) or activity reinforcer (privileges or special events) because of inappropriate behavior. For example, a child who breaks a prized vase by playing ball in the house (inappropriate behavior) is not allowed to go to a movie with friends (removal of reinforcing activity).

Time-out

Time-out procedures serve as punishment for students/clients by removing them from a positive environment for a fixed period of time, essentially denying them the opportunity to receive reinforcement. This system of punishment is popular, though often misused. Time-out is properly titled *time-out from positive reinforcement*. This title is the key, for if the environment is not positive, students/clients will prefer time-out. Different levels of time-out range from a momentary break in activity to regain composure (e.g., "everyone put your heads on your desks and close your eyes") to removing a student/client from the environment for a period of time. Usually if a person is to be removed from the environment, the environment itself controls how and where this is done.

Because time-out can be misused, a review of concerns and guidelines is appropriate. Most concerns revolve around time-out procedures where people are put in seclusion. Research indicates that the duration of time-out should probably not exceed 2 minutes. If a longer period of time is needed, then the teacher/therapist should approach the student/client after 2 minutes and review the reasons for time-out. Another 2 minutes may then be added to the punishment.

When the person is excluded from the positive environment, the new environment should not present any danger; alternately, it should not provide any interest. A secluded area overlooking the playground will not function appropriately. When an inappropriate behavior occurs, the teacher must identify the misbehavior and send the student directly to time-out, without discussion. Any protest should be ignored. At times, the most appropriate response when students protest is to add more time to the time-out. "It appears that you have more to think about; I'm adding 15 seconds to your time-out." Once the time-out is finished, the teacher/therapist must not reinforce the student/client for good behavior during time-out; the student/client should be returned to the activity in which he/she was engaged prior to time-out.

Time-out will only be effective if: (a) the regular environment is reinforcing, (b) the time-out is not a fun/happy place, and (c) students/clients do not avoid the activity in which they were engaged prior to the misbehavior.

Presentation of Aversive Stimuli

The presentation of *aversive stimuli* is what is commonly known as punishment. Though not recommended as a first, second, or even third alternative to correcting behavior, this technique is effective in many ways. First, it quickly stops the occurrence of the inappropriate behavior and often has long lasting effects. Second, it provides a clear discrimination between appropriate and inappropriate behavior. Finally, when administered in the presence of others, vicarious learning often takes place.

Disadvantages to the presentation of aversive stimuli are numerous. Some of the more obvious ones include respondent (student/client) aggressive behavior or respondent escape and avoidance behaviors. There are two other less obvious problems as well. First, because presentation of aversive stimuli generally "works," the societal agent is reinforced for using it. Therefore, when an inappropriate behavior recurs, instead of reexamining the conditions of the original decision to use punishment, the societal agent may decide to resort to punishment again. Secondly, one must consider the issue of *Negative Modeling*. When a societal agent uses presentation of aversive stimuli, the societal agent also teaches students that the delivery of aversive consequences is "acceptable." This ramification alone may be more deleterious than all of the advantages of this method.

Unconditioned Aversive Stimuli

Unconditioned (primary) *aversive stimuli* result in pain, discomfort, or physical annoyance for the person. Unconditioned aversive stimuli do not require any prior experience to be effective. The unconditioned punishers can include (a) substances such as water, lemon juice, or ammonia generally sprayed in face; (b) items such as an air horn or a bright light; or (c) physical control or restraint which could include aversive holding or even corporal punishment.

In addition to the pitfalls of using any aversive stimuli, unconditioned aversive stimuli may not be universally punishing. If the person likes lemon juice, or receiving a spray in the face, these stimuli will not decrease the probability of the behavior reoccurring. Even access to restraint has been used as a "reinforcer" in some studies. Therefore, what seems to be obviously unpleasant is not necessarily so.

Conditioned Aversive Stimuli

Conditioned (secondary) *aversive stimuli* result in social unhappiness. These stimuli may have been learned in pairing with primary aversive stimuli, but more likely, in conjunction with other social behaviors. They can be directly associated with secondary social reinforcers, but used negatively. The categories for conditioned aversive stimuli are words, expressions, proximity, and touching (although most touching is unconditioned).

Verbal reprimands are the most common form of conditioned aversive stimuli, followed by expressions of displeasure. These are both more effective if delivered in conjunction with a gentle but firm grasp (touching) or close proximity. When administering this method, rules must be clearly defined; for example, "if you do this (_____), then this (_____) will happen." Second, the societal agent should avoid a lengthy episode of verbal punishment. It should be quick and to the point. Third, the episode should be intense. If the punishment is not intense enough, there could be an escalation effect whereby the reprimands must become more caustic, escalating to a greater magnitude than would be necessary had they been strong enough in the first place. Finally, the societal agent should never demonstrate any emotion. Emotional demonstration allows the student/client to give the societal agent the problem and also allows individuals to be reinforced by the societal agent's lack of control. In addition, if the teacher/therapist shows emotion, students/clients learn that through negative modeling, verbal punishment is acceptable when they are angry or frustrated. Maintaining composure when delivering punishment is critical for success and provides much less to imitate. Additionally, when keeping composure, students/clients learn that it is not acceptable to *lose one's temper* and verbally strike out.

Overcorrection

Overcorrection involves more than one principle of behavioral change. The basic premise of overcorrection is that it teaches correct behaviors when inappropriate behaviors are exhibited. Although overcorrection is rather time consuming, it teaches the appropriate behavior, and therefore, provides the student/client with an alternative to the inappropriate behavior previously demonstrated. Overcorrection is generally considered educative.

Restitutional Overcorrection

The definition of *restitutional overcorrection* is requiring the person who has disturbed the environment by his/her misbehavior to return the environment to a state that is much improved over the initial environment. For example, a student caught placing used chewing gum on the bottom of a desk is required to clean the gum off all the desks in the building. In restitutional overcorrection, the punishment is purposely "out of proportion with the crime." Any disturbance in the environment can be addressed with this method, including objects that are moved and places that are vandalized. Even disturbing a study environment can be compensated with long-term silence.

Positive-Practice Overcorrection

In *positive-practice overcorrection*, persons who demonstrated inappropriate behavior are required to demonstrate the appropriate behavior in an exaggerated manner, or to overly correct practice, or to engage in the behavior for an extended period or number of times. The educative nature of positive-practice requires that the behavior practiced is the preferred alternative to the original behavior demonstrated. For example, a teacher tells a class to line up for lunch, and the students run from their seats to the door in an effort to be first. The teacher tells the students sit down, explains how they are to line up, and then has them do it. However, in order for it to constitute positive-practice overcorrection, once the students line up correctly, the teacher instructs them to do it 10 more times without positive reinforcement.

There are a few issues relating to overcorrection that must be considered. Overcorrection generally requires teacher attention and can rarely be done independently, especially in the initial stages. Second, overcorrection procedures take time. Lining up (as in the above example) will definitely have a class arrive 10 to 15 minutes late for lunch. Cleaning numerous desks can take hours. Finally, if the teacher delivers positive reinforcement during positive-practice or restitutional overcorrection, students might engage in inappropriate behaviors in order to re-engage in overcorrection and receive more reinforcement.

Negative Practice to Satiation

Negative practice to satiation is not overcorrection and is not educative. It does not teach a new behavior to replace an inappropriate one. Negative practice requires the student to perform the inappropriate behavior repeatedly until satiation occurs. Returning to the above example, instead of lining up correctly 10 times (the positive-practice example), the class must run from their seats to the door until they are too tired to go to lunch. Another example could concern smoking. After a parent caught a child smoking a cigarette, the parent might put the child in a room until they had finished smoking an entire pack of cigarettes. This example demonstrates a situation where negative practice might be most applicable, because satiation is plausible and there is not a topographically opposite behavior other than the non-behavior to positively-practice.

STUDY GUIDE FOR CHAPTER 9

1. Explain "task analysis." Why is it important that every teacher understand how to sequence information?

2. What is the function of a prompt? In what ways can a prompt be detrimental?

3. Explain "errorless learning" and give an example. Do you think that this is the best way to teach a new task? Why? Why not?

4. Why is "modeling" so important in learning? Can you describe some cases where unwitting modeling resulted in behavior that was inappropriate?

5. What is the definition of "positive reinforcement"? Is there a difference between positive reinforcement and "reward"? Does "feedback" constitute positive reinforcement?

6.   What are the *necessary* ingredients in establishing a "token economy"? To what does "back-up" refer?

7.   What would be your reasons for setting up a token economy? How would you terminate a token economy?

8.   In what circumstances would you use "group contingencies" to modify behavior?

9.   What is the Premack principle? What are some common uses of this principle?

10. Specify in what situation or circumstance you might use punishment. What is the difference between punishment and "negative reinforcement"?

LEARNING ACTIVITY 17— SPECIFYING A SHAPING PROCEDURE

Choose one learning (academic) task in your specific subject area:

Specify the following for the above task:

Terminal behavior:

Criterion for measuring terminal behavior:

A shaping procedure for learning including at least five steps:

An example of contingency contracting with the student for above task:

LEARNING ACTIVITY 18—
DETERMINING BEHAVIORAL PRINCIPLES

Read the following excerpts and determine which principles are being used in the underlined passages.

A four-year-old hyperactive child attends a session where the objective is to stay in the area of activity. A large hula-hoop is placed on the floor and is a cue for working since all activities take place inside of the hoop. (1) The child's favorite songs are tape recorded and played while the child has two feet in the hoop. Music is turned off when at least one foot is out of the hoop. (2) By the end of six weeks, the child knows that when he/she sees the hoop it means that two feet should be placed inside of it. (3) Then the volume of music is gradually decreased (4) until the child can stay in the hoop without the aid of the music.

1.
2.
3.
4.

A four-year-old girl is learning to sing a song. The music teacher sings the first line first while the child listens. (1) A different musical note is associated with each word syllable of the song. (2) When the child repeats the verse correctly, the teacher smiles, (3) but when the child simply babbles, the teacher stops the music, sits back, and waits 10 seconds before continuing. (4) At this point, the teacher decides that there are too many mistakes and that the song must be taught differently. The teacher decides to sing the first line leaving out the last word, then leaving out the second to the last word and last word, (5) and continues in this manner. After every single response (6) from the child, the teacher lets her know how she has done. (7) Thus, the song has been taught so that each step is progressively learned. (8)

1.	5.
2.	6.
3.	7.
4.	8.

CHAPTER **10**

An Introduction to Behavioral Designs and Terminology

DESIGNS FOR CHANGING BEHAVIOR

In most field settings a minimal program of behavioral techniques is all that is necessary to effect acceptable change in behavior. All behavioral programs must include four phases: **pinpoint** the behavior to be modified, **record** the occurrences of the behavior (baseline), **consequate** the behavior by establishing new contingencies (intervention treatment), and **evaluate** the effectiveness of the newly established contingencies. This design is recognized as the **AB design** (A = baseline, B = treatment; see Figure 1). Though the four phases of the behavioral design seem complete in and of themselves, some special situations and all scientific investigations require validation demonstrating that the treatment selected was in fact what effected the behavioral change and that the contingencies selected were indeed the most effective. There are four basic designs: (a) reversal, (b) alternating treatments, (c) multiple baseline, and (d) changing criterion.

REVERSAL DESIGN

Austin is a fourth-grade student who has had difficulty finishing his multiplication assignments during the regularly allotted 45-minute math period. Ms. Williams has noticed that, while most students normally finish 65 problems in the allotted time, Austin only finishes 18 or so. She believes that if she can get Austin to have more success with the multiplication problems, she can also get him to enjoy mathematics. Ms. Williams has noticed that although Austin does not enjoy math, he does like recess. She decides to start a program to help motivate Austin to complete more multiplication problems during the regular math period. For 1 week she records the number of mul-

AB Design

FIGURE 1

tiplication problems he completes daily, and finds that he is actually completing about 21 per day. This example demonstrates the importance of taking baseline data. If data are not known, intervention results might be misinterpreted. Ms. Williams then introduces the behavioral program.

For each pair of problems Austin completes correctly above 20, he will get to stay at recess for 1 extra minute (intervention). The next day, Austin correctly finishes 24 problems and is able to stay at recess for 2 extra minutes. On the following days, Austin finishes 35, 39, 44, and 49 problems, again earning extra recess time. The subsequent Friday, Ms. Williams tells Austin how proud she is of his accomplishments, but states that next week he will need to return to class with the other students. The next week, Austin's mathematics performance gradually returns to the baseline level. During the fourth week, Ms. Williams reintroduces the extra recess time (intervention), and Austin's performance returns to its higher level. Ms. Williams has established that additional recess time was motivating Austin's mathematics behavior and that this contingency (extra recess time) would need to be continued for Austin to make adequate progress in Mathematics (see Figure 2). She then devised a plan to slowly begin thinning the recess time reinforcement and to create a more intrinsic reward system for math achievement.

A reversal design entails measurement of a pinpointed behavior during four phases and is probably the easiest behavioral design to conceptualize. The first phase is referred to as the baseline phase. In this phase, the pinpointed behavior is observed and recorded without any intervention. During the second phase, an intervention is introduced such that a behavioral change will likely result. In the third phase, the intervention is removed; often the behavior of the subject is likely to return to baseline levels. In the fourth phase, intervention is reintroduced in order to replicate the second phase. This design is commonly identified as an ABAB design.

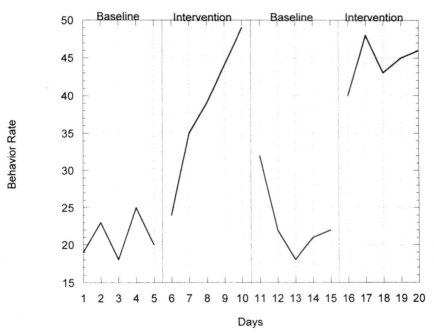

FIGURE 2

The rationale for this design is that if the rate of observable behavior changes with the introduction and removal of an intervention, then the intervention treatment is deemed effective. One advantage of this design is that it represents a straightforward and powerful illustration of a direct cause-

and-effect relationship. There are, however, two distinct disadvantages to this design. First, some behaviors are irreversible (e.g., newly introduced skills) and once modified by an intervention, are not likely to return to baseline when the independent variable is removed. Second, the use of a reversal design may reestablish certain undesirable behaviors (e.g., illicit drug usage) during the return to baseline condition. Other behavioral designs allow for change without a "return to baseline."

ALTERNATING TREATMENTS DESIGN

Mr. Dimon has found that his students are completing an unacceptable number of grammar problems. After one week of counting, he has found that with a class of 20 students, he only receives an average of 104 correct sentences per day. Mr. Dimon has noticed that the class really enjoys a geography game and music class, so he decides to use these two activities to motivate grammar acquisition. He tells the class on Monday that for every 20 correct grammar

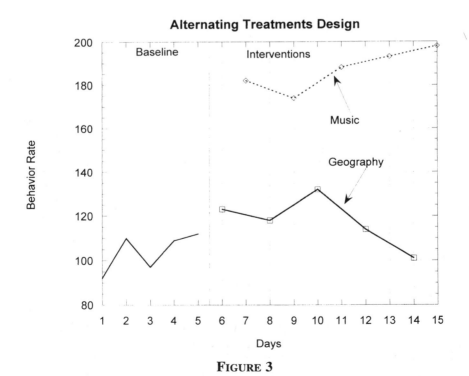

FIGURE 3

problems he receives that day, they can play their favorite geography game for 1 minute at the end of the day. Monday he receives 123 correct responses and the class plays the geography game for 6 minutes. On Tuesday he tells them that for every 20 correct grammar responses, they can sing one of their favorite songs from music class at the end of the day. Tuesday he receives 182 correct responses. He continues to alternate these two treatments for 2 weeks, and the data continue to indicate that music is the activity that motivates a higher level of grammar skill acquisition (see Figure 3). Following these 2 weeks, Mr. Dimon decides that the opportunity to sing motivates his class more than the opportunity to play the geography game, so he decides to use only music to motivate grammar acquisition.

The alternating treatment design is exactly what the name implies: two or more interventions that are suspected to effect behavioral change are selected and are either rotated or placed in some predetermined order such that data can be collected as to the effect each has on a targeted behavior. They can be used sequentially in a single session, or if more appropriate, each can be used for a given period of time (i.e., a given treatment for each day) in order to determine effectiveness. It should be noted that a distinctive cue or discriminative stimulus immediately preceding each treatment will aid in the differential effects of each treatment (i.e., "For each correct response, today you will receive . . . ").

The advantage of the alternating treatments design is that it is an efficient technique for teachers or therapists to determine which specific treatment will modify a pinpointed behavior more quickly and with an economy of effort. Two possible problems can occur when this design is used. The first problem pertains to the residual effects that may generalize from one intervention to the other. The second problem occurs if the two treatments have a confounding effect, whereby results could not be attributed to a specific intervention.

MULTIPLE BASELINE DESIGN

Ms. Bailey has noticed that Virginia's marks are suffering in three of her subjects: Math, English, and Science. She has also found that Virginia enjoys choir. She sets up a program with Mr. Parrish to give her one 15-minute private voice lesson before school if she earns satisfactory daily reports from her Math teacher. After one week, Virginia receives five satisfactory daily reports and a marked improvement in Math. She then receives an individualized voice lesson. During this time, Virginia's marks in English and Science remain poor. The second week, Ms. Bailey changes the contingencies for the private voice lesson such that Virginia must make satisfactory progress in Math *and* Science. Virginia does indeed comply, but English remains the

same. Ms. Bailey then adds Virginia's English class to the contingency and
finds that Virginia enjoys her private music lessons with Mr. Parrish enough
to continue making progress in her three other classes (see Figure 4).

Multiple baseline design is a widely used and highly flexible design in
behavioral research. This design allows the societal agent to establish contingencies for the change of a pinpointed behavior in one isolated setting,
but not in others. While contingencies are implemented in one setting, mon-
itoring for behavioral changes should be completed on that setting and baseline data should also be collected in all other settings. In this manner, any
change noted in the modified setting can be attributed to the change in contingencies (if no differences are noted in the other settings). At a later time,
interventions are introduced (one at a time) for each of the other settings.
This design is flexible because a multiple baseline design can be used across
different settings (e.g., first period, second period, third period, and so on),
across different behaviors (e.g., work problems completed, language usage,
fighting), or across subjects.

Probably the greatest advantage to using a multiple baseline design is

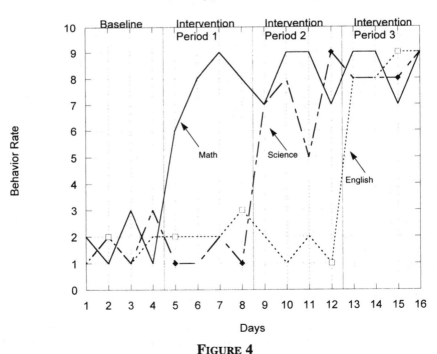

Multiple Baseline Design

FIGURE 4

that the societal agent is not required to withdraw a seemingly advantageous set of contingencies (intervention) in order to demonstrate that the change in behavior is indeed due to the change in contingencies. As the pinpointed behavior is modified in the area or setting where the intervention has been introduced, no change in behavior is noted in the baseline setting. Therefore, there is no need to return to baseline, because effectiveness is established by the other baseline settings. The previously illustrated weaknesses of the reversal design (i.e., possible reintroduction of something that could be harmful to the subject, or trying to establish effectiveness of a method on a behavior that is not reversible) are avoided.

One reason against using a multiple baseline design should be mentioned. While an intervention strategy is introduced in one setting, all of the other settings remain in a baseline condition. Thus, if the targeted behavior is dangerous, allowing that behavior to continue is questionable. A further consideration against the efficacy of using a multiple baseline methodology would be if several behaviors are being modified that are not completely independent of each other (i.e., off-task and work assignments completed). In this case, modifying one behavior may have an effect on another.

CHANGING CRITERION DESIGN

In the first example, Ms. Williams found that Austin did indeed work harder in math if he was allowed to stay in recess for additional time. However, there were two problems: (a) as Austin completed many more problems he stayed so long at recess that recess time began to lose its reinforcing effect (satiation), and (b) he could never be allowed to stay long enough in recess to get him up to the class average. She decided to implement a program where if Austin finished 40 problems in a day, he was allowed to stay in recess for an additional 10 minutes. Once he was able to consistently reach that goal, the contingency was raised to 45 problems in a day. If he completed those, he was again allowed to stay in recess an additional 10 minutes that day. This program, illustrated in Figure 5, represents stepwise progress that continued each time. Austin was successful in attaining the target level until he was completing 65 problems per day, which was the class average.

The changing criterion design is used to shape a student's/client's behavior by requiring a gradual stepwise change in behavior in order to receive reinforcement. The general design is similar to the AB design, but the B phase is divided into many sub-phases, each moving in a stepwise fashion successively approximating the level of the desired terminal behavior. Successful use of this design necessitates determining the appropriate levels of each sub-phase and modifying the criterion at appropriate times. Generally a steady baseline level is used to determine steps in the sub-phases. Changing from one step to the next is usually determined by the success of the subject at each level.

This design is good in carefully establishing a cause-and-effect relationship between behavior and reinforcement, while continually improving the targeted behavior. This design should be selected with pinpointed behaviors that are not dangerous (hence needing immediate change) as well as those behaviors that need to be modified over an extended period of time.

FIGURE 5

GLOSSARY OF BEHAVIORAL TERMINOLOGY

This introduction to terminology is included to serve as a transition from the present volume to the published research found within scientific journals dealing with aspects of behavior modification. Indeed, the entire growth of behavior modification represents a scientific approach to the control and/or modification of behavior. The goal of behavior modification is to predict and influence the behavior of an individual organism through scientific laws and procedures. *Laws* are statements concerning the empirical scientific relationship between independent and dependent variables. The *dependent variable*—the response—is the behavior the scientist is interested in controlling. The *independent variable(s)* represents events or occurrences within the environment, or things that will effect change in *dependent variables*. This is the variable that is manipulated or treated with consequent changes on the dependent variable noted. The relationship between these two represents the cause-and-effect relationship in behavioral science. Thus, behavior modification functions on a scientific basis. The cause-and-effect relationship constitutes the primary realm of concern for the behavioral technician. In essence, behavior modifiers maintain that behavior is a result of its consequences. Therefore, if the independent variable (cause) is known and its effect on the dependent variable is known, the behavior modifier is in a more certain position to control and predict behavior. In summary, perhaps the most important contribution of the behavior modification movement is its emphasis on an operationally defined, readily observed, and easily measured dependent variable: behavior.

Abscissa: The horizontal reference axis on a graph (chart). In behavior modification the abscissa is usually labeled with a scale that represents the passage of time in some form such as minutes, days, observations, or trials.

Accountability: Providing an objective demonstration in measurable terms of the effectiveness of given programs. Ex: An increase in reading scores following the introduction of contingency contracting with students.

Adaptation: The gradual reduction of responses or responsiveness as an organism adjusts to the introduction of new stimuli into the environment. Ex: Sensory adaptation to a bright light; students tuning out a teacher's loud (or soft) commands when there is no contrast.

Adaptation Period: The phase (time period) in any behavioral program during which the subject (or subjects) adjusts to any novel stimuli that have been introduced into the environment. Ex: The time necessary for a class to adapt to observers prior to collection of baseline data.

Adaptive Behavior: Behavior that serves to ensure survival or is considered appropriate in specified societal contexts such as school.

Addiction: A condition in which cessation of reinforcement (usually physiological) produces physical or psychological problems of abstinence.

Alternating Treatments Design: Two or more interventions suspected to effect change are selected and either rotated or placed in a predetermined order such that data can be collected as to the effect each has on the targeted behavior.

Applied Research: Research that is directed toward an analysis of variables that can be effective in improving behavior under study. Applied research is often conducted in natural settings.

Approval: Any observable endorsement of behavior.

Aversive Control: The withdrawal or presentation of an aversive stimulus, which then maintains or increases the frequency of a response. Three types of aversive control exist.
1. Escape, in which the organism terminates the aversive stimulus after it has begun.
2. Avoidance, in which the organism postpones the beginning of aversive stimuli.
3. Punishment, in which responses are followed by an aversive stimulus.

Aversive Stimulus: Any stimulus that an organism will escape from, avoid, or terminate.

Back-up Reinforcer: An object or event that has already demonstrated its reinforcing effect on an individual that is received in exchange for a specific number of tokens, points, or other more generalized reinforcers.

Baseline: A stable, usually recoverable, performance (five or more observations) upon which the effects of experimental variables can be assessed. (Record phase.)

Behavior: Any act of an organism, either internal or external, that can be observed and/or measured. Any behavior may have one of four relationships to the environment.
1. Dependent, when the event must, by nature of the situation, occur following the behavior. Ex: Because the water must cease running from the faucet when the handle is turned, the subsequent cessation of the flow of water is said to be dependent upon behavior of turning the handle.
2. Contingent, when the event does follow the behavior but need not do so. Reinforcement is generally contingent upon behavior. After reinforcement has occurred, a contingency is said to have been established. Ex: If one is asked to turn off the water and does so, the behavior is said to be contingent.
3. Superstitious, because behavior has nothing to do with the reinforcer.

Ex: The fondling of a "good luck piece" does not cause "good luck," but is occasionally reinforced with chance good fortune.
4. Random, when the behavior has no logical relationship to the environment and all stimuli are neutral. Ex: Tuneless whistling while daydreaming.

Behavior Modification: The changing of behavior (increasing or decreasing frequency of occurrence) using a combination (schedule) of reinforcement (positive and/or negative) and/or non-reinforcement. Generally represents the programmed use of techniques based on scientifically derived principles of learning to produce observable changes in behavior.

Behavior Therapy: The application of learning theory techniques for the purpose of changing maladaptive behavior.

Behavioral Approach: An approach in which values and/or ideas, in order to be considered, are operationally defined into directly observable and measurable behaviors. The assumption is made that most behavior, including behavior defined as abnormal, is learned.

Behavioral Contrast: A phenomenon that may occur if a behavior is placed on one reinforcement schedule under one stimulus condition and on another schedule under a different stimulus condition. In such a situation a decrease in the rate of the behavior under one stimulus-correlated condition may be accompanied by an increase in the rate under the other stimulus-correlated condition.

Behavioral Dimensions: Measurable descriptive characteristics of behavior such as frequency, intensity, duration, and topography.

Behavioral Goal: The specification of the set of responses to be emitted by the subject at the completion of a given behavior modification program. Usually the criteria for achievement of the goals and conditions under which the responses are to be emitted are also specified. When limited to academic instruction, this is often referred to as the behavioral objective.

Chaining: A series of two or more responses joined together into a complex behavioral sequence by stimuli that act as both discriminative stimuli and conditioned reinforcers. For instance, discriminative stimulus—response—reinforcement—response to reinforcement—reinforcement for last response—etc. Therefore, one operant response leads to another in a linking of the three-term paradigm (discriminative stimulus, response, reinforcement) which permits the development of a series of operants of indefinite length. Ex: Child is offered candy—takes candy and says "Thank you"—Child given a smile and "You're welcome"—Child engages in eye contact and smiles—Child is given a hug. *Forward chaining* begins with teaching the first task in a chain and then adding additional sequences (links) in order. *Backward chaining* reverses the additive process. It begins with the entire sequence and removes the ending links one by one until the entire chain has been learned.

Changing Criterion Design: Design used to shape behavior by requiring a gradual stepwise change in behavior in order to receive reinforcement.

Cognitive Behavior Modification: The application of behavioral principles and techniques of behavior therapy to problems of a primarily cognitive nature. Most behavior therapists are presently concerned with cognitive as well as overt behaviors.

Conditioned Aversive Stimulus: (See Conditioned Stimulus.)

Conditioned Reflex: A reflex that is elicited by a formerly neutral stimulus that has been paired with the naturally eliciting stimulus.

Conditioned Reinforcer: Some stimuli acquire the power to reinforce (strengthen or maintain) behavior through being paired with the delivery of primary, or stronger conditioned reinforcers, within the experience of the organism. These are called secondary or conditioned reinforcers. Ex: Money is useless, unless one can exchange it for goods. To many people, however, money is a *conditioned reinforcer* because it has become the reward.

Conditioned Stimulus: A formerly neutral stimulus that has been paired with an unconditioned stimulus or a reinforcing stimulus (either positively or negatively) and has taken on the reinforcing properties of the stimulus with which it has been paired.

Conditioning: A neutral stimulus may acquire reinforcing properties through temporal association with another reinforcer. This process is called conditioning. (See Operant Conditioning and Respondent Conditioning.)

Confounding Variables: Variables that are operating in an experimental study, which make the effects of the experimental manipulation on the independent variable difficult to evaluate precisely.

Consequate: To apply consequences (reinforcement) following the occurrence of behavior.

Contingency: The relationship between the behavior of an organism and environmental events (generally reinforcing) that follow the behavior and either increase or decrease the probability of similar behavior in the future.

Contingency Contract: A written contract specifying subsequent behavioral contingencies between persons involved. Ex: Completion of school assignments will result in money and special privileges from parents and free time in school.

Contingency Control: The ability to manipulate the environmental consequences of a given behavior in order to achieve a specific behavioral goal.

Contingent: The relationship between a specific response and environmental consequence is said to be contingent if the consequence follows the behavior and subsequently has the effect of increasing, maintaining, decreasing, or eliminating behavior. (See Contingency.)

Continuous Field: A continuum of stimuli.

Continuous Response: A response that does not have a clearly discriminable beginning or end.

Contract: A contract provides written documentation regulating contingencies.

Counterconditioning: Structuring responses that are incompatible with one another.

Criterion: Specification of a predetermined level of behavioral performance that is to be achieved. Criteria are used to specify goals and to evaluate the success of behavioral programs.

Cue: A stimulus used to help an individual remember to produce any specified response, which may then be reinforced. (See Discriminative Stimulus.)

Dependent Variable: A phenomenon that varies in any way (appears, disappears, or changes) as a function of any application, removal, or variation in other variables (independent). A dependent variable is usually monitored or measured in behavior modification studies.

Deprivation: The removal of the occurrence of a stimulus.

Desensitization: A process of eliminating anxiety-stimuli through extinction and reconditioning. The process generally involves three operations: (1) training muscle relaxation, (2) constructing anxiety hierarchies—i.e., arranging specific stimuli from least to most anxiety provoking—and (3) counter-posing relaxation and anxiety-evoking stimuli from the hierarchies.

Differential Punishment: The extinguishing of certain behaviors while others are being reinforced. (See also Differential Reinforcement.)

Differential Reinforcement: The strengthening of certain behaviors while others are being extinguished. A programmed contingency whereby specified responses are reinforced while others are not. (See also Differential Punishment.)

Differential Reinforcement of Alternative Behavior (DRA): A procedure in which a reinforcer follows a behavior that is an alternative to a targeted behavior. DRA and DRI schedules are similar. A DRA schedule differs from DRI schedule in that the targeted behavior is not physically impossible but topographically dissimilar.

Differential Reinforcement of High Rates (DRH): A schedule that involves the selective contingent reinforcement of a grouping of responses that occur in rapid succession. High rates are differentially reinforced while low rates are not.

Differential Reinforcement of Incompatible (DRI): A procedure in which a reinforcer follows a response (usually a physical response) incompatible with a targeted behavior.

Differential Reinforcement of Low Rates (DRL): A schedule in which responses that are spaced relatively far apart in time are selectively reinforced. Low rates are differentially reinforced while high rates are not.

Differential Reinforcement of Other Behaviors (DRO): A procedure in which a reinforcer follows any response an individual makes, except for one particular response. Thus, the individual receives scheduled reinforcement except when he engages in a particular specified behavior. This procedure results in a decrease of the specified behavior.

Disapproval: Any observable consequence to behavior defined negatively by the organism receiving it.

Discrete Stimuli: Separate presentation of stimuli.

Discriminative Stimulus (S^d): An environmental event that sets the occasion for responses that are followed by reinforcement. The probability of the response is high only when certain environmental events (discriminative stimuli) are present. Whenever the discriminative stimulus (S^d) is present, specific responses may then be reinforced. (See Stimulus Control.)

Eliciting Stimuli: Environmental events that regularly precede responses. They elicit relatively fixed and stereotyped responses. Ex: The bell in Pavlov's classic dog experiment.

Emotion: A complex response elicited and occasioned by environmental conditions and composed of both operants and respondents. Ex: Love or sadness.

Environment: The sum total of an organism's surroundings (stimuli).

Errorless Discrimination Procedure: Teaching the acquisition of a discrimination by carefully arranging a sequence of discriminative stimuli so that only correct responses are occasioned.

Event Sampling: An observational procedure in which the frequency or duration of a specific discrete behavior, such as times tardy or number of pages completed, is recorded over a specific extended period of time. The specific time interval may be, for instance, a classroom period or day.

Extinction: A procedure in which the reinforcement for a previously reinforced behavior is discontinued. The process whereby a conditioned response is reduced to its preconditioned level or strength, often approaching or reaching zero magnitude or frequency. The process of extinction in the case of respondents involves continuing presentation of the conditioned stimulus without any further pairing with the unconditioned stimulus. With operant responses, extinction results when responding is no longer followed by reinforcement.

Fading: The gradual removal of discriminative stimuli such as cues and prompts.

Fixed Interval Reinforcement: (See Schedules of Reinforcement.)

Fixed Ratio Reinforcement: (See Schedules of Reinforcement.)

Frequency: The number of occurrences per given time period.

Functional Analysis: The determination of the external variables of which behavior is a function. (See also Functional Relation.)

Functional Relation: A relation in which the occurrence of event B consistently follows the occurrence of event A or is dependent upon the previous occurrence of event A.

Functional Relationship: A lawful relationship between two variables. In behavior modification, a dependent variable and a given procedure are functionally related if the behavior systematically varies as a function of the application of the procedure.

Generalization: Responding to two or more discriminatively different stimuli as if they were the same. Generalization involves the following components:

1. Stimulus Generalization—the spread of the effects of reinforcement (or of other operations) in the presence of one stimulus to other stimuli that differ from the original stimulus along one or more dimensions.
2. Response Generalization (induction)—the spread of effects of reinforcement to responses outside of a specific response may be accompanied by other responses that are similar but not identical to the reinforced response.
3. Generalization Training—a procedure designed to facilitate the occurrence of generalization.

Generalized Reinforcer: A conditioned reinforcer that is effective over a wide range of deprivation conditions as a result of having been paired with a variety of previously established reinforcers.

Group Contingencies: Establishing contingencies for a defined group that result in both positive and negative outcomes.

Habituation: A gradual decline in the magnitude of a respondent over repeated occurrences. Ex: A nurse's aversion to the sight of blood decreases as she is exposed to repeated viewing of open wounds.

Imitation: Matching the behavior of a model.

Incompatible Behavior: Any two or more behaviors that, by the very nature of one, cannot exist with the other. Sometimes the term is used to include not only behavior that cannot occur simultaneously with another, but also behavior that interferes with other behavior. Ex: Speaking and being quiet.

Incompatible Response: A response whose occurrence precludes the simultaneous occurrence of another response. Ex: A musician cannot be both flat and sharp at the same time.

Inconsistency: Not applying the previously specified consequences to the occurrences of a behavior, applying the consequences when the behavior has not occurred, applying inappropriate consequences (approval following inappropriate behavior or disapproval for appropriate behavior), or applying appropriate and inappropriate consequences simultaneously.

Independent Variable: The factor purposely manipulated in a behavior modification program to ascertain its relationship with the dependent variable. Sometimes thought of as the "cause" of the "effect" on the dependent measure.

Intermittent Reinforcement: (See Schedules of Reinforcement.)

Interresponse Reinforcement: The amount of time that passes between two responses.

Interval Reinforcement: (See Schedules of Reinforcement.)

Latency: The time between the occurrence of the stimulus and the occurrence of the response.

Learning History: The sum of an individual's behaviors that have been conditioned or modified as a result of environmental events.

Link: Each unit of a chain, composed of a discriminative stimulus, response, and a reinforcer.

Modeling: A technique whereby the behavior that is to be taught is demonstrated for the learner and any semblance of the goal behavior is initially rewarded. The criterion for reinforcement is then gradually increased until the goal behavior is obtained. Sometimes no shaping is required.

Multiple Baseline Design: An experimental design (usually single-subject) that involves:
1. Obtaining base rates on several dependent behaviors
2. Applying the independent variable to one of the dependent behaviors until it is substantially changed while the other dependent behaviors are left free to vary
3. Applying the independent variable to a second dependent variable as in No. 2 above. This procedure is continued until it is demonstrated that each behavior systematically changes when the independent variable is applied to it.

Negative Reinforcer: A stimulus whose removal, if paired with the occurrence of a behavior, will increase the probability of occurrence of the behavior. Many times the term aversive stimulus is used in place of negative reinforcer. (See also Aversive Control.)

Negative Transfer: (See Transfer.)

Neutral Stimuli: All those environmental events that at any given moment do not elicit any behavior change, whether they precede, accompany, or follow responses.

Off-Task: Any behavior that interferes or is incompatible with previously defined situational expectations.

On-Task: Behavior consistent with definitional classes of behavior previously defined.

Operant: A behavior emitted by an organism that operates on or changes the environment in a very particular way.

Operant Behavior: Operants have the potential to produce stimulus events that alter the behavior's future occurrence. Operant behavior is behavior that is controlled by consequences. Operant behavior is mediated by the central nervous system and involves, primarily, the skeletal musculature. Operant responses act on, and interact with, the environment and are controlled and modified by the principles of operant conditioning. Operant responding includes not only the gross motor movements of the organism, but also its verbal behavior. Most of the daily, ongoing behavior of the individual as he interacts with his environment and other people is operant in nature.

Operant Conditioning: The changing of the frequency of an occurrence of a behavior by modifying the consequences of that behavior.

Operant Level: The strength of an operant before any known reinforcement; the unconditioned level of an operant (response), or the rate at which responses occur before they have been reinforced. Generally, baseline or base rate recording is a record of the operant level.

Operant Reinforcement: The potential of operants to produce events that will strengthen their future occurrence; following operant behavior with consequences of a reinforcing nature.

Ordinate: The vertical reference axis on a graph. In behavior modification, the ordinate is usually labeled with a scale that measures the dependent behavior, for example, frequency, percentage of responses, or rate.

Overcorrection: Procedures used to teach correct behaviors when inappropriate behaviors are exhibited. *Restitution overcorrection* involves returning the environment to its original state. *Positive-practice overcorrection* requires demonstration of the appropriate in an exaggerated manner or engaging in the behavior for an extended period of times.

Oscillation: Alternation of emotional responses usually found during the process of extinction.

Pairing: The act of associating one stimulus with another.

Pavlovian Conditioning: (See Respondent Conditioning.)

Pay-Off: That which rewards the occurrence of a behavior.

Pairing: Combining primary reinforcers with secondary reinforcers.

Positive Reinforcement: A stimulus that, when presented as a consequence of a response, results in an increase or maintenance of that response.

Premack Principle: The principle that contingent access to high frequency behaviors serves as a reinforcer for the performance of low frequency behaviors.

Primary Reinforcers: Reinforcing stimuli that have the effect of maintaining or perpetuating life, such as food, water, elimination, and warmth.

Probe: A phase in a behavior modification experiment designed to test the effect of a given procedure. A reversal is a probe since it removes the behavioral procedure for a brief period of time to test the procedure's effects. (See also Reversal Procedure.)

Programmed Instruction: The selection and arrangement of educational content based upon principles of human learning.

Prompt: An auxiliary discriminative stimulus that is applied to help occasion a given response. Prompts are usually faded before the terminal goal is judged as having been achieved.

Punishing Stimulus: A contingent stimulus that, when presented, results in a reduction in the occurrence of the dependent behavior.

Punishment: The potential of all operants to produce events that will *weaken* their future occurrence. There are two broad types of punishment:
1. Positive punishment—those events that will weaken an operant's future occurrence by the presentation of stimuli; and
2. Negative punishment—those events that will weaken an operant's future occurrence by the *removal* of stimuli.

Rate of Responding: The number of occurrences per unit time of the response.

Ratio Reinforcement: (See Schedules of Reinforcement.)

Reflex: A physical response (behavior) mediated by the autonomic nervous system.

Reinforcement: The contingent use of a stimulus resulting in an increase or maintenance of behavior. All operants have the potential to produce events that will strengthen their future occurrence. There are two broad types of reinforcement:
1. Positive reinforcement—those events that will strengthen an operant's future occurrence by the *presentation* of stimuli; and
2. Negative reinforcement—those events that will strengthen an operant's future occurrence by the *removal* of stimuli.

Reinforcement Density: Frequency or rate with which responses are reinforced. The lower the ratio or shorter the interval required by a given reinforcement schedule, the denser the reinforcement.

Reinforcement History: The sum total of an organism's past.

Reinforcer: A stimulus, the contingent use of which results in the increase or maintenance of the dependent behavior. The stimulus will increase the probability of the response that precedes it (see Approval, Disapproval, and Reinforcement).

Reinforcing Incompatible Behavior: A behavioral procedure that increases the occurrence of a behavior or behaviors that cannot coexist with another, usually "undesired," behavior.

Reliability: Refers to consistency of measurement. It is usually calculated by comparing how well two or more independent observers agree among themselves. It is often calculated and reported in percentages by dividing the number of agreements by the number of agreements plus disagreements and then multiplying the fraction by one hundred. Reliability measures should be reported for each phase of a single-subject design.

Replicate: To repeat an experimental procedure or finding.

Respondent: A regular response from all normal organisms of the same species to the same eliciting stimulus. Ex: Salivation.

Respondent Behavior: All respondents are a function (elicited or maintained) of antecedent stimulus events.

Respondent Conditioning (Classical or Pavlovian Conditioning): The process whereby eliciting stimuli increase the frequency of respondents (usually a physiological change). A neutral stimulus, when associated repeatedly with an unconditioned stimulus that reliably elicits a specific response, comes to elicit a "new" response, which is similar in some respect to that produced originally by the unconditioned stimulus.

Response: A physical reaction in time and space to an environmental event, generally synonymous with behavior and, in behavioral research, both observable and measurable (fines, etc.)

Response Cost: A procedure in which there is contingent withdrawal of specified amounts of available reinforcers.

Response Differentiation: The process whereby reinforcement alters some specific property of an operant such as its duration, intensity, or topography; a procedure that reinforces a subset of specific behavior, conforming to specified behavioral dimensions.

Reversal Procedure: A technique that involves the removal of the procedure in order to test the effectiveness of the procedure. For instance, one frequently utilized experimental design involves: (1) obtaining a base rate of the dependent variable; (2) applying the independent variable until a substantial change in the dependent variable is recorded; (3) the reversal, a discontinuation of the independent variable and a reintroduction of the conditions in effect during the baseline period, until a substantial reversal in the value of the dependent variable is obtained; and (4) a reapplication of the independent variable to reinstate the change (Often abbreviated as **ABAB** design.) Such a procedure is used to demonstrate a *functional* relationship between the *independent* and *dependent* variables.

Satiation: The process whereby a reinforcer temporarily ceases to strengthen an operant. A reduction in performance occurs generally after a large amount of reinforcement.

Scallop: A pattern on a response record that is characterized by a sequence of positively accelerating curves.

Schedule of Reinforcement: The rule followed by the environment in determining which among the many occurrences of a response will be reinforced. Schedules include three general types: ratio, interval, and mixed.

   1. **Ratio Schedule of Reinforcement:** A schedule in which reinforcement is made contingent upon the emission of a number of responses

before one response is reinforced. One version is the Fixed Ratio (FR) schedule, when a specific number of responses must occur prior to the reinforced response. For example, a FR-3 schedule indicates that each third response is contingently reinforced. The other type is the Variable Ratio (VR) schedule, when a variable number of responses must occur prior to the reinforced response. The number of responses usually varies about a specified average. For example, a VR-6 schedule means that six performances on the average are required prior to each reinforcement.

2. **Interval Schedule of Reinforcement:** A schedule in which reinforcement is made contingent upon the passage of time before the response is reinforced. It could be a Fixed Interval (FI) schedule, when a particular response is scheduled for reinforcement following the passage of a specific amount of time, and that time is held constant. For example, an FI-3 indicates that reinforcement follows the first occurrence of the primed response after three minutes have passed. Or one might establish a Variable Interval (VI) Schedule in which a variable time interval must occur prior to the reinforced response. The time interval usually varies within a specified average. For example, a VI-6 indicates that an average of six minutes passes before the primed response receives contingent reinforcement.

3. **Mixed Schedules of Reinforcement:** Combinations of interval and ratio schedules. Most school and home reinforcement, of necessity, is mixed.

Shaping: Taking the behaviors that the organism already has in his repertoire and reinforcing those that are similar to the goal behavior, gradually requiring that the organism's behavior be more and more similar to the goal behavior to be reinforced. This is continued until the goal behavior is obtained. New behaviors may be developed by systematic reinforcement of successive approximations toward a specified goal. (See also Successive Approximations.)

Single-Subject Experimental Designs: Research designs developed for evaluating the effects of one or more independent variable(s) on the behavior of a single organism.

Social Reinforcer: A conditioned reinforcing stimulus mediated by another individual within a social context.

Spontaneous Recovery: The reappearance of a response previously eliminated by means of an extinction procedure following a time interval without any intervening reinforced responses.

Stimulus: An environmental event.

Stimulus Change: A behavioral procedure that employs discriminative stimuli, or stimuli that occasion or inhibit specific behaviors.

Stimulus Control: After an operant has been reinforced in the presence of a particular stimulus a number of times, that stimulus comes to control the operant. Control of this sort is achieved when responses are reinforced in the presence of a specified stimulus and not others and the stimulus controls the probability that the response will be emitted.

Stimulus Delta ($S^\wedge$): A stimulus in the presence of which a given response is not reinforced. This kind of discriminative stimulus, like S^d, is said to be established when, after several pairings with the occurrence or nonoccurrence of reinforcement, its presence or absence is accompanied by reliable changes in response.

Stimulus Deprivation: The process whereby the reinforcing power of a stimulus is restored by depriving the organism of it for a period of time.

Stimulus Discrimination: The process whereby an operant is emitted only in the presence of certain stimuli.

Stimulus Generalization: Responding to similar stimuli that approximate the original stimulus.

Stimulus Overload: When a response decreases in frequency because of too large a frequency or magnitude of reinforcement, stimulus overload has occurred.

Subject Confounding Variables: Subject characteristics (demographic, previous learning history, and present behaviors) that have not been controlled in an experiment but may effect changes in the occurrences of the dependent variable. Single-subject designs control for subject confounding variables by comparing the subject's performance under one condition with his performance under other conditions.

Subset of Behavior: The group of simple response components that compose a more complex behavior.

Successive Approximations: Behavioral elements or subsets, each of which more and more closely resembles the specified terminal behavior. (See Shaping.)

Superstitious Behavior: Behavior that is not based on contingencies that are actually in existence but is reinforced by chance. Ex: A child might wish on a star for a bicycle and believe that his wish caused him to get it for his birthday.

Supplementary Reinforcers: Reinforcers used in addition to the major contingent reinforcer.

Target Behavior: A behavioral goal.

Terminal Behavior: The behavior that is achieved at the end of a behavior modification program. The terminal behavior is described according to all its relevant behavioral dimensions and is usually assigned a criterion by which an acceptable level of performance is to be judged.

Task Analysis: A process of breaking down a complex behavior into its smallest parts.

Tic: An habitual spasmodic movement of particular muscles.

Thinning: The process of gradually decreasing reinforcement given for a particular behavior.

Time Sampling: A direct observational procedure in which the observer records the presence or absence of the behaviors to be changed, within uniform time intervals. For example, an observer may observe for 10 seconds and record during the following 5 seconds the occurrence or nonoccurrence of the subject's behavior. This procedure may continue for a specified 30 minutes each day. Observers may sample any predetermined time periods.

Time Out: Time out from positive reinforcement is a procedure in which access to the sources of various forms of reinforcement are removed for a particular period, contingent upon the emission of a response. The opportunity to receive reinforcement is contingently removed for a specified time. Either the individual is contingently removed from the reinforcing environment or the reinforcing environment is contingently removed from him for some stipulated duration.

Time Out Room, Time Out Booth: A facility that is arranged in such a manner that the individual placed therein has little likelihood of receiving reinforcement from the environment. The place in which time out from positive reinforcement occurs.

Token Economy: A system requiring two components: tokens and back-up reinforcers. Many token economies are widely used in schools and other institutional settings.

Token: An object that can be exchanged at a later time for another reinforcing item or activity. The extent to which tokens are reinforcing or take on the properties of a generalized reinforcer is dependent on the individual's experience and on what back-up items are available.

Topography: The physical nature of the responses that compose the operant. Ex: How hard the lever was pushed, by which hand, and how long a time it stayed depressed, the movement of the body during observed motor off-task.

Transfer: The effect that learning a task has on the learning of another task. If having learned the first task facilitates learning the second task, it is called *positive* transfer; if learning the first task interferes with learning the second task, then it is called *negative* transfer.

Unconditioned Reinforcer: When a stimulus can reinforce a behavior without the organism having had any previous experience, the reinforcer is said to be a primary or unconditioned reinforcer. Ex: The smell of food produces salivation.

Unconditioned Response: A response that nearly inevitably follows a specific stimulus. This is the *unconditioned* stimulus of that response.

Unconditioned Stimulus: (See Unconditioned Response.)

Variable Interval Reinforcement: (See Schedules of Reinforcement.)

Variable Ratio Reinforcement: (See Schedules of Reinforcement.)

STUDY GUIDE FOR CHAPTER 10

1. Describe the basic AB design. Why is this design so popular with most teachers?

2. Why do most people want to start an intervention without taking baseline? Why is it important to establish baseline before attempting "to do something" in order to change behavior?

3. What might you tell a person who starts their question with the statement: "Tell me what to do with my problem son, who misbehaves . . . ?" List all of the information that one might get from baseline data that might help in determining the intervention strategy.

4. Describe a complete reversal design. Why would a behavioral scientist not "just stop the intervention" after the first AB if the behavior is getting better?

5. What is unique to the alternating treatments design? How can the derived information be useful? What might constitute drawbacks to using this design?

6. What advantages are there to using a "multiple baseline design" compared to a reversal design? Explain how the multiple baseline would be implemented in various facilities (i.e., a school, a sheltered workshop, and at home).

7. What is a "changing criterion design"? In what ways can this design be used? How does it relate to the development of a long-term task analysis?

8. Why do most parents and teachers not ask the question: "What is it that *I am doing* that causes the child to misbehave?"

9. How can studying behavioral terminology help in reading the applied research literature?

10. Why is it important that researchers in various fields have an "agreed upon" technical language?

LEARNING ACTIVITY 19—TEST OVER GLOSSARY

I. True or False

1. _____ A negative reinforcer will decrease the behavior.

2. _____ In classical conditioning, food is the conditioned stimulus for salivation.

3. _____ Removal of tokens for inappropriate social behavior in a class is an example of response cost.

4. _____ A consequence is non-contingent if it decreases a specific behavior.

5. _____ Successive approximation of speech might initially include reinforcement of any vocalization.

6. _____ Observer reliability is the measurement of agreement between independent observers.

7. _____ A schedule of reinforcement refers to the type of primary or secondary reinforcers used in the shaping process.

8. _____ A multiple baseline controls for subject confounding variables.

9. _____ Negative transfer refers to a lack of stimulus generalization.

10. _____ Replication is an important aspect of behavioral research.

11. _____ The multiple baseline design is generally an example of a single-subject design.

12. _____ Placement in a juvenile detention house may be a time-out procedure.

13. _____ Punishment will frequently result in escape and avoidance behavior.

14. _____ The effectiveness of behavioral techniques may be accountable without data.

15. _____ A rising baseline is an indication of the operant level of a behavior.

16. _____ A classroom with continuously available record player, TV, and games may cause "stimulus overload."

17. _____ Money is a back-up reinforcer.

18. _____ Laws are statements concerning empirical scientific cause-and-effect relationships.

19. _____ A teacher giving a high amount of approval is responding to a "good class."

20. _____ One of the most important contributions of behavior modification is its emphasis on operationally defined dependent variables.

II. Circle the answer that best completes the statement:

21. One process through which a conditioned respondent can be eliminated is:

a) desensitization
b) negative reinforcement
c) punishment
d) extinction
e) positive reinforcement

22. A student being reinforced for any behavior except for hitting other students is on a _____schedule of reinforcement.

a) continuous
b) variable interval
c) DR
d) DRO
e) FR

23. Criteria are generally used in behavioral programs to:

a) decide what to teach
b) structure the program in sequential steps
c) provide the student with feedback
d) evaluate the program
e) all of the above

24. Programmed instructional texts use:

a) positive reinforcement
b) an errorless discrimination procedure
c) learning principles
d) fading techniques
e) all of the above

25. Behavior is the result of:

a) mental ability
b) a person's emotional state
c) its consequences
d) premeditation
e) all of the above

26.   Counterconditioning refers to:

a) desensitization
b) confounding of certain behavior modification principles
c) structuring incompatible responses
d) two of the above
e) three of the above

27.   Counting the number of problems completed during a 20-minute math period is an example of:

a) time sampling
b) continuous response measurement
c) event sampling
d) variable interval observation
e) a continuous field

28.   Removal of tokens until a behavior increases is an example of:

a) response cost
b) DRL
c) punishment
d) negative reinforcement
e) two of the above

29.   If a teacher adjusts his teaching to compensate for a student's learning, the teacher's behavior is a(n)

a) respondent behavior
b) operant behavior
c) positive reinforcer
d) neutral stimulus
e) conditioned reflex

30.   A child who acts similarly to a parent has usually acquired those behaviors through

a) transfer
b) modeling
c) stimulus generalization
d) adaptation
e) discriminative stimuli

III. Complete the following statements:

31.   Singing a song, hitting a ball, and participating in class discussion are all examples of _____ behavior.

32.   The process of causing a student to transfer from a specific situation to another similar situation is called _____

33.   To decrease piano performance anxiety, _____ may be used to recondition anxiety-stimuli.

34.   The use of rock music listening time as a reinforcer for increasing math scores is often an example used to illustrate the _____ principle.

35.   Rewarding a child with frequent large quantities of food will probably result in_____

36.   Spanking a child after a child misbehaves is an example of _____ if the child's misbehavior decreases.

37.   A parent gives a child weekly allowance contingent on completion of assigned work tasks. The dependent variable is_____

38.   All teaching involves the establishment of _____ where there previously existed nondiscrimination.

39.   Reinforcement should be contingent; however, a consequence of a behavior could be contingent but not_____

40.   The principles of behavior are functional. This is true because the behavioral principle operating can only be defined by the _____ of that consequence.

LEARNING ACTIVITY 20—LEGAL, MORAL, AND ETHICAL RESPONSIBILITIES FOR THE TEACHER

Write an essay dealing with the issues relating to the legal, moral, and ethical responsibilities in regard to teaching. Be sure to include such aspects as: What is fair? What behaviors should be referred to professionals in other areas? What type of potential approvals/disapprovals will be ethically and morally correct? What aspects of discipline represent legal considerations?

The following questions might help stimulate ideas for writing an essay (or facilitating class discussion).

1. Can humans modify their behavior to be more free?

2. Can humans really avoid controlling others (through the ongoing exchange of rewards and punishments) even if they wish to?

3. Under what circumstances and for what types of behavior is negative reinforcement and/or punishment appropriate/necessary?

4. In what ways can behavioral techniques be abused? Is the potential for abuse greater for the behavioral approach than other approaches?

5. Should *behaviorists* be allowed to "experiment" with humans? What criteria should be established to determine the permissible areas of behavioral intervention? Should some populations (mentally ill persons who are institutionalized, persons who are mentally retarded, or prisoners) be immune from experiments? Should they have less right to informed consent because of diminished capacity or status?

6. What limits should we place on the teaching of others? Can an acceptable standard be developed that allows for the proper treatment of chronic problems while somehow preventing "brainwashing" and unwarranted deprivations of rights and freedoms?

7. Should parents be granted the right to informed consent before a student is admitted to a behavior modification program? When do behavior modification practices (deliberate or unwitting) constitute a "program" subject to special consideration?

8. What kinds of reinforcers are really proper for the school environment (for "adjusted" or "maladjusted" children)?

9. Are structured techniques such as token economy system too mechanistic to be used in the schools? What better alternative, if any, is available for dealing with reluctant learners?

10. How might behavioral principles be employed to improve or reform the educational system (increase motivation, reduce disruption, promote individuality and creativity, provide instructional alternatives, and promote racial harmony)?

References

Example
number:

1   Jersild, A. T., & Holmes, F. B. (1935). "Methods of overcoming children's fears." *Journal of Psychology*, 1, 75-104.

4   Reynold, N. J., & Risley, T. R. (1968). "The role of social and material reinforcers in increasing talking of a disadvantaged pre-school child." *Journal of Applied Behavior Analysis*, 1, 253-262.

5   Harris, F. R., Johnston, M. K., Kelly, C. S., & Wolf, M. M. (1964). "Effects of positive social reinforcement on regressed crawling of a nursery school child." *Journal of Educational Psychology*, 55, 35-41.

8   Brown, R., & Elliott, R. (1965). "Control of aggression in a nursery school class." *Journal of Experimental Child Psychology*, 2, 103-107.

10   Allen, K. E., Hart, B. M., Buell, J. S., Harris, F. R., & Wolf, M. M. (1964). "Effects of social reinforcement of isolated behavior of a nursery school child." *Child Development*, 35, 511-518.

12   Harris, F. R., Wolf, M. M., & Baer, D. M. (1964). "Effects of adult social reinforcement on child behavior." *Young Children*, 20, 8-17.

13   Kobasigawa, A. (1968). "Inhibitory and disinhibitory effects of models on sex-appropriate behavior in children." *Psychologia*, 11, 86-96.

15   O'Leary, K. D., O'Leary, S., & Becker, W. C. (1967). "Modification of a deviant sibling interaction pattern in the home." *Behavior Research and Therapy*, 5, 113-120.

16   Hawkins, R. P., Peterson, R. F., Schweid, E., & Bijou, S. W. (1966). "Behavior therapy in the home: Amelioration of problem parent-child relations with the parent in a therapeutic role." *Journal of Experimental Child Psychology*, 4, 99-107.

17   Madsen, C. K., & Geringer, J. (1976). "Choice of televised music lessons versus free play in relation to academic improvement." *Journal of Music Therapy*, 13, 154-162.

20   Zeilberger, J., Sampson, S. E., & Sloane, H. N., Jr. (1969). "Modification of a child's problem behaviors in the home with the mother as therapist." *Journal of Applied Behavior Analysis*, 2, 47-53.

21   Wahler, R. G., Winkel, G. H., Peterson, R. F., & Morrison, D. C. (1965). "Mothers as behavior therapists for their own children." *Behavior Research and Therapy*, 3, 113-124.

23   Poche, C., Yoder, P., & Miltenberger, R. (1988). "Teaching self-protection to children using television techniques." *Journal of Applied Behavior Analysis*, 21(3), 253-261.

24   Dickinson, D. J. (1968). "Changing behavior with behavioral techniques." *Journal of School Psychology*, 6, 278-283.

25   Kennedy, W. A. (1965). "School phobia: Rapid treatment of fifty cases." *Journal of Abnormal Psychology*, 70, 285-289.

26   Baer, P. E., & Goldfarb, G. E. (1962). "A developmental study of verbal conditioning in children." *Psychological Reports*, 10, 175-181.

27   Becker, W. C., Madsen, C. H., Jr., Arnold, C. R., & Thomas, D. R. (1967). "The contingent use of teacher attention and praise in reducing classroom behavior problems." *Journal of Special Education*, 1, 287-307.

29   Hall, R. V., Lund, D., & Jackson, D. (1968). "Effects of teacher attention on study behavior." *Journal of Applied Behavior Analysis*, 1, 1-12.

31   Schutte, R. C., & Hopkins, B. L. (1970). "The effects of teacher attention on following instructions in a kindergarten class." *Journal of Applied Behavior Analysis*, 3, 117-122.

32   O'Leary, K. D., & Becker, W. C. (1967). "Behavior modification of an adjustment class: A token reinforcement program." *Exceptional Children*, 9, 637-642.

34   Patterson, G. R. (1965). "An application of conditioning techniques to the control of a hyperactive child." In L. P. Ullman and L. Krasner (Eds.), *Case Studies in Behavior Modification* (pp. 370-375). New York: Holt, Rinehart and Winston.

36   Madsen, C. H., Jr., Becker, W. C., Thomas, D. R., Koser, L., & Plager, E. (1968). "An analysis of the reinforcing function of sit-down commands." In R. K. Parker (Ed.), *Readings in Educational Psychology*. Boston: Allyn and Bacon.

37   Madsen, C. K. (1979). "The effect of music subject matter as rein-forcement for correct mathematics." *Council for Research in Music Education*, 59, 54-58.

38   Holland, C. J. (1969). "Elimination by the parents of fire setting behavior in a seven year old boy." *Behavior Research and Therapy*, 7, 135-137.

39   O'Leary, K. D., & Becker, W. C. (1968). "The effects of the intensity of a teacher's reprimands on children's behavior." *Journal of School Psychology*, 7, 8-11.

40   Ellison, D. G., Barber, L., Engle, T. L., & Kampwerth, L. (1965). "Programmed tutoring: A teaching aid and research tool." *Reading Research Quarterly*, 1, 77-127.

43   Madsen, C. H., Jr., Becker, W. C., & Thomas, D. R. (1968). "Rules, praise and ignoring: Elements of elementary classroom control." *Journal of Applied Behavior Analysis*, 1, 139-150.

44   Ferritor, D. E., Buckholdt, D., Hamblin, R. L., and Smith, L. (1972). "The non-effects of contingent reinforcement for attending behavior on work accomplished." *Journal of Applied Behavior Analysis*, 5, 7-17.

45   Ollendick, T. H., Matson, J. L., Esveldt-Dawson, K., & Shapiro, E. S. (1980). "Increasing spelling achievement: An analysis of treatment procedures utilizing an alternating treatments design." *Journal of Applied Behavior Analysis*, 13(4), 645-654.

46   Wagaman, J. R., Miltenberger, R. G., & Andorfer, R. E. (1993). "Analysis of a simplified treatment for stuttering in children." *Journal of Applied Behavior Analysis*, 26(1), 53-61.

50   Doubros, S. G., & Daniels, G. J. (1966). "An experimental approach to the reduction of overactive behavior." *Behavior Research and Therapy*, 4, 251-258.

52   Olympia, D. E., Sheridan, S. M., Jenson, W. R., & Andrews, D. (1994). "Using student-managed interventions to increase homework completion and accuracy." *Journal of Applied Behavior Analysis*, 27(1), 85-99.

53   Holmes, D. S. (1966). "The application of learning theory to the treatment of a school behavior problem: A case study." *Psychology in the Schools*, 3, 355-358.

55   Madsen, C. K., Smith, D. S., & Feeman, C. C., Jr. (1988). "The use of music in cross-age tutoring within special education settings." *Journal of Music Therapy*, 25(3), 135-144.

63   Hall, R. V., Panyan, M., Rabon, D., & Broden, M. (1968). "Instructing beginning teachers in reinforcement procedures which improve classroom control." *Journal of Applied Behavior Analysis*, 1, 315-328.

67   Chadwick, B. A., & Day, R. C. (1971). "Systematic reinforcement: Academic performance of under-achieving students." *Journal of Applied Behavior Analysis*, 4, 311-319.

68   Grandy, G. S., Madsen, C. H., Jr., & DeMersseman, L. M. (1973). "Effects of individual and interdependent contingencies on inappropriate classroom behavior." *Psychology in the Schools*, 10, 488-493.

69   Hall, R. V., Cristler, C., Cranston, S. S., & Tucker, B. (1970). "Teachers and parents as researchers using multiple baseline designs." *Journal of Applied Behavior Analysis*, 3, 247-255.

75   Ninness, H. A. C., Fuerst, J., Rutherford, R. D., & Glenn S. S. (1991). "Effects of self-management training and reinforcement on the transfer of improved conduct in the absence of supervision." *Journal of Applied Behavior Analysis*, 24(3), 499-508.

70   Polirstok, S. R., & Greer, R. D. (1977). "Remediation of mutually aversive interactions between a problem student and four teachers by training the student in reinforcement techniques." *Journal of Applied Behavior Analysis*, 10, 707-716.

77   Bailey, J. S., Wolf, M. M., & Phillips, E. L. (1970). "Home-based reinforcement and the modification of pre-delinquent classroom behavior." *Journal of Applied Behavior Analysis*, 3, 223-233.

80   Hall, R. V., Panyan, M., Rabon, D., & Broden, M. (1968). "Instructing beginning teachers in reinforcement procedures which improve classroom control." *Journal of Applied Behavior Analysis*, 1, 315-328.

84   Green, B. F., Bailey, J. S., & Barber, F. (1981). "An analysis and reduction of disruptive behavior on school buses." *Journal of Applied Behavior Analysis*, 14(2), 177-192.

87   Davison, G. C. (1969). "Self-control through 'Imaginal Aversive Contingency' and 'One-downmanship' enabling the powerless to accommodate unreasonableness." In J. D. Krumboltz and C. E. Thoresen (Eds.), *Behavioral Counseling: Cases and Technique* (pp. 319-327). New York: Holt, Rinehart and Winston.

88   Madsen, C. K., & Forsythe, J. L. (1974). "The effect of contingent music listening on increases of mathematical responses." In C. K. Madsen, R. D. Greer, and C. H. Madsen, Jr. (Eds.), *Research in Music Behavior*, New York: Teachers College Press.

89   Kirby, F. D., & Shields, F. (1972). "Modification of arithmetic response rate and attending behavior in a seventh-grade student." *Journal of Applied Behavior Analysis*, 5, 79-84.

92   Madsen, C. K., & Madsen, C. H., Jr. (1968). "Music as a behavior modification technique with a juvenile delinquent." *Journal of Music Therapy*, 5, 72-76.

93   Marlowe, R. H., Madsen, C. H., Jr., Bowen, C. E., Reardon, R. C., & Logue, P. E. (1978). "Severe classroom problems: Teachers or counselors." *Journal of Applied Behavioral Analysis*, 11, 53-66.

96   Miller, L. K. (1965). "A note on the control of study behavior." *Journal of Experimental Child Psychology*, 1, 108-110.

102 Budney, A. J., Higgins, S. T., Delaney, D. D., Kent, L., & Bickel, W. K. (1991). "Contingent reinforcement of abstinence with individuals abusing cocaine and marijuana." *Journal of Applied Behavior Analysis*, 24(4), 657-665.

104 Wagner, J. L. & Winett, R. A. (1988). "Prompting one low-fat high fiber selection in a fast-food restaurant." *Journal of Applied Behavior Analysis*, 21(2), 179-185.

107 Houten, R. V. (1988). "The effects of advance stop lines and sign prompts on pedestrian safety in a crosswalk on a multilane highway." *Journal of Applied Behavior Analysis*, 21(3), 245-251.

111 Cope, J. G. & Allred L. J. (1991). "Community intervention to deter illegal parking in spaces reserved for the physically disabled." *Journal of Applied Behavior Analysis*, 24(4), 687-693.

112 Schwitzgebel, R. L., & Kolb, D. A. (1964). "Inducing behavior change in adolescent delinquents." *Behavior Research and Therapy*, 1, 297-304.

113 McSweeny, A. J. (1978). "Effects of response cost on the behavior of a million persons: Charging for directory-assistance in Cincinnati." *Journal of Applied Behavior Analysis*, 11, 47-51.

115 Scott, D. S., Scott, L. M., & Goldwater, B. (1997). "A performance improvement program for an international-level track and field athletic." *Journal of Applied Behavior Analysis*, 30(3), 573-575.

116 Fitterling, J. M., Martin, J. E., Gramling, S., Cole, P., & Milan, M. A. (1988). "Behavioral management of exercise training in vascular headache patients: An investigation of exercise adherence and headache activity." *Journal of Applied Behavior Analysis*, 21(1), 9-19.

Index

Behavioral goals, 42–43, 313
Behavioral objectives, 32–45
Boredom (*see also* Academic apathy):
    example, 169
Bothering teacher at desk,
    example, 132
Boy Scout program, 37
Brain damage: temper outbursts, 108–109
Bribery, example, 127
Bus, disruption on school, 158–159

C

Cause-and effect relationships, 105–106,
    158–159
Censorship:
    example, 177–178
    lack of, 117, 137, 171
Chaining, 282–283, 313
    examples, 177–178, 185–187, 282–283
Changing criterion design, 309–310
Chewing gum problem, example, 152
Classroom, out of control, examples,
    141–142
Cognitive Behavior Modification, 64–66, 314
Communication (*see also* Talking
    Verbalizations): low frequency, 99–100
    lying, 139–141
    refusal, 160–161
Computer, 113
Cooperation with teachers, rewarded, 102
    (*see also* Parents)
Conditioned reinforcer, 314
    examples, 119–120, 122–123, 127–128,
    138–139
Conditioned reflex, 314
Conditioned reinforcer, 314
Conditioned stimulus, 314
Conditioning, 314
Confounding variable, 314
    example, 103
Consequate, 314 (*see also* Payoff,
    Reinforcement, Rewards)
    explained, 79
    examples, 214–218
Consistency, 56, 74–76, 102 (*see also*
    Payoff, Reinforcer, Reinforcement)
Contingency, 314
    control, 151–152, 314
    contract, 159, 314
    contingent, 57–60, 314
    group vs. individual, 147–148
    techniques for structuring, 62–64
Continuous field, 314
Continuous response, 315
Contracting: contingency contract, 289, 314

    example, 158–159
Cross-age Tutoring, 136
Counseling (*see also* Behavior therapy):
    behavioral, 166–167
    greater effect if teacher is approving,
    127–128, 166–167
    client-centered, 166–167
    program with parents and teachers, 168
Counterconditioning, 295, 315 (*see also*
    Incompatible behavior)
    examples, 98, 143
Crawling, during school, 100
Criterion, 315
    example of choosing 148–149
    changing criterion design, 309–310
Crying (*see also* Verbalizations)
    example, 99
    reinforcement of, 10, 75–76
Cue, 315
    examples, 108–109, 127–128, 169

D

Dawdling,
    excessive example, 139, 148–149, 151, 153
    in work completion, 153
Delinquency, examples, 157–158, 180
Demerit approach, 36–38
Dependent variable, 315
    examples, 116, 132–135
Deprivation, 315
Desensitization, 295, 315
    in vivo, 98
Desire vs. behavior, 3–5, 19–20, 34–36
Differential punishment, 315
Differential reinforcement, 292–294, 315
    high rates (DRH), 315
    low rates (DRL), 315
    other behavior (DRO), 316
    alternative, (DRA), 315
    incompatible, (DRI), 315
Disapproval, 62–64, 316
    activities and privileges list, 212
    closeness, 212
    expressions, list, 211
    group, 57–59, 151
    ineffective use, 78–79
    responses, list, 208–211
    as reward, 154
    things, 212
    threat of (fear), 62–64
Discipline, 5
    courage required, 11
    external/internal, 8
    importance of consistency, 74–76
    relationship to lose, 5–7, 82–83

School failure, 168 (*see also* Academic failure)
School phobias, 115–116
Secondary Reinforcers, 286
Self–concept, examples, 116, 170
Self–control, 160–161
Self modification, 192
Sex:
asking about, 117
role behavior, 105–106
Sex education, and parents' values, 117
Shaping, 322
class control, 141–142
contingencies for, 62–64
initial steps in, 18, 57–58
precision in, 40
Sharing, example, 98
Showing off, maintained by peers, 115–116 (*see also* Attention-seeking)
Single–subject designs, 322
must structure for individual, 112–113
Skinner, B.F., 41
Social reinforcer, 322 (*see also* Approval)
Socialization,boy-girl, 169–170
Special education, 21–23
Spelling, 130–131
Spontaneous recovery, 322
Standing (*see also* Inappropriate behaviors)
example, 117, 122–126
reinforcing inappropriate, 122–126
and walking around, 122–126
Stealing, 140–141
Stimulus, 322
change, 322
control, 323
deprivation, 323
discrimination, 323
overload, 323
stimulus delta (S^), 323
Street, walking in, example, 104
Striking children with objects, 118–119 (*see also* Aggressiveness)
Study:
developing a routine for, 185–187
disturbing others during, 153–154
Stuttering, 131
Subject confounding variable, 323
Subset of behavior, 323
Successive approximation, 323 (*see also* Shaping)
Superstitious behavior, 323

T

Talking (*see also* Inappropriate verbalizations)
blurting out noise inattention, 117
constant, 153–154
disruptive social, 155–156
disturbing others, 153–154
fear of, 143
low frequency increased, 99–100
in lunchroom, 137–138
out of seat and standing, 147–148
refusal to talk, 160–161
and standing, 117
Tardiness, following recess, 148–149
Target Behavior, 323
Task analysis, 278–280
Teacher (as reinforcer):
abdication of responsibility, 23, 53–54, 80, 84
consistency, 74–76
contingencies of, 57–59
determining payoff, 55–57, 83, 99
examples, 99, 117, 124–125, 166, 181–182
good, 80
handling problem where occurs, 166
imposition of value system, 26–28, 82–83, 91–94
initial step for teaching, 26–28, 82–83, 151
power of, 26–28
practicing positive approach, 197–198
using behavioral approach, 32–44, 78–79, 82–83
Teaching:
beginning reading, 125–126
contractual agreements, 159
lying, 139–141
responsibility in, 26–27
Teasing other children, example, 133
Television as reward, 123–124
Temper outbursts (*see also* Verbalization)
Talking, Inappropriate verbalizations):
example, 108–109
Terminal behavior, 323
Test, 218–227
Thumb–sucking, high level 127
Tic, 323
Time:
importance of, 69–70, 138–139, 168
sampling, 323
structuring activities in, 71–73
Time log, 49–50
Time-out, 297, 324 (*see also* Isolation)
Time-out room, or booth, 324